Doris Roberts Takes On:

LIFE—

"I love Marie because I understand her. If things had turned out differently in my life, I might have been Marie."

LAUGHS—

"The real anxiety about aging begins when you turn forty, the gateway to middle age. Some women grow into maturity. Those who don't, have it thrust upon them . . . A few years ago, I turned seventy and decided I was finally ready to celebrate my fortieth birthday."

LASAGNA—

"I've been on dozens of diets, and I can safely say that none of them have worked, at least not for long . . . I have no patience for skinny people who wag their fingers at us sensualists and explain that the problem is that we associate food with love. Of course we do. Food *is* love."

Are You Hungry, Dear?

Life, Laughs, and Lasagna

DORIS ROBERTS

with Danelle Morton

ST. MARTIN'S GRIFFIN ✦ NEW YORK

I would like to dedicate this book to

Michael, Jane, Kelsey, Andy, and Devon,

who make it all worthwhile.

www.stmartins.com

Book design by Donna Sinisgalli

Library of Congress Cataloging-in-Publication Data

Roberts, Doris, 1925–
   Are you hungry dear? : life, laughs, and lasagna/ Doris Roberts with Danelle Morton.
      p. cm.
   ISBN 0-312-31226-1 (hc)
   ISBN 0-312-31227-X (pbk)
   EAN 978-0312-31227-5
    1. Roberts, Doris, 1925– 2. Actors—United States—Biography. 3. Cookery, American. I. Morton, Danelle. II. Title.

PN2287.R626A3 2003
791.45'028'092—dc21
[B]
                                       2003043121

First St. Martin's Griffin Edition: May 2004

10 9 8 7 6 5 4 3 2 1

Contents

Acknowledgments

Many people contributed to making this book, and I'm going to try to thank all of them, but I'll probably forget someone and for that I apologize. I'll start at the very beginning. I want to thank my grandparents and my mother for passing on the DNA that gives me the courage and stamina to write this book and to keep working into my seventh decade. I would like to thank everyone who touched my life and made it better. Those who didn't, you're not in the book. I thank Jennifer Lasselette, my charming and thorough assistant, for her invaluable contribution to making the scattered notes in my recipe file into real, workable recipes. I'd like to thank my son Michael for his brilliant management of my career, for his lifelong tolerance and acceptance of his mother and the love that I always know is there. I want to thank my coauthor, Danelle Morton, for giving this book its shape and clarity. I want to thank everyone connected with *Everybody Loves Raymond*: my brilliant and hilarious fellow actors, the fabulous Phil Rosenthal and his troupe of wonderful writers, and the entire crew, who make coming to work each week a joy.

I want to thank the extraordinary playwrights who have given me the opportunity to be in their plays: Edward Albee's *The Death of Bessie Smith*, Neil Simon's *Last of the Red Hot Lovers*, Terrence McNally's *Bad Habits*, Paul Zindel's *The Secret Affairs of Mildred Wilde*, Michael Jacobs' *Cheaters*, Irene Marie Fornes' *The Office*, and Eve Ensler's *Vagina Monologues*. (And I'm not mentioning the plays that lasted only one night.) I thank my friend and acting teacher, the incredible Milton Katselas, for his insights, wisdom, and inspiration, which have helped make me the actress that I am. I'd like to thank my doctor, Richard Wulfsberg, for keeping me healthy; my business manager, Gary Haber, for helping me stay solvent; and my housekeeper, Teresa Ayala. My friends in New York, my friends in California, and my friends in Europe continue to make this journey so exciting and entertaining, and I thank them for that.

Lastly, and most important of all, I want to thank Jane and my grandchildren Kelsey, Andrew, and Devon for their nurturing and love.

Preface

It all started when Eve gave Adam the apple—and we've been feeding them ever since. I don't completely agree with my grandson Andy who, at the age of nine, saw a painting of Adam and Eve being ejected from Paradise. "Nanny, if Eve gave Adam the apple *she* should get thrown out and Adam should get a time out," he said. Shows how men think!

That legendary snack Eve served Adam in the Garden of Eden set up the eternal relationship between the sexes, one centered around love, hunger, shame, and guilt. Let's call them the four maternal food groups. You all remember the story. Adam and Eve were hanging around the Garden of Eden. She was probably trying to get him to mow the lawn and prepare for the Fall but he was ignoring her. She tried whining, cajoling, and even a little guilt and finally hit on the universal language women use to communicate with men—food. She wanted to know the same thing that Marie Barone and all women want to know about their men:

Are *you* hungry, dear?

Marie Barone, my character on *Everybody Loves Raymond,* asks that question of every man who enters her home. She doesn't ask: How are you? How was your day? Marie has a lot of advice to hand out. Some of it is good and some of it is bad, but all of it comes from a mother's love. She starts with the offering she knows can immediately salve whatever wounds he may have suffered. He may have just endured a humiliation at work, been disappointed in love, or simply got frustrated in the checkout line at the supermarket. No matter what fate might have befallen them when they ventured into the world outside her kitchen, her answer to almost every question is food.

Marie's got it right.

"Are you hungry, dear?" is a female version of asking, "Is there anything I can do for you?" When a loved one drags into the house, battered by a difficult day, you can't go back and fight his battles for him. All you can offer is your continued love, ready sympathy, and unquestioning acceptance, all of which is communicated immediately through food.

Women invest so much emotion in food that it becomes a symbol for many other things. We're hungry for comfort, sex, validation, praise, security. Probably a better question than "Are you hungry, dear?" is "What are you hungry for?" Someone to listen to you, to share with you, to assure you that whatever it is, it will pass. That is what we all want out of those close to us, and that is a theme I come to again and again in the pages of this book—a book that describes my life, my hungers, and the way I've fed them and those I've loved through the years.

When you love someone you feed them, either quite literally with food or through other forms of nurturing. The question "Are you hungry, dear?" is as much a greeting as an embrace.

When I decided to write a book about my life, I realized I couldn't pen a Hollywood tell-all because I'm one of the few stars in Hollywood who has no scandals to expose. The title of that book would have to be *I Slept With No One.*

Despite my modest roster of exploits, I've lived a rich and varied life full of incredible struggles, unexpected triumphs, unforgettable people, and great meals. I've pulled myself out of a hard-scrabble existence and made my way slowly but surely up the ladder of success until I hit the top while in my seventies. I deeply loved several men in my life, including my son whom I raised mainly alone. Some of the greatest actors of my generation have been my close friends and work mates. I have been more than blessed, I've worked hard, played hard, loved hard, and fallen hard, and yet I kept coming back for more. Still hungry.

When I think about my life so far, I remember the laughter first. But I want to be completely honest about my life and it hasn't all been funny. The best stories contain both the laughter and the sorrow. They show how the main character started in one place and ended up somewhere she never expected as well as all the obstacles she overcame along the way. Of course you always struggle to maintain your sense of humor when fate throws wrenches in your path. Every story in this book is a mixture of the dark and the light, just as in life.

With me, what you see is what you get. Although it was sometimes painful to describe moments of my life that were very personal, I believed that I owed you nothing less. I wanted to share moments with you and relate some of the lessons I've learned, the revelations that came to me along the way. I'm happy to say that through all of life's ups and downs I maintained my sense of humor and a gift for providing a good meal at just the right moment.

Part of the challenge in writing this book was trying to match the right recipe with each story. In some places I had three or four ideas for a recipe, and with some it was pretty hard to find the one that fit just right. But it amused me to discover how important food was to almost every phase of my life. Food was the occasion for peacemaking, laughter, lovemaking, and friendship. The time when those I loved could get together and put aside what divided us. In the presence of a great meal, the problems somehow seemed solvable and the things that tied us together seemed most important of all.

Now that I've come to the end of writing this book about my life, I can turn that timeless question, the Eve and Marie question, on myself. If I were to look in the mirror and ask myself, "Are you hungry, dear?", I still answer yes. I'm hungry for life and all it has to offer. I don't want to settle or give up or give in. Life is still exciting to me and I would like to think that when I leave this planet I will have seen everything and felt everything that there is for a human to experience. I know I've eaten practically everything in the course of this extraordinary journey. And yes . . . I'm still hungry, dear.

Part One

Life with Raymond

Chapter 1

Marie and Me

When fans come up to me on the street to hug me these days, I'm not sure that they love me, or my television alter ego, Marie Barone. The popularity of the show proves that *Everybody Loves Raymond,* but I know that just as many of them love Marie, the woman who has come to personify everything we adore and dread about family. Marie clearly loves her family with all her heart, worries about them more than she should, and would do anything to keep them fed, happy, and safe. The problem is that her version of what's good for them differs in a lot of ways from what most of them want for themselves. In this way, she is like me—like every mother, in fact. In short, Marie is one of the world's all-time most meddlesome mothers.

I know a lot about being a meddlesome mom. Not only have I played that role in my life off screen, I've been cast as the mother of many stars of stage and screen. In fact, I keep a list in my purse of those I've mothered. The list includes Billy Crystal twice *(The Rabbit Test* and *My Giant),* Bette Midler *(The Rose),* Tony Danza *(Mama Mia),* Donna Pescow *(Angie),* Robbie Benson *(California Girls),* Marlo Thomas *(It Happened One Christmas),* Charles Grodin *(The Heartbreak Kid),* Linda Lavin *(Alice),* Chevy Chase *(National*

Lampoon Christmas Vacation), Valerie Harper's mother-in-law (*Rhoda*), David Spade (*Dickie Roberts, Child Actor*), and of course Brad Garrett and Ray Romano. Of all the mothers I've portrayed, Marie is the one who has solidified my reputation as "The Mother of Them All." The mother of all Mothers, or, as they said in *Shaft* "one Badd Mother."

Since I have been spending four days a week every week for seven years with a group of people who all are pretty good at pretending to be a family, it's no wonder that it has begun to feel as though I really am the mother of the cast of *Everybody Loves Raymond*.

The home-like atmosphere of the set is part of what reinforces my maternal instincts. The set of *Everybody Loves Raymond* is a family-friendly place where the cast is permitted to bring their children. I know the many children of all of my colleagues quite well. When we're working on a show, it's not unusual to see one of Ray's four kids sitting tall in the big director's chair observing his daddy at work. And when I go upstairs to the playroom and school room the show maintains for the Sweeten children—Madylin Sweeten, who plays Ray and Debra's oldest daughter, and her twin brothers Sullivan and Sawyer Sweeten, who play the twins—I never know whose children might be among the toys and games. During a break in filming, the kids have the free run of the set and all of us feel responsible for their welfare, something that makes the set a very loving place.

This family feeling extends all the way through the crew as well, as was evidenced a few seasons back when my sitcom husband Peter Boyle had a heart attack. I had been at a benefit with Peter the night before and had noticed something different about him. He was quiet, which is not his normal social style, and his face was ashy. When I asked how he was feeling, he told me it was nothing. Men are so terrible when it comes to illness. They never want to admit to any weakness and always believe they can just ride it through.

The next day, on the set, Peter complained of chest pains. The first assistant director, Randy Suhr, had been on the set of a movie with Jack Lemmon when he had a heart attack. He spotted similar symptoms in Peter and called for an ambulance without asking him if he wanted one. He knew Peter well enough to realize that if he'd asked him if he wanted to go to the hospital, Peter would have said no and tried to tough it out. When the ambulance arrived, it turned out that Randy was right. Peter was actually having a heart attack when the ambulance came. Fortunately this came at the end of the season and he was able to do his recuperation during our hiatus.

The show has definitely benefited from the fact that almost all of the staff are very involved in their own families and the writers exploit their family dilemmas for comic effect on the show. Another thing that blurs the line between where Marie ends and I begin is the way I dress on the show, a way that is unique for my body type but also greatly influenced by the clothes worn by producer Phil Rosenthal's mother.

From the very beginning Marie has had a particular look about her, a look I developed with the help of years of experience with this particular body and the costume designer Simon Tuke. It's based on the fact that I look best with dark colors underneath and wonderfully colorful tops. Less for me is better. I don't like a lot of material on my body because it just makes it look huge. He also knows he can't use drop shoulders or dolman sleeves because they make me look too bulky. All the blouses are over blouses that are long enough to cover up and minimize my behind.

It's camouflage and fashion at the same time. The outfits are fashionable and slimming without looking like old lady muumuus. I cannot tell you how many people send me fan mail asking where I got my outfits. At Phil's insistence, I always wear a pin because his mother does. My favorite is the one with little cherries and matching little cherry earrings. Marie is a great fan of seasonal jewelry, as are many women my age. I've always got a pin that reflects the holiday:

a Christmas wreath or tree during the holidays, a shamrock for St. Patrick's, or an Easter Bunny in the spring.

As with the wardrobe, the episodes are based on reality and nothing is really forced. For example, the famous episode where I drove my car through Raymond's living room was based on something that happened with one writer's cousin and aunt. When the car smashed through the front door in that episode, we got the longest laugh I'd ever heard on television. When I emerged as the driver of the car, that laugh topped the previous one. Although it was my foot that stepped on the gas instead of the brake with the car in reverse, I came out blaming Frank for not getting the brakes fixed. Frank was much more concerned about the damage to his car than he was about the fact that it was parked in his son's living room and quickly developed a scheme to bilk the insurance companies out of money with the repairs.

I love the *Raymond* set, which the set decorators have outfitted just like a real house. I've always adored the clutter of Ray and Debra's home, with its masses of toys and stuffed animals heaped on the stairs, just like the living room of anyone raising three young children. I also love Frank and Marie's place for its whiff of great sitcom scenes past. The kitchen is the kitchen that was used in *All In The Family* with only a few minor changes to update it. Marie's living room is very evocative for me, a place that blends my real family and my sitcom one. I was delighted by the plastic slipcovers on the living room upholstery when I saw them for the first time. I had an aunt who covered her furniture the same way to save it for mythical "good company" who never arrived. In fact, we did an episode about these slipcovers. Debra convinced Marie she had to take them off because they were so unstylish and uncomfortable. When the boys sat down on the naked sofa for the first time, they looked more uneasy than they ever did on the plastic covers.

The piano at Frank and Marie's has a special place in my heart as well. It's a real piano, the one I taught Raymond to play on. Listen to me! You'd think I actually did teach him and he was my son. I can be forgiven, I suppose, because of the episode we did where I tried to refresh his mind about his childhood musical education. Marie was a music teacher when her kids were young and when she tried to remind Raymond of all he knew, that part of her returned with a vengeance. She chided him for his posture and his finger positioning and continually made him stand up so she could get him a simpler lesson book to start on because his form was so bad. It was a funny episode, but it also said something about Marie and the world of art and culture she tried to bring to her family.

I love Marie because I understand her. If things had turned out differently in my life, I might have been Marie. Women of my age group were told by society to get married early and have babies. After the kids were grown, their usefulness was fulfilled. That was pretty much all they could expect from life. I have another life, but the Maries of the world don't. They have spent their whole lives caring for their families.

A lot of these women are brilliant, but haven't had a chance to use those smarts on anyone except their poor families. They have husbands they've been feeding for forty years, and in the last twenty serving as a short-order cook for anyone who came into the house. You know the women I'm talking about. They've got an incredible instinct for the regular order of things. They can walk into a room and notice that a chair is just a little out of place, and from that one observation know instantly that something is not right in the household. It's almost an animal instinct. Like when a dog can predict an earthquake or smell fear. Or pees on the carpet so everybody knows it's her territory. The house is her realm, her seat of power, and she always knows when something is amiss.

When little kids think that their mothers have eyes in the back of their heads, those are the eyes of Marie. She can hear when someone is opening the refrigerator. She knows the sound of a milk carton being taken out of its slot on the refrigerator door, and she can guess, because of the sequence and the timing, that her son has not bothered to get a glass to put his drink in. So, as Raymond lifts the carton to his mouth to take a swig, he is completely unnerved by the voice from the living room that yells out: "How many times do I have to tell you, we don't drink out of the carton? We're not animals. Get a glass!" This is a voice that remains in their heads long after they've moved out, and well into their third or fourth year of therapy.

How did she know?

How could she *not* know?

Every room of the house is wired into her central nervous system. It's a place she's ruled for forty years, and she doesn't need motion detectors to know where everyone is and exactly what they are doing. Part of it is instinct, and part of it is experience. She's made a lifelong study of the characters in her house and she knows their habits and flaws, especially the latter. I'm sure even Jesus would have gotten his share of nagging, if Marie had been his mom. "You'll heal a leper, sure, but your room looks like a manger."

She knows that if it's four o'clock on a Sunday afternoon she'll find her husband Frank, played so brilliantly by my friend Peter Boyle, parked in front of the television watching the game. From the kitchen, where she's fixing the ziti that he'll be craving in about fifteen minutes, she can yell to her husband (without walking into the living room to verify that it's true): "Frank, stop scratching yourself and wash up. The ziti's almost ready."

Does this make her irritating, or loving? (Or perhaps she's just sure that Frank still has that rash?)

It doesn't matter. In most families, one comes with the other.

It's irritating to have another person know you so well that she anticipates what you're going to do before you do it (it can cause a rash). To you, a decision seems carefully thought out. To Marie, it seems inevitable. It offends your self-image to realize that you are so predictable, and to hear "I told you so." On the other hand, it's com-forting to realize that, despite this, she loves you anyway. She feeds you before you say you're hungry and puts ointment on the rash when no one else will come near.

When their sons have gone off into the world and out to chase down the women that will be their wives (not that they're running), the Maries of the world know they've lost a lot of their power. I don't think there is any mother who gives up her son completely. I remem-ber the mourning I went through when my son Michael went off to college and I faced the realization that, from that moment on, he would always be a guest at our house, even though he would never be allowed to use the guest towels. We would never again have that casual intimacy that comes from living together as a family and knowing all the little ins and outs of each other's day. From then on, he would be *presenting* his life to us, describing it, instead of living it with me as the primary witness (and occasional alibi).

Any mother mourns that transition, but particularly Marie. She doesn't know what do to with herself. But, give her a void and she'll find a way to fill it. After the housecleaning is done, the cooking com-pleted, and the gossip re-circulated, she has many hours left to calcu-late how to get her hooks back into her sons' lives. One way she can feel important is to advise them on what they should be doing. She wants them to use the benefit of her experience to avoid making poor choices and mistakes. We all know how well it goes over, giving your children advice. They tune you out the moment your voice hits that special note, the advice tone, like it was the whir of a dentist's drill. The other phrase their ears simply cannot hear is: "I told you so."

Like Marie—who is every mother in the world—how we get them back is with food. It's like a culinary hostage trade-off. Take the manicotti. Give me my son. Nobody gets hurt.

I have a friend whose son lives in Germany. When he comes to visit, you do not see her for two weeks before, or during the week or so that he is here. The two weeks before he comes is completely devoted to cooking. She makes all of his favorite dishes in advance and stores them in the freezer. She numbers the sequence of them so that she can produce them magically while he's home, and sit beside him and watch him eat. When your role in life has been to take care of the husband and the children, the years after they leave you're lost. When one of them returns, it makes you feel important again, young again. I don't know many young men who will sit and talk to their mothers about their problems, but I also don't know many who will refuse to sit down when their favorite pot roast is on the table.

Marie has won the biggest battle. Her son lives across the street from her. She has a way to feel needed and important every day.

I really feel for Raymond's wife Debra, the character played perfectly by Patricia Heaton. She's running a fine house. Her husband loves her, and her kids are happy and well-fed (when she follows Marie's recipes). Every time Marie comes in, it all suddenly seems a little shoddy, not quite up to snuff. As much as she'd like to tell her mother-in-law to get lost, she knows that that is not possible because of the incredible power Marie wields over Raymond. When Marie is unhappy, no one else in the family can be happy. So, as subservient as Marie's role appears to be, she is actually the most powerful person in the family, the real godfather.

As crazy as she gets, as intrusive and controlling as she is, everyone understands that she wants to make their lives better and strengthen the bond of the family, by any means necessary. When I read Marie's lines I believe in my heart that nothing she is saying is mean-spirited.

At the end of last season, we had a series of shows where Marie and Debra had stopped speaking to each other. These were some of the funniest shows that our writers ever came up with and it was a challenge for Patricia and me to make sure the tone of this battle between two powerful women came off exactly right.

For as much as the men in the family are constantly complaining that they want the women to shut up, it's total chaos when they do.

There are few things more powerful than a silent woman. Just try not speaking for one single solitary day. You'll get apologies for things that haven't even been done, confessions for things that were done, and lots of flowers. Sometimes you even get jewelry, which is where I think the expression "Silence is Golden" comes from.

In one of the episodes, Marie arrives unannounced (Why knock? I know you're there) at Raymond's house in the late afternoon with a few of her friends because she wants the kids to tell them a knock-knock joke. The place is in an uproar with the kids running all over the living room, ignoring Debra's efforts to get them to calm down and sit still. Finally, she turns to Marie and in a frustrated and very sharp tone of voice explains how it is not a very good time for a visit and she and her friends should leave.

The harsh tone of her voice in response to such a playful, harmless request felt like a slap in the face to Marie, particularly when delivered in front of her friends. "Well," Marie said, aghast. I held that "well" for a long time, with a look of wide-eyed incredulity on my face that showed both her horror at the rebuke and how hurt she was. Marie was at a rare loss for words in this circumstance. She apologized for bringing her friends over without a warning. "I should have known that by this point in the afternoon you've lost complete control of the children."

This kind of line in a script is potential dynamite. If I say it too quickly, or the wrong way the audience won't laugh. A shocked *"Ooohhhhh!"* comes from their mouths, as if I'd just taken out a dagger. If I played Marie mean, I bet *Everybody Loves Raymond* wouldn't be on the air today. The humor comes from the fact that her apology, which I delivered in her sweetest voice and with total sincerity, is a horribly insulting indictment of Debra's skills as a mother. Her intention is to soothe over a bad situation, but, in fact, she's just made it much, much worse. That's what makes the show so funny; you laugh simply because it's not happening to you.

In life, many of the things we do intending to help those that we love will backfire, despite the sincerity of our efforts. Some of what we think we're doing for another person ends up being something that we're really doing to preserve our role in the family and our hold on whatever position we may have staked out. The truth is that, because of the great advances in medicine, my generation is hanging around long past the time that our grandparents did. We're still trying to figure out what do to with all that extra time we've been granted. Men have always had golf to occupy their time, and now they have Viagra to keep them going. Great, just what we need—a retired guy with a sex pill and the day off. *Please* go play golf.

We, like Marie, want to be involved without becoming a pain in the ass. We want to be respected, but we don't need to be revered. We want to remain useful, and for many women a sure-fire way to remain useful is through feeding the troops.

The problem is that the food we make with such love and care can be used as a weapon against us. If you are a bad cook, you could be considered a double agent. We make those comfort foods from childhood, and our children turn up their noses explaining they don't eat red meat anymore. Or they waste precious eating time worrying about the fat content of my fettuccini carbonara with the heavy cream, butter, prosciutto, and two kinds of cheese. The kids complain: "But Mom, these meals are not in *The Zone Diet*." Yes they are. They're in *the flavor zone*, where all the meals are delicious, as far I'm concerned. My fettuccini has my cardiologist's seal of approval. He's always looking for new business.

Of course, like the food Marie offers as love, everything has hidden dangers that strike at the heart. As irritating as Marie can be, we cannot help but love her. She is human and she demonstrates the flaws that a lot of us and those we love have in the complicated interactions of family.

For all these reasons, Marie is a character who is very dear to my heart, and the source of some cheap therapy. Marie is my friend and my teacher, in how she shows me what *not* to do. For that, my son and daughter-in-law are eternally grateful and hope that the lessons continue for a few more years. (Don't worry kids, Mom's in syndication.)

Marie is famous for her lasagna, and I'm pretty renowned for mine. Here it is.

My Lasagna

This is best served with passive-aggressive questioning and subtle innuendo.

4 Italian sausages

1 pound fresh white button mushrooms, sliced

1 cup frozen peas

2 packages lasagna noodles

6 hard-boiled eggs, sliced into disks

meatballs (see recipe, which follows)

1 large container ricotta cheese

1 pound mozzarella cheese, shredded

1 cup Parmesan cheese, grated

meat sauce (see recipe, page 193)

1. In a sauté pan, fry sausages until cooked through. When cool, slice and set aside. Sauté mushrooms and peas in butter, salt, and pepper until soft and mushrooms are starting to brown. Set aside.
2. Cook noodles according to package. Drain, separate, and set aside.
3. Slice eggs and set aside.

4. In a fairly deep baking dish, ladle a thin layer of sauce on the bottom. (The layer of sauce should be only enough to keep the first layer of noodles from sticking to the dish.) Line the dish horizontally with noodles, allowing a generous overhang. Spoon on a bit more sauce and arrange another layer of noodles vertically, as you would do if you were making a lattice pie crust. You'll use the noodles that hang over the sides of the dish to wrap the lasagna when you're finished building the layers. Scatter a layer of meatballs onto the noodles. (Be sure to mind the amount of residual sauce that is spooned with the meatballs, as too much sauce will make the dish runny and unable to maintain its shape on the dinner plate.) Add sliced sausage, egg slices, mushrooms, and peas on top of the meatballs. Drop generous dollops of ricotta, followed by a handful of shredded mozzarella and a sprinkling of the Parmesan cheese. Repeat layers until the dish is full. This should give you three substantial layers. When construction is complete, fold the horizontal noodles over the top of the dish. Finish with a layer of sauce and some more Parmesan. Beat one egg vigorously and pour it over the finished lasagna to keep your masterpiece together. Tap dish on countertop to settle layers. Bake at 325 degrees for 30–40 minutes.

Serves 6–8.

My Meatballs

Note: In the spirit of Marie, if you're giving this recipe to your daughter-in-law, leave out the peas, mushrooms, and hard-boiled eggs. She will be unable to answer your son's questions about why it doesn't taste as good as Mom's.

2 pounds ground sirloin

4 cloves garlic, minced

1 cup Parmesan cheese

1 handful chopped Italian parsley

2 eggs

vegetable oil

salt and pepper to taste

1. Thoroughly mix all ingredients (except oil) in bowl and form into balls about the size of a quarter.
2. Heat 1–1½ inches of vegetable oil. When oil sizzles as a drop of water is added, add meatballs and fry until brown.
3. Transfer to meat sauce (see page 193).

Serves 6–8.

Chapter 2

The Greed Party

Christmas is the season of giving, but it's also the season of greed, no matter how much we don't want to admit it. People always say Christmas is for the children. They think of those shining eyes that light up as the kids race down the stairs early Christmas morning. That light in their eyes isn't because they are overjoyed at the prospect of celebrating the birth of Christ. They're just on fire for the big haul. I don't want you to think that I'm only criticizing children here. We adults are just as guilty, something that is very clear to me every year when I throw a "Greed Party" with the cast of *Everybody Loves Raymond*.

I've have been giving the Greed Party at Christmas time for more than twenty years. My guest list has included Neil Simon, Marsha Mason, Pierce Brosnan, Stephanie Zimbalist, Bruce Vilanch, Jimmy Coco, Michael Gleason, and Linda Lavin. The party has taken on a new energy with the cast of *Everybody Loves Raymond*, though. It's one of the cast's annual traditions, and we look forward to it every year.

We are lucky that we have as many social traditions as a real family. After the show wraps, we all go home for a wonderful three-day weekend. Frequently I end up seeing one or another of the cast members during my free time. I probably see Brad most often because we play cards together. We usually play at his house because since his marriage to Jill and the arrival of their two children, it's just easier for them if I go there. We usually play *Onze*—the French word for *eleven*—a game with eleven different versions of rummy. Then there is Sunday movie night at Phil's house. Pizza and beverages and dessert and then a wonderful either new or old movie in the most comfortable seats you'll ever find to watch from. All of us look forward to the great open house Patty holds on Boxing Day, as the British call the day after Christmas. Her home is beautifully decorated, and she opens the doors to her and her husband's friends as well as everyone's kids. The place is happy bedlam with children running everywhere and great food served in abundance.

Ray is a great host, too. He recently had a huge party to celebrate completion of his new 10,000-square-foot house, which was featured in *InStyle* magazine. More than his skills at socializing, what always impresses me about Ray is his generosity. Although he is an extremely busy family man with a skyrocketing career, he always finds time to help his friends. I'm very active in a charity called Children Affected With AIDS, and Ray has always agreed to do whatever I've asked of him to help raise money for this cause, whether it's playing in a celebrity golf tournament or performing at a comedy benefit.

The size of my house forces me to limit the Greed Party guest list to forty people, so it's a very tight-knit group. We all remember how each of us behaved at the last party: who cheated who out of what and who walked away with the best gift. There are grudges, vendettas, and plots worthy of a Shakespearean tragedy—all against a tinselly backdrop of holiday cheer. In short, it's like Christmas at your house.

The plan is simple: six weeks before the Christmas holiday, I send out invitations to some of the *Raymond* bunch for a lavish holiday party at my house. The invitation specifies that each guest must bring a wrapped gift. This is no run-of-the-mill office "Secret Santa" party where you might end up taking home a light-up reindeer tie. I won't let anyone into the party until they've surrendered their gift, that the invitation specifies, must cost approximately fifty dollars.

Fifty dollars seems like a pretty high-end present to me. At the first *Raymond* greed party seven years ago, I said the gift had to cost thirty dollars, a price I'd set fifteen years earlier, and that still seemed reasonable to me. In the years since, under intense pressure from the boys—Ray, Brad Garrett, and our executive producer Phil Rosenthal—I was forced to increase the price to fifty dollars, because they swore that you couldn't buy anything worth giving for less than that. Men! They just don't know how to shop.

The reason I dictated how much the gifts should cost is because I wanted them all to be of more or less equal value. I hope the guests take the time to choose something that they might want to have themselves. I send the invitation out early in the holiday season, so that people who are serious shoppers can spend some time considering what they want to contribute to this festivity.

Some of my guests rummage through the antique stores and flea markets for months before the party, and haggle aggressively with shop owners to get the price down to fifty dollars, because most of them want to contribute a highly desirable gift. Others just suck at gift giving. One year I remember someone contributed an industrial-size chafing dish from Costco. What did that person think? In case you had to feed the First Battalion?

The bar off the living room opens at 7 P.M., and the house is decked out with the many Christmas decorations I've collected over the years. After all the guests have arrived and most of them are on to their second drink, I invite them into the dining room for a catered holiday dinner. When they've all been well fed and adequately loosened up by holiday grog, the greed begins.

Once the guests have gathered before the heap of presents in the living room, I pass around a hat filled with numbered slips of paper. In this game, the bigger your number, the better off you are. Number one can pick any present that's there, open it, and it's his or hers. Number two on down can pick any present that's there, or take one away from anyone who went before. Once a gift is taken away from you, you cannot take it back, but you can go under the tree and get another gift. If someone with a higher number likes your present, it's fair game and you'll be forced to select another from the pile.

As each number comes up, the person goes to the center of the room and opens the gift in front of an audience. Murmurs of approval fill the room when someone gets a good one. Shrieks and moans erupt when a gift is snatched away. The more snapping and groaning the wilder the party becomes. The irony is that all of us can easily afford to buy ourselves something that costs fifty dollars. Yet, faced with the prospect of getting stuck with something you don't want when there are other things in the room you *do* want leads instantly to manipulation, pouting, thievery, and duplicity. It's as if in this one party we're all going to get revenge for the dozens of miserable holiday gifts we've been stuck with over the years. There are few things more entertaining than observing a room full of rich people haggle over a $50 gift certificate to the Olive Garden.

The rule is that you have to show your wares, but many people try to get around that rule. People who have received something they'd like to hold on to try to hide it behind their backs hoping that those who get a higher number than that person will forget about the one he or she has concealed. Then there will be others hawking their gifts. "Anybody want this beautiful, convenient, and very soothing foot warmer? What am I bid for foot warmer? How can I get rid of this damn foot warmer?" There is also the internal drama, of deciding to risk what you have and go for something that might be worse. Or am I just doing this to piss off my boss? Do I really want to trade up for the two-CD set of *Charo Live from Honolulu*?

Another hilarious feature of the evening is the giant platter of *schadenfreude,* a German word that means taking pleasure at others misfortunes. The taunting and the heckling are right out of the schoolyard: "Sorry, loser. Might as well box it up and take it home now. No one's coming back for that."

There are also threats. One time I held the Greed Party in New York, and the actress Colleen Dewhurst attended, as did Gary Nardino, who was then the head of Paramount television. Gary had received a lovely cheese board with a beautiful tile inset. As Colleen approached him with a gleam in her eye that warned him she was about to take it away, Gary grabbed the cheese board and twisted his trunk around to keep it as far out of Colleen's reach as he could manage. "If you take this, you'll never work at Paramount again," he said. And he meant it. One year I let someone's children come to the Greed Party. Jimmy Coco managed to grab onto one child's huge Godiva chocolate bar. Jimmy's gluttony in the presence of his favorite food reached across the generations. He grabbed the bar with glee in his eyes and the kid got very upset. "I don't care if you're a kid," Jimmy said. "This is for me."

During the first few years of the *Raymond* edition of this party, most of us were too scared to take away anything from Phil. He is the boss, after all, and holds our jobs and our salary increases in his hands. If he wanted the flying pig cereal bowls I had, I'd give them to him cheerfully. (Or at least I appeared to be cheerful while he was still in the room.) But as we've gotten closer and more secure in our jobs over the last six years, that politeness has fallen away. Anything that Phil has is as acceptable a target as whatever the rest of the cast and crew may have snagged from the pile, if not more so. All power and status is dwarfed by greed.

Last year one of the big items was cordless headphones for television watching. It was such a hot item that two people brought exactly the same gift. Phil got one and right away one of the producers took it from him. Then it went from that producer to one of the writers. Those headphones started bouncing around so much that I lost track. When they reached their final destination, the next person went to open a gift. He'd received exactly the same thing.

This new set of headphones was fair game for all those people who had lost the first one. When that second set had passed around so many times that we'd all lost track, the spouses got involved. Plots were hatched, conspiracies were conceived, and evil pervaded the festivities. Ray cheered when the darn thing were stolen *again* from his boss. The irony of it all? At the conclusion of the evening, *both* sets ended up with a husband and wife, the smug victors of this fierce battle. We all laughed at this couple, who clearly had no desire to talk to each other.

The fun is as much in the performances as the rivalries. Brad's number came up. He rose slowly and paused to survey the room.

When Brad opens his gift, if it's not to his liking the sorrow that drips down the corners of his mouth as he sulks back to his seat is hilarious. He looks like a St. Bernard who lost his bone. If you're hiding a gift and Brad wants it, having that big face coming toward you followed by those big hands coming at your person forces you to surrender without thinking twice.

This is the most painful holiday party I attend every season, because by one in the morning when everyone has finished chasing cheese boards around and accepted that what's in their hands really is their final answer, my sides ache from laughter. And of course it's funny how much the gifts matter when we are all in the room fighting over them, and in the end—when everyone has gone home—how little they matter. The only gift I can remember from the last seven years is that silly industrial-size chafing dish. What I do remember is the evening, the holiday, and the time spent with the cast of the best job I've ever had in television. I savor the party as my gift to my beloved co-workers much more than I ever will another George Foreman Lean-and-Mean Grilling Machine.

If *you're having* a Greed Party, be greedy yourself and hire a caterer. Here's the menu from the last Greed Party we had at my house.

A Selection from
Our Southern Christmas Menu
by John Connelly Catering

Smoked Turkey Salad on Corn Rounds

Calvados Pâté w/ Apple Slices and Hazelnuts

Grilled Shrimp with Remoulade Sauce

Parmesan Cheese Puffs

Honey Glazed Ham

Sweet Potato Casserole

Apple Cranberry Stuffed Patty Pan Squash

Red Beans and Rice

Maple Glazed Carrots

Turnips and Greens

Sautéed Okra

Peach Cobbler

Sweet Potato Pie

Double-Decker Pumpkin Pie

Pecan Pie

Persimmon Pudding w/ Caramel Custard

Chapter 3

Think Pink

Seven years back, just before I got the part of Marie Barone in *Everybody Loves Raymond*, I directed my first play. My good friend Jack Betts had written a play called *Screen Test, Take One*, about the difficulties of a director trying to cast a movie and the complicated lives of the actors involved. There are a lot of plays about backstage in the theater, but I'd never before read one about the world of movie auditions. Jack's was a three-scene play where the same scene was done by three different groups of actors. It was very complicated to pull off. It required twenty-three actors and four hundred and sixty-three lighting cues. It was a huge undertaking for anyone, but particularly for me, a first-time director.

I was a bit fearful when Jack asked me to do it. Over the years I'd spent taking direction, I developed very strong feelings about what made a good director and what made a poor one. Having strong opinions about something doesn't necessarily make you capable of performing up to your own standards when the tables are turned, though. I surprised myself by how good I was at it and how much I loved being in charge. The table turning began right from the first audition.

In my nearly five decades in the theater, I'd been through hundreds of nerve-wracking auditions where I performed before a room full of people whose stony faces never gave me a hint what they were thinking. Was I too much? Too little? Too short? Too blond? You rarely can tell from the professional poker faces of that audience of producers and directors, all of whom are under tremendous pressure to make the right decision. Everybody's a little frightened about making choices, and in the entertainment business there's a lot of money riding on every single decision. Casting the wrong person can throw the whole production off and hand you a failure when you could have had a success.

When I was finally sitting in the casting chair, I saw how the performance was only one part of what had to be considered. Not a single red flag could be ignored. Many times, an actor revealed a lot simply by the way he entered the room. The scowl you bring into the room can make or break your chances of getting the job. Nothing ruins an audition more than getting a traffic ticket on the way there, or being told to zip up your fly. (Or even worse, to zip it down.)

The first meaning my dictionary lists for the word *audition* is "the sense or power of hearing." I listened very carefully to everything the actors did when they came in to read for a part. A *part*, the dictionary says, "is one's proper or expected share in a responsibility," but it's also "one of the melodic lines in a piece of music." I was looking for talent, but I was also looking for harmony.

I asked an actor who I thought had made the wrong choice in reading a line with anger to come in again and try it a different way.

"This is as good as it's going to get," he responded.

That actor didn't get the part. I could see that there was no way he would take direction.

When another actor walked in, I asked him where he was coming from.

"Stage left," he said.

"Yes, and you were very boring," I said. "Where is your character coming from in his life? Is he about to miss a mortgage payment? Did he have sex last night, or did his wife refuse him again? Is his child sick? Where is he coming from?"

Clearly this guy hadn't done his homework. He'd just showed up.

When we were only two weeks away from opening the play, my agent called to tell me I had an appointment to read for the part of a mother in a sitcom. The sitcom was with some comedian named Ray Romano, and would be about his family life on Long Island. I've auditioned for dozens of pilots, most of which go no further than that. After viewing a single episode of the series, the network usually decides that the chemistry of the actors or the quality of the script isn't good enough to justify spending the money to place the program on the broadcast schedule.

Or if it makes the first cut and goes into production, sometimes it only lasts a week or two. I was cast as the friend in a very short-lived Erma Bombeck sitcom called *Maggie.* You'd think with a great comedy writer such as Erma Bombeck at the helm, the show would go on season after season, just like her humorous columns. Erma didn't take the quick defeat too personally, though. She thought it was just the difference between writing for the page and writing for the screen. She sent a telegram to the head of ABC that said: "If I'd realized I only had twenty-four minutes to prove myself, I would have had all of them in bikinis and a lot of car chases." You know you shouldn't put a down payment on a new car if they put your show in the 8:30 Friday night slot. I was in a show called *The Boys* with Chris Meloni and Ned Beatty that earned that unenviable slot. We lasted five weeks, too.

The idea of setting myself up for another one of these didn't appeal to me, because I was so wrapped up in directing *Screen Test, Take One* at that moment. I had convinced a good friend, the Academy-Award-winning set designer, Brian Savegard, who had designed the sets for *Room With A View,* to design our production.

My son Michael, who had worked on *The Bob Newhart Show,* used his connections to get Paramount Studios to lend us cameras and other backstage furnishings so we could create a perfect replica of a soundstage. I'd also hired a first-rate lighting designer I knew from the movies, and my dear friend Buffy Snyder to help with the costumes, which she did brilliantly.

The momentum was going in the right direction and I sensed that it was important for me to stay on top of things to keep it going that way. There were so many details to check and recheck. I was still making choices on lights, sound, songs, entrances and exits, so I knew that I wouldn't have time to properly prepare for an audition. Besides, did they really need me to audition to know if I could do the part? I'd appeared on at least a dozen different television shows, and had often played somebody's mother. Couldn't they just review a few of the hundreds of hours of film of me and decide if I was right for their plot or not?

No, they could not, my agent said. They needed to see my chemistry with this Ray Romano, and my agent wasn't buying any of my excuses. He checked with my producer and cleared me to skip rehearsal the next Monday at 3:30 P.M.

That weekend I read the *Everybody Loves Raymond* pilot script and thought it was awfully funny. The episode centered around Ray and his mother Marie, and their dispute over his birthday present to her. He'd signed her up as a member of the Fruit of the Month Club, a club that delivers a big box of top-quality seasonal fruit to your door every month. Marie had received the first shipment—a huge box of forty-eight pears.

"It came this morning," the script said. "It was a lot of pears."

"Yeah, Ma," Ray said proudly.

"Well, what am I going to do with all those pears?"

"Eat them."

"How can I eat all those pears?"

"Go give them to Robbie."

"He can't eat all those pears."

"Well, give them to your friends."

"They buy their own fruit."

"Well . . ."

"Please, do me a favor. Don't buy me any more fruit, okay? I thank you very much, but don't buy me any more fruit."

"Mom, there's another bunch coming next month."

"What, more pears?"

"No, it's the Fruit of the Month Club."

"A club? Is it some kind of a cult? Oh my god! What are you doing?"

I loved Marie and the genuine quality of her frustration with her son, but I simply didn't have time to go through my normal preparation routine. Usually, I read a script and jot my first reactions to my lines in the margin. Then I read the whole script again and note what the other people say about my character, so that I can understand her context. Then I put the script down and think about her: the world she lives in, where she is coming from when she enters the scene. I never read for a part without having everything going for me. If my character's background isn't written into the script, I write one for her, so all the choices I have to make as an actress come from knowledge. This is a very time-consuming process, but also one that gives me a lot of confidence when I enter a room. This time I barely had a minute to myself before my appointment.

As I was driving over to CBS for the audition, I was not in the best of moods. I had heard that more than a hundred actresses had read for the part of Marie. If that was true, why were they just getting to me now? As I pulled into the parking lot, I mustered all my discipline and experience as an actress to banish resentment from my mind. If the producers got a whiff of that, I might as well not have come at all.

Decades earlier, during a time when I was angry that I wasn't getting the kinds of parts I believed I should, I took a class in singing for actors. At the first class, the teacher, David Craig, told us to stand center stage and sing "Happy Birthday." Then he asked the class to describe what color the singer was emitting. I thought he was off his rocker. It sounded so New Age, as if we were trying to pick up on that undetectable aura psychics talk about. Would we be channeling the voices of dead singers next? It turned out to be a valuable exercise. As my fellow class members took the stage, it was very clear that some people were gray, some were blue. After my solo, the class said I was red.

All my resentment about not getting work was clear, even when I was singing a simple happy song like "Happy Birthday." Who would want to work with me? When you come in red, nothing else of you shows, just the anger. If you come in gray and colorless, you have the opposite effect. You drain the energy from the room. Either one of these colors gives you only half a chance of getting what you want, instead of a full one.

The teacher taught us to *think pink*. Pink is fresh and open. Pink says I'm not coming here to start a war. I'm not going to be a difficult human being. I'm not bringing in my anger from not having gotten a job five months ago. I have trained myself over the years to reflect pink. Before I put my hand on the door of the room where I'm going to read for a part, I think: "I'm coming here to give you the best I've got and I hope you like it. I'm not here to be validated. I validate myself." (And I hope you validate my parking. Otherwise, I get red again.)

As I put my hand on the door to the room where Ray and the producers were waiting, I put aside my preoccupation with the play and my shakiness about the fact I hadn't prepared very well. I tossed away my resentment that I had to read at all, let alone as one of a hundred actresses. None of that would help me do a good job, and none of that was useful to bringing Marie Barone to life. I took a deep breath and thought: Pink!

Despite my lack of preparation, my instincts were right. I could have played Marie as angry and irritated, but I knew that in comedy, anger doesn't work (unless you're Don Rickles, but he never gets asked to play a mom). Frustration *does,* and it did with Marie. Everyone in the room broke up laughing. The next day I did the scene before a group of network executives, who gave us the go-ahead to do the pilot. The day we filmed the pilot, Les Moonves, the head of CBS, came by the set to compliment me.

Fortunately my peers at *Raymond* are some of the most generous and interesting co-workers I've ever had. Of course I knew the work of Peter Boyle—his incredible performances in *Joe* and *Young Frankenstein.* Such distinctly different characters and both so memorable. As we got to know each other, Peter was one surprise after another—an exceedingly intelligent, well-read man and a history buff. We quickly bonded over family, love of New York, and theater. Sometimes it feels like we really have been married for forty-five years.

The other gem awaiting me on the set was Patricia Heaton, who really is the character she plays—a strong-willed woman with a big heart. She, like Debra, balances career, church, children, and family. I was so impressed with that as well as with her comic timing. As the show has become a hit, I've really enjoyed watching Patty evolve from cute to glamorous even as she's produced two more children. It's great to see a woman in her forties getting more beautiful all the time. She's in her prime.

Then there were my boys. It's hard not to think of them as my sons because they work so beautifully as a pair. Brad Garrett, the goofy cutup with the hangdog face of deep sorrow, made the rehearsals so much fun. Out of nowhere he would become Gregory Peck or Bill Cosby. Or even Charles Nelson Reilly. But the person in the center of all of it is Ray. Truthful and genuine, he was and is the fresh-faced, self-deprecating kid who doesn't quite believe all this is happening to him. I've watched him grow as an actor and it's a pleasure working with him.

How could I not want to give them both a hug and make them a sandwich? Phil Rosenthal and his band of writers had found in Ray a way to express something about the true nature of family—and not just the Hallmark-card version. And Phil had found a cast that really felt like a family.

While *Raymond* moved forward to regular production, *Screen Test, Take One* premiered to very appreciative reviews. One of the reviewers said I had directed the play so smoothly that it went down like buttered popcorn on a Saturday afternoon. My son told me he thought I was wasting my time as an actress. I should launch my career as a director.

It was enormously gratifying to accomplish these two milestones in such a short period of time. I love the fact that, now into my seventh decade, I'm still learning. With a lot of fear and insecurity, I threw myself into directing a play. With resentment, substantial doubts, and shaky preparation, I threw myself into the audition for the part of Marie Barone.

A simple truth of life is that, if you are going after the things you want, you're always auditioning. When you put your hand on the doorknob, leave all negative emotions aside and say to yourself: I'm giving you the best I can and I hope you like it. Think pink! If you can manage to do that, you can come into the room as the real you: a person who is open to life and keeps growing and moving forward.

Here are a couple of ideas for what Marie could do with "all those pears."

Poached Pears

1 bottle white dessert wine, such as Riesling or Muscat

½ cup sugar

6 pears, peeled, halved, and cored

6–8 fresh basil leaves

vanilla ice cream

1. In a large saucepan, bring wine and sugar to a boil, stirring until sugar dissolves.
2. Reduce heat to simmer and add pears to pot in one layer. (You may have to do this in batches to accommodate the size of your saucepan.) Cover and let cook until the pears are fork-tender.
3. Remove pears from liquid and let cool.
4. Stack the basil leaves and roll into a cigar. Slice into thin ribbons. Set aside.
5. To serve, place two halves in a dessert bowl. Top with a gluttonous scoop of vanilla ice cream and sprinkle a few ribbons of basil on top.

Serves 6.

Pork Tenderloin with Caramelized Pears and Onions

1¼ pound pork tenderloin, trimmed and cut into 1-inch-thick
    slices
4 tablespoons butter
4 firm pears, peeled, halved, cored, and sliced
1 large yellow onion, halved and sliced
the leaves from 1 sprig thyme or 1 teaspoon dried thyme
salt and pepper

1. Pound pork to ¼-inch thickness between plastic wrap or wax paper.
2. Melt 3 tablespoons butter in a large sauté pan and add pears, onions, and thyme. Salt and pepper to taste. Let cook until pears turn golden and onion is soft.
3. In another pan, melt 1 tablespoon butter and add one layer of pork slices. Salt and pepper pork. Cook pork about 2 minutes per side, or until just cooked through and a nice crust starts to form. (You will have to cook the pork in batches.)
4. Arrange pork on a serving platter and slather the pear-onion mixture over the top.

Serves 6.

Part Two

Motherhood

Chapter 4

Ta-Ta, Mommy

That moment when an infant wobbles unsteadily, but with great determination, to his or her feet, is an event that a mother never forgets. I remember with incredible clarity the frown of concentration on my son Michael's face as he scanned the familiar living room of our brownstone on St. Mark's Place planning his route. He plotted his course carefully, making sure that he was never more than half a step from a solid object, as he launched his first unassisted voyage on uncertain toddler feet. He let go with a fearful look in his eyes, but as he took that first step, his confidence returned. His foot hit the ground solidly, not on the edge or on crumpled toes, and then the other foot repeated the miracle. With each step he took, he got cockier.

Encouraged by my applause, he ventured another step, turning back to make sure I was watching and not far away. As he made his way across the room to the sofa, he tossed back a sweet-but-newly-independent: "Ta-ta, Mommy!" I saluted him back an enthusiastic: "Ta-ta, Michael."

Twisting his torso to deliver his farewell was too much for his balance. Just as he reached the sofa, his feet clenched like fists and he tumbled into the cushions with a terrified look in his eyes. A soft landing, though, is always a triumph in toddlerhood. I gathered him up in my arms and nuzzled my nose in his chest, cooing and baby-talking about what a good boy he was and how proud I was of him. He cooed back, and then kicked in my arms to get free to try it again.

I cherish that memory, yet I hold it with a certain sweet sadness. From that moment on he was forever walking away from me. From that moment on, he said bigger and bigger good-byes.

I had struggled so hard to bear a child, and it was tough for me to imagine that he would ever move away from me. From the first few years of my marriage, I had tried to get pregnant, but we were not blessed with a child. Doctors couldn't offer us much in the way of fertility treatments in the 1950s. They all seemed to say that the solution was to lessen stress, relax, keep at it, and let nature take its course. Nature, on the other hand, seemed to be busy with something more important. As the months piled up with no pregnancy, it became more and more difficult for me to relax.

I should have known that I would have a difficult time getting pregnant. My mother and father had been married for seven years before I came along, seemingly by accident. My mother had resigned herself to the fact that she was incapable of bearing children. When I was finally conceived, my mother and father were traveling the country promoting a prizefighter who was a client of my father's. They had come to visit my Aunt May in St. Louis, when my mother complained of terrible constipation. She went to the doctor for a high colonic. After the procedure offered her only minimal relief, the doctor discovered that what Mom really needed was an obstetrician.

A high colonic five months into the pregnancy might have finished another baby off, but I was tenacious, like a little superhero: stronger than a high colonic and more powerful than a long rubber hose. The pregnancy was precarious, though, and for the health of both mother and baby, the doctors ordered us to stay put. My mother was elated by the sudden pregnancy, but my father was upset at being forced to stay in St. Louis, which to him was as bad as a high colonic. The stress affected my mother's appetite. Just at the point in life when most women are piling on the pounds, my mother started losing weight. If only we could have marketed the Pregnancy Weight Loss Diet! She told me more than once that, when she was carrying me she was so thin that her stockings fell off her legs.

The doctor insisted on bed rest for my mother from the seventh month, and at the first sign of labor she was admitted to the nearest hospital, which was Catholic. The labor was slow. The nuns who tended to my mother believed our chances were so poor that on All Saints Day, a few nights before I was born, they started a novena— nine days of prayers and devotions directed toward a specific out- come—for my mother and me. They prayed for the health of the mother and the baby, because, in the 1930s, with that primitive medical technology, it would have been difficult to save both of us if the birth became complicated. The nuns' prayers were answered— on November 4th Doris May arrived without complications.

I pieced together this story by eavesdropping on my mother's conversations with her sisters, and it produced tremendous guilt in me. I gave my mother an abscess when she was breastfeeding me (I'm sure she thought it was payback for that high colonic). I was a colicky baby, and my crying drove my father out of the house and into the arms of another woman. Within a few months, he left alto- gether, and my mother returned to New York to raise me on her own.

The heavy burden of this sad story seemed a lot to bear at times, but like many tragedies from our youths, it served as a motivation for me. If I ever had a child, I promised myself, I would ensure that the birth was a beautiful event, a day that my husband and I experi- enced together as pure joy, and continued to celebrate for years to come.

The fact that I couldn't get pregnant disturbed this dream. I felt like a failure as a woman, and I worried that my eggs were damaged in some way. All sorts of fears and disappointments crowded my head every time I longed for a child, which made it very difficult to follow the doctor's orders to relax. After all that trying and failing, tears and frustration, I know for certain which night I got pregnant. That night I had the greatest orgasm I ever had in my life. I thought: if something doesn't break loose because of that, honey, it never will.

Well, it did, and I began my perfect pregnancy. I asked my doctor for things that are commonplace today but were considered bizarre in the 1950s. You might say I was ahead of my time. At that time, the standard procedure was to knock out the mom when she went into labor and present her with a clean, swaddled baby when she woke up. During labor and delivery, husbands paced the waiting room of the maternity ward smoking cigarettes, just as they are pictured doing in old movies.

First I shocked them by saying that I didn't want to take drugs. I didn't want to be knocked out. I wanted to see my baby being born. I asked if there was a way that I could manage the pain without medication. The doctors offered me a breathing technique called Lamaze, which was just gaining some popularity in America. I also wanted my husband Michael with me the whole time. Neither the doctor nor my husband were wild about that idea. The doctor agreed that he could attend the birth. But no, he could not have the drugs I had refused.

My pregnancy was surprisingly trouble-free. I stayed trim and worked steadily, hiding my swelling body in bulky outfits and big coats. In fact, I worked on a movie two days before Michael was born, even though I had been suffering labor pains for several days. I would have contradictions five minutes apart, and I'd call the doctor to warn him that he should get ready to meet me at the hospital. Then I'd call him back to inform him that, sadly, the contractions were decreasing in frequency. They'd gone from one every seven minutes to one every nine minutes. This would continue for a while, and then they'd speed up again.

By Sunday night I was fed up. I yelled at the doctor: "This is not false labor, this is a false pregnancy." He told me to hang in there and it would happen when it was supposed to happen, a surprisingly passive attitude for a doctor. I took matters into my own hands. I didn't want advice. I wanted comfort. I wanted pasta!

I marched into the kitchen and made the biggest pot of pasta I've ever made and I ate every single bite. I wrestled the spoon out of my husband's hand when he tried to get even one noodle. I thought it would help me to relax, but I now think it did even more. I believe that the weight of all that food put pressure on Michael. The pasta version of a high colonic is a highly underrated birthing technique. There wasn't any more room in the inn, so the baby had to come out like a bank robber in a foiled heist. "We have you surrounded. Let the water go and come out of that womb with your hands up."

The next morning my water broke and Michael and I grabbed a taxi to the hospital. Far from the loving and tender scene I'd crafted so carefully in my imagination, where my husband held my hand as we worked together to bring our precious baby into the world, *my husband* was overcome with fear. He tried to hang in there, but each time a contraction peaked and I looked up to his face I saw nothing but panic. His anxiety was making *me* anxious. Finally, I suggested he go get himself a cup of coffee. I suspected he was going to Brazil to get it, from the way he dashed out.

Then I was suddenly alone in the room and I was afraid. A sweet and very experienced nurse came in to hold my hand. Her presence really calmed me down, and my contractions began to increase in strength and frequency. Just at the moment when Michael's head was cresting, my husband returned to hold my hand and watch as Michael entered the world. I had asked the nurses to set up a mirror so I could see Michael being born. It's a memory that still overwhelms me today.

The nurses washed the baby off and handed him to me swaddled in a white blanket. I looked up at my husband as I held Michael to my breast, and I said, in the low voice of Yvonne De Carlo in *Dragonwick*, "I bore you a son." *What?* What the hell was *that? Whose voice had I just heard?* With all my years of acting, here I am with one of the most dramatic scenes I'd ever play and my performance sucked. Suddenly, I was acting like a woman possessed. Motherhood will do that to you.

From the moment I brought my son Michael home I was a different woman. I had a new and fierce pride at accomplishing the everyday act of bringing a life into the world. I looked at my body in a new way. It was not just an ornament, an instrument of my pleasure, or a shape that needed to be fed and clothed. It created life.

That unbelievable feeling of power was reinforced by my enhanced senses. My hearing was clearer. I could hear Michael before he started to cry. My vision was different, too. Colors looked sharper. It was as if everything in the world had been masked behind a thin film of fog and my baby's birth had lifted that fog away. When I looked at him, I looked at the totality of him, bathing him with my heart and my emotions. My thoughts were of all the things that I was going to do to make sure that Michael's life was never as hard as mine, or, if it had to be hard, at least it would be in ways different than those I had endured as a child. For starters, I promised never to force-feed him pasta again.

Those first months heightened life beyond the limitations of words. Those of you who have been mothers know what I'm describing. The way I looked at him was an embrace, and I never begrudged him any amount of time or love. Life had always seemed frustratingly slow to me, but suddenly I had infinite patience. Nothing was really happening in the room with me and the baby. But, on the other hand, everything was happening, and I didn't want to miss a minute.

I understood that my husband was jealous of this connection, and he had every right to be. A mother's focus on a new child is so consuming, enormous, and gratifying, that when you finally put him down to bed at night, you just collapse. I know I did. I had given so much all day that there was very little left for my husband.

And then came the day when Michael started to toddle away, barely a year after he filled up my life in ways I never could have imagined. It was a game at first, a test of his independence, as he moved hand over hand around the objects in the living room. Even while he was holding something solid, he made sure that I was in the room. Something solid in his hand and the steady presence of Mom observing him made him understand that what he was doing was right.

Gradually, he became more interested in the world in front of him than the mother he was leaving behind. Of course, I didn't want to hold him back. I couldn't really. It would have been a disservice to him and to me to try to keep us locked in the bliss of that first year. When we celebrated his "Ta-Ta, Mommy," I had no idea we were saying good-bye to that precious year we spent together.

As life evolved and we faced hardships and disagreements, Michael's first year was something I returned to again and again in my mind, a memory of a time when I could be there for him completely, and all his pains and sorrows were solvable. The memory of him walking away contains comfort, too. He was walking away, but he was still looking back to make sure it was all right. Although he hardly ever stumbles now, I still flatter myself that I could catch him if he did, even though he's much more likely to be the one who rescues me. The tables have turned. Michael is my son, but he's also my manager. He's in charge of everything now, but I can still threaten to hold his check back until he cleans his room.

This is the pasta I made the night before I gave birth.

Penne Marinara with Ricotta Cheese

Hint: If, when you check the dish, the pasta
looks as if it's drying out, add more sauce.

2 tablespoons olive oil

1 onion, chopped

3 cloves garlic, minced

handful fresh basil, chopped

salt and pepper to taste

two 28-ounce cans whole tomatoes

½ teaspoon sugar

2 pounds penne pasta

one 16-ounce container ricotta cheese

Parmesan to sprinkle

1. Heat oil in large pot, add onion, garlic, basil, salt and pepper.
2. Cook until onions are translucent.
3. Add tomatoes, stir, and let simmer for half an hour.
4. Add sugar, then mash with potato masher until desired consistency. Let simmer until ready to use.
5. In another pot, bring water to a boil with salt and a dash of olive oil. Undercook pasta by 1–2 minutes less than the suggestion on the box (to al dente).
6. Drain and rinse. Dump pasta into a large baking dish. Ladle sauce and toss until pasta is coated with sauce.
7. Plop generous dollops of ricotta cheese evenly over the pasta, sprinkle with Parmesan and bake at 350 degrees until heated through.

Serves 4–6.

Chapter 5

Break Down the Door

If you love someone, you would do anything for her—even break down a door—or so I believed when I was a little girl. In my early childhood, my mother was a single mom who left me with my grandparents, because she had to focus completely on work during the week. Work was God in that household, a Jewish home where no menorah was visible and the family did not observe any religious holidays. Work meant money, and money meant everything, because the family economy hung by such a slender thread. If any member of the family said he or she had to work, that was a reason no one argued with.

My grandparents' apartment in the South Bronx was crowded with people. My mother was the oldest of seven children and had her own apartment in the same building. Several of my teenage aunts and uncles, who hadn't yet finished high school, were living with my grandparents, too. The only place to put my bed was in the kitchen, a very strange place for a child to watch the life of a household. The only advantage was that I did have first dibs on the leftover matzoh balls.

Most kids wake up with the sounds of the world coming to life. I, on the other hand, heard the crackling sounds of frying smelt, a foul stinker of an East River fish that was my grandfather's daily breakfast. That would put anybody off fish for life. I know it did me.

My first sight was not the flowerbeds out the window, but my wirey, bantam-weight grandfather, who buzzed around the kitchen like a giant gnat. His tinny voice cautioned me not to make a peep or I'd wake the rest of the family. From between the slats of my crib I'd watch my aunts and uncles struggling to wake up as my grandmother cooked breakfast. After the family left, the house was quiet and my grandmother began her chores, including trying to get rid of the smell of smelts, a futile battle fought with lemon juice, Borax, and prayer. A wrecking ball finally got rid of the stench, years after we moved.

My grandmother was a large woman whose sad face reflected a lifetime of hard work and unspoken disappointments. She and my grandfather left Russia to make a better life for themselves, but found the America they dreamed of was out of reach for a family of nine. My grandfather's salary as a furrier didn't stretch very far, and my grandmother's full-time preoccupation was trying to scrape by. That, and my grandfather's infidelities.

My grandfather was an energetic little charmer whose appeal was lost a long time ago on my grandmother, who was weary from her work and wearier still of his philandering. She hadn't completely given up on love, though. She was in love with the movies, and most specifically with Rudolph Valentino, who didn't cheat on her and never smelled like fish. She built a shrine to him in her bedroom—a shrine of pages clipped from the movie magazines and memorabilia from his hits.

I was an accomplice in her fantasies. In fact, the only happy memories I have of my grandmother were when she brought me along to the local movie palace and hand-fed me Hershey Kisses as she sat transfixed by Valentino. (No wonder I think food means love.

My most exotic fantasy is to have Sean Connery feed me candy in the dark.) I witnessed her rapturous affair with her screen idol, an affair that seemed much more romantic and consuming than my grandfather's sleazy doings down at the local bar.

Little did grandmother know that while I may have been her accomplice, I was also my grandfather's beard. My grandfather would tell my grandmother that he was taking Little Doris for a walk around the neighborhood. I wondered if Grandma was suspicious when Grandpa would put on his best suit and trim his nose hair to take me on our "walk." Instead of a stroll around the neighborhood, he'd make a gnat line right for the bar down the street where his flashy mistress awaited.

They'd order me a non-alcoholic drink called a Shandygaff. A traditional Shandygaff is beer and ginger ale. Mine was a "virgin" one, ironically: ginger ale mixed with club soda. As I sipped, I'd watch this strange woman flirt with my grandfather. She'd start off like a coquette, with her head held at a coy angle and a big smile plastered on her face. Gradually, the distance between me and my grandfather increased as the gap between the mistresses and him closed. Her hand would touch his forearm and linger a bit longer than was absolutely necessary, especially for a fishy-smelling old man accompanied by his granddaughter. She'd twist toward him and lean close so he could get a better view of her blouse, which was cut extremely low to match her self-esteem. Even at my young age I knew this was not kosher. This whole walk started out as a treat for me and ended up as a treat for Grandpa. He got the sex and I got the smelts.

I never saw my grandparents fight over his cheating, but I did observe my grandmother's secret form of revenge. She did his laundry on the stove in my bedroom, boiling it in a big pot. When she was doing his long johns, she'd put hot red peppers in the wash water, driving a poker right into the crotch of his underwear. Absolute voodoo. What my poor grandmother didn't realize was that she was actually spicing up his life, because this affair went on for years.

These two adults formed my notion of love, and a pretty pathetic notion it was, too. I never saw my grandparents holding each other or showing any kind of affection, and I certainly didn't get any. I don't remember ever being hugged or invited to snuggle on their laps, and no one ever told me I was a special little girl. As far as I could see, love was either worship or voodoo, there was always a price to pay. Every Friday, which was payday for my mom, she would come into the kitchen and I would see her lay a wad of dollars on the table to pay my room and board. It was obvious that my grandparents weren't taking care of me because they loved me. I knew they were in it for the money.

All this combined made me think my existence was an imposition on the family. I learned very quickly not to cry or speak out. If I did, from somewhere down the darkened hallways of the apartment I'd hear an adult bellow: "Tell that brat to shut up!" Living in the room that everyone passed through on their way out the door was like living in a hallway. I never felt secure there. I believed that if I caused trouble or got too noisy, they might actually toss me out. If I was really unhappy and cried, I cried into a pillow.

When I started school the family decided to experiment with me actually living with my mother. She was making more money, and she'd snagged a man, who was later to become my stepfather. They were able to afford a bigger apartment. It seemed like things were finally looking up for Little Doris. My mother actually hired someone to pick me up after school and stay with me until she arrived home around 6:30.

The woman who tended to me was a dried-up, mean-spirited old woman whose mouth was turned down at the corners in a perpetual scowl. Her name was Miss Sweet, my introduction to irony. In my childhood mind I came up with a different name, but I don't use that kind of language anymore, so let's just call her Miss Sour. Things in the apartment had to be exactly the way she wanted them or I would get a scolding. I was not allowed to bring home friends from school because Miss Sour didn't want the noise or the confusion. Apparently "noise and confusion" was the sound of me being happy. At night, by around six, Miss Sour would put me to bed.

In this apartment, I'd moved from the kitchen to the dining room. (Why food? Why always food? Well, at least I wasn't in the bathroom.) The dining room was separated from the rest of the apartment by French doors covered with sheer curtains. Six o'clock was an absurd time to put a five-year-old child to bed. I didn't have to become a mother to realize that. But Miss Sour would insist, and she would pack me off to bed and close the French doors. Miss Sour liked the peace and quiet of sitting alone with her meanness.

When the front door opened, I could see the form of my mother through the sheer curtains as she greeted Miss Sour. I would sit up, staring hard at those French doors, holding my breath with the hope that my mother would come into my room and pick me up to hug and kiss me.

"How's my little girl?" my mother would ask Miss Sour.

"She's fine, but she's asleep," Miss Sour would say as she collected her things to get on her broom and fly away.

For whatever reason—either my mother was so intimidated by this woman or so exhausted from her day at work—she didn't open the door to greet her little girl. I was too shy and too withdrawn from my years being stifled at my grandparents' apartment to say what I longed to say: "I'm not asleep. Mommy, come and get me."

Children are very cunning, and I was the most cunning of all. I wasn't only shy, I was testing her. If she cared enough, I thought, she'd open the door. I had a terrible knot building in my stomach, but I didn't express anything until the afternoon I locked myself in the bathroom.

At first Miss Sour pleaded with me, then she threatened to call my mother at work. Little did she know this was exactly what I hoped for. In fact, I thought she was taking far too long to act on her threat as there was no way I was going to budge out of that room until my mother came home. I remember the intense satisfaction I felt when I heard her hang up the phone from delivering the news to my mom.

"You're in big trouble now, young lady," she announced. "Your mother is coming home."

I remember very clearly every object in that bathroom, as I had a lot of time to look them over. I put the toilet seat lid down and sat on top of it surveying the cracks and chips in the enamel of our old-fashioned bathtub, the kind with claw feet grasping a ball. I remember the soap in the dish on the bathroom sink, the white towels with their flowered embroidery, and the toothbrushes hanging from the rack on the wall. The tile could have used some new grout, and I thought about recommending that the bathmat go to the laundry. I also had a lot of time to think about my mother.

I pictured my mother sitting on the subway with her little purse in her lap and her jaw clenched. She was most likely rehearsing what she was going to say to me. But I had accomplished my objective. Every single thought she had was about me. This is what all children want, even if they have to do something drastic, such as locking themselves in the bathroom (or going into show business).

Of course, I was also extremely satisfied by the other outcome of this stunt. This spelled big trouble for little Miss Sour. Wasn't she supposed to control me? How could Miss Sour have let me lock myself in the bathroom?

After what seemed like forever, I heard the familiar sound of my mother's key in the door. For several frustrating minutes I could hear my mother trying to find out how this had happened. What was she doing out there? I wanted her to break down the door and come and get me. Then my mother began her pleadings and threats at the bathroom door. I held my ground and kept silent. I had a lot of experience with that from the gnat. Break down the door, furious Little Doris thought, break it down and come and get me.

After an hour, my mother lost patience and called the fire department. Even while we were waiting for the firemen to arrive, she continued begging me to let her in. I heard the clamor of the firemen in their clunky gear entering the apartment. The fireman warned me that he was going to break the door down and told me to stay as far away from it as I could get. I cowered by the window in the corner, watching as his big axe made a gash in the center of the door, and then another cut, and then another, until the center of the door was shredded and he could reach his hand around and unlock the doorknob.

When the fireman ushered me out I was still furious, and so was my mother. We didn't hug, nor did we argue. There was only silence. Silence answered by silence. Although I'd gotten Miss Sour fired, I accomplished nothing with my mom.

Odd how the events of life have a way of repeating themselves across the generations. My grandfather was a philanderer and my mother married one. My mother was a determined single mother and I also became one. And one day, when my son Michael was eight years old, he locked himself in the bathroom and refused to come out.

We'd had an argument, but I can't recall what it was about. Whatever reason Michael locked himself in the bathroom, it was clear his anger at me matched the anger I'd harbored for my mother decades before. Of course, at first I tried all the expected things—the pleading, cajoling, threats, and bribery—but I didn't waste much time on them. I could see myself in that bathroom nearly thirty years earlier, and I knew exactly what Michael wanted me to do.

I'm no superhero, and to be honest with you, only recently have I started going to the gym. I'm singularly unathletic and top out at five feet four inches tall when wearing heels. Yet, as any mother will tell you, during a crisis involving her child, a mother could kick the ass of any superhero. After about only fifteen minutes of pointless pleadings, I took a swift, powerful kick at the weak center of the plywood bathroom door and punctured a hole in it with a single blow. My only mistake was to forget to warn Michael to step back. When I finally opened the door, he was plastered against the wall with a horrified look on his face. He didn't realize I had just joined the mothers' SWAT team. He was getting a hug whether he liked it or not.

The whole episode was as frightening for him as it was for me. Once I got him in my arms, I never reprimanded him. I stroked his hair and we rocked back and forth while I told him how much I loved him. I loved him enough to do what I wanted someone to do for me. I loved him enough to break down that door. To this day, when he goes to the restroom, he often says, "Don't worry, Mom, I'll be right out."

This recipe is quick and comforting—the way I hope my hug felt to Michael after his bathroom vigil.

Leftover Vegetable Soup

The bulk of the ingredients will vary, depending
on what is in your refrigerator that has to go.
The only mandatory ingredients are:

6 cups whatever vegetables you have on hand: celery,
    broccoli, carrots, squash, cauliflower, etc. cut into ½-inch
    pieces
2 medium potatoes of any creed, color, or taste

1 medium onion

2 cloves garlic

1 tablespoon oil

1 tablespoon thyme

salt and pepper

1 bouillon cube for every cup of water used

1. Cut up vegetables and potatoes to a uniform size to ensure even cooking.
2. Place them all in a big pot and cover with enough water so that the vegetables are covered by 1 inch. Cook over a medium flame.
3. Meanwhile, chop onion and garlic coarsely. Heat 1 tablespoon oil in sauté pan and add onion and garlic.
4. Add thyme, salt, and pepper to onion and garlic and sauté until brown. Add to vegetables.
5. Ladle 1 cup of cooking liquid into the same, now-empty sauté pan. Let the bouillon cubes dissolve in the liquid and return to soup.
6. Let the soup simmer for a few minutes to allow the flavors to get to know each other.
7. Puree with a hand mixer, or in batches in a blender.
8. Serve with a splash of lemon juice in bowl—delicious.

Serves 10 as a first course and 8 as a main dish.

Chapter 6

My Miracle Child

When a child is born, parents spend the first few weeks of the baby's life staring in astonishment at the miracle they've created: this tiny, perfect creature that sprang from a single act of love. A person who is tied to you forever, wholly dependent now, but also independent of you, with a destiny all its own. As the child grows, the parents' romanticism fades, but the real miracles are just beginning. Given the pressures and dangers of life, continued survival into adulthood is a miracle, something I think of frequently when I look at my grown son Michael.

Besides the drama of his birth, which took more than twenty-six hours of labor, there was his adolescence. Adolescence, from a parent's point of view, is a dangerous mix of hormonal changes and physical daring. It's a time when children demonstrate a perilous mix of arrogance and incompetence, which constantly places their lives at risk. It's a time when they had better learn how to survive, because otherwise you just might kill them.

During his teenage years, Michael spent a portion of each summer with his crazy pack of cousins at the Jersey shore. The cousins were from his father's side of the family, a family with a strong jock culture of stunts, pranks, and athletic competition. One of the boys' favorite pastimes was waterskiing. They had their own speedboat and several pairs of skis, and an irresponsible crew of teenagers eager to drive the boat as fast as possible. This combination was so terrifying to me that I decided the less I knew about what they were really doing down there, the better off I was.

Michael was the best waterskier of the bunch, the summer of his eighteenth year. He'd bought his own equipment and spent weeks perfecting a particular trick, similar to the kids' game of Crack the Whip. The boat would take an abrupt turn in the water and he would pull the line hard at just the right moment to be whipped around with such force that he would more than double the boat's speed as he moved past it. I was glad I was never there to see him perform this trick, as I think my heart would have stopped, watching him go from skimming the water at a brisk twenty knots, to being snapped forward at forty. My precious baby was not designed to go at warp speed.

Quite literally break-neck speed, as Michael found out that summer. The Fourth of July weekend, 1977, he and some college buddies had spent most of the night before drinking, when Michael's cousins roused him at 6 A.M. for a spin on the waterskis. Hung over, his motor coordination wasn't at its best. He didn't pull on the rope at the crucial moment. When the jolt of the boat taking up the slack hit, his arms were locked down at his sides and he took the full impact on his neck. His head snapped back, compressing his vertebrae into his spine and fracturing his neck in six places.

The first miracle in this story is that he didn't die at that moment. The second miracle is that he isn't paralyzed. His cousins, one of whom had smacked his head against the boat's windshield upon impact, turned around to get Michael, who was lying on his back treading water. The third miracle is that he didn't drown, considering the fact that he had forgotten, in his stupor, to put his lifejacket on. The fourth miracle was that he was able to climb into the boat. But the miracles were just beginning.

Once ashore, Michael walked off the boat and went back to the beach house to lie down. A few hours later he wasn't feeling quite right. His skin was all red, as if he'd just gotten a bad sunburn, and he was going numb at the extremities. Apparently, his brain was asleep, too, because I found out later that, in this tip-top condition, he made the genius decision to ride his motorcycle to the Seaside first-aid station and have the paramedics take a look at him. My choice would have been an ambulance and a spinal cord consultant, but I hadn't been asked. When he tried to put his helmet on his head, his arms went completely numb. At this point, more than an hour after the accident, his father insisted he was going to drive him rather than let him walk.

No one, not even Michael, knew what an extremely vulnerable state he was in. It didn't take long for the paramedics to figure it out, though. They checked his reflexes and asked him to stand by for another round of tests. Michael was belligerent. He'd decided that all he really needed was more painkillers. When you're eighteen, beer and painkillers seem to be the cure for any medical condition: cold, flu, hangnail, backache, paralysis. The staff hadn't explained to Michael the full extent of his injuries, because they feared he wouldn't believe them, since he could still walk. They thought he might decide that they were incompetent and walk out of the first-aid station.

As he waited, three police cars and an ambulance pulled up to the first-aid station and attendants came out on the double with a stretcher. Michael later told me he thought that someone must have gotten mauled in a shark attack, because what else could justify such an extreme response. Was he ever surprised when they headed straight for him and hustled him onto the gurney.

Michael, displaying his true Italian stubbornness, began to argue with them. He wanted his father to drive him to the hospital. The paramedics finally persuaded him that at least, with an ambulance, they wouldn't have to fight through Fourth-of-July traffic. When they finally got him in the ambulance, the driver sped at ninety miles an hour, traveling against traffic on the causeway, and got him to a hospital ten miles away in eight minutes. As they wheeled him in, Michael realized he had no reflexes left. Later, he was told that his blood pressure was dropping fast and they were extremely concerned about the swelling in his spine.

By the time they got him into X-ray, the swelling in his spine was so severe that Michael's brain had stopped communicating with his body. Actually reviewing his behavior that summer, it was clear to me that that communication had ceased months or even years earlier. He could no longer use his arms or legs. The X-ray showed he had a compression fracture between vertebrae four and five and another between five and six. They rushed him into the intensive care unit and put him in cervical traction, the medical equivalent of grounding him.

I was in Los Angeles, filming a Marlo Thomas television remake of *It's a Wonderful Life,* when I got the call from his father that Michael was in the hospital. I am grateful he didn't explain to me just how serious his injury was, as that would have made the excruciating plane trip I took to Newark Airport and the endless taxi ride to the hospital seem even longer. I spent the whole plane ride chanting to myself: "He's going to be okay. He's going to be okay." I wouldn't let a single negative thought enter my head.

Michael later told me he could hear me charging down the hallway, the sound of my high heels tapping a thunderous beat on the linoleum. Then he heard a series of gurneys being shoved aside, wheelchairs flying for the exits, and the sound of concrete meeting cranium, as patients tumbled to the floor. This of course was his fantasy of how I came into the room. Truth is, I don't remember any of that walk. I was powered by the kind of strength that allows mothers to lift a car when their child is trapped underneath. If he'd been inside a mountain, I would have clawed my way through the earth to get to him. Still, nothing could prepare me for the sight of him in the ICU.

He was pale and disheveled, not the brawny weight lifter I'd seen only a few weeks before. Probably some of the intense physical training he'd been doing that summer allowed him to survive this horrible accident. It had to be more than that. As his doctor observed when we met, "When he gets out of that bed, you'd better get on your hands and knees and pray to Whoever it is you pray to, because we've never seen anyone with a break like that who was able to walk."

I stayed at his bedside for four days, hardly able to take my eyes off him, the miracle of his survival always foremost in my mind. I knew he was going to survive, because his spirit was still incredibly strong. His father's family was streaming in and out of the room at all hours, and Michael was never alone. In fact, his cousins were still playing jokes on him. One night, when I had gone to his aunt's for a nap, the cousins pulled aside his covers and his hospital gown exposing him for all the world to see, pressed the nurse call button, and made a hasty retreat.

Michael was a difficult patient, the kind that survives. He swore he would make it to his cousin's wedding on July 21st. He forged the hospital release papers to do so, but he did attend the wedding.

The doctors insisted Michael needed surgery to repair the damaged discs, but once again he refused. Failing to persuade him, they prescribed an intensive course of physical therapy. He stayed in the house in Seaside for the rest of the summer, wearing his halo brace, which is essentially a cage that rests on the shoulders. The brace supported the weight of his head via a halo attached to the top of his skull, so that there would be no pressure on his shattered spine. He spent the summer sleeping through his physical therapy appointments, as if it was summer school, and he could study later.

Whatever he was doing worked well enough that he was back skiing within a year, and up to his old daredevil stunts with no decrease in his range of motion or stamina. He graduated from college, built himself a career in the entertainment industry, married, and fathered three children with no apparent need to have his neck repaired. In 1998, he was skiing in Utah when he took a bad fall. He felt tingling in his fingertips, and after that the numbness wouldn't go away. When he arrived back in Los Angeles, he decided to see a neurologist, who recommended a MRI the next morning.

He was on his way to work after the MRI when the doctor called him and told him to return to his office immediately. Michael was ushered into an examining room to the grim faces of the doctor and the radiologist, who said the phrase Michael would hear over and over again in the next year and a half: "It's a miracle you are walking."

The MRI showed he had again severe spinal trauma. The discs that cushion and separate the vertebrae when healthy are like jelly donuts: a pliable exterior and a jelly-like interior. His donuts looked like squished pieces of noodle. The disc were so compromised, the bone was cutting into the sheath of the spinal cord and starting to impinge on the nerves. Even a minor car accident or a surprise leap on his back by one of his children could turn him into a parapalegic.

Stubborn as always, Michael refused surgery. If he'd survived without it this long, he didn't see why he'd need it now. His wife Jane and I begged him to get a second opinion, a third opinion. He ended up seeing seven doctors, all of whom wanted to schedule him for surgery immediately. His original doctor was still trying to help him, within the limits that Michael would tolerate. He gave him a neck collar and put him on steroids, which made him so full of rage that he was even more irrational on the subject of surgery. I was frantic. Every time he drove up to meet me, my heart was in my throat, imagining what could happen to him if he stopped short to avoid hitting a child who ran out into the street after a ball. During visits to his family, I cringed as he roughhoused with the children. There was no talking to him on this subject, however.

Clearly, someone was watching out for Michael, who seemed incapable of watching out for himself. We were in a pet food store one day when his pager went off. The number on the pager was one he didn't recognize. He called the number back and the person on the other end of the line didn't recognize Michael either. Some technological glitch brought him together with a top UCLA neurologist, Dr. Bruce Dobkin. Michael joked that he might be needing the doctor's services some day, and Dr. Dobkin persuaded Michael to come see him the next week. I consider that one of the most important achievements in medical history: persuading Michael.

Dr. Dobkin took one look at Michael's MRI and expressed incredulity at the by-now-commonplace miracle that Michael could walk. He, too, wanted to schedule surgery, and recommended one of the top surgeons in the world, UCLA colleague Dr. Ulrich Batzdorf, whose specialty was Michael's exact problem. Michael continued to resist, but Dr. Dobkin had an answer for him. It took six months to a year just to get an appointment to see Dr. Batzdorf, who only took referrals from doctors he knew. There was no harm in Dr. Dobkin getting Michael on the list. He could decide a year from now when his turn came.

Miraculously, Michael agreed. He's shown over the years that he only agrees with insane logic and happenstance. Three days later, Dr. Batzdorf himself called Michael and said he was so intrigued by Michael's case that he wanted to schedule an appointment three days hence. I was overcome with the miracles piling up for my boy. He had refused to deal with his problem, and now events bigger than he were creating a momentum that was sweeping him toward a solution. After the initial appointment, Dr. Batzdorf agreed to schedule surgery immediately.

The operation had to go just right for it to succeed. I think of the top of spine as God's country, such a tiny and extremely delicate area, that, if the doctor so much as sneezed at the wrong moment, Michael might never walk again. Dr. Batzdorf had to remove the discs and drill out more space around the spinal cord to give Michael more room there, and then reinforce the discs. He used a sort of Roto-Rooter for the spine. The operation took six excruciating hours, hours Michael's wife Jane, her parents, and I spent pacing the waiting room. I sure could have used the drugs I refused during his labor.

Jane's parent came up to help take care of the kids. Her mother stayed with them, while her father, Jane, and I stood vigil by Michael's bed in those first few days after surgery. I had the day shift. He was terribly drugged up, and supported by an elaborate brace to keep him upright, with pillow wedges at his sides to steady him. With all the swelling in his throat, he couldn't breathe or swallow very well. He was receiving fluid intravenously, and, with a half dozen machines monitoring him, he looked like a fly caught in a spider's web. His mouth and throat were still so dry that he gagged frequently and could barely whisper.

I sat at his bedside hour after hour as he came in and out of consciousness. It seemed my anxiety would never ebb. First it was about him resisting the operation, then the operation itself, and then the recovery. Every time he moved, I sprang to attention. At one point he made some noise and I jumped up to get to him. Unfortunately the heel of my foot had rested on his medication IV, and when I stood up the tubing went taut. The tape snapped and the needle came springing out of his arm. Luckily for me he was still unable to move. I knew instantly he was hurt. His eyes burned with fury at me. I apologized profusely and looked down at his arm with the tape hanging from one side. He raised his other arm and pointed to the door.

"No, you're drugged," I responded, refusing to leave. "You don't really know what you are saying."

His part of the conversation was to repeat his gesture. I wasn't going anywhere. Then he attempted to say the word "out." I knew what he said. I just pretended not to understand.

To this day he will not let me live that one down. Any time he wants to needle *me* he raises his left arm and rubs the area where I ripped the needle out.

I really don't care. No one could have gotten me to leave that room. I was staring at him with the same kind of wonder and amazement young mothers have for their miracle babies. I still looked at him as my little baby. That's the kind of statement mothers make that never fails to annoy their children. He's made a complete recovery, despite trying with all his might not to, and once again he is skiing and running around just like he did years ago.

The great irony is that he now has three of his very own thrill-seeking, daredevil, insubordinate, stubborn, miracle babies of his own. Still he continues to be a miracle to me.

I include my pizza recipe here, because, like Michael, the dough rises, gets punched down, and rises again.

Pizza Dough

3 cups flour

1 teaspoon salt

1 cup warm water

1 packet active dry yeast (2¼ teaspoons)

2 tablespoons olive oil

1. Mix flour and salt in large bowl.
2. Mix warm water and yeast separately, then add. (Make sure the water is warm, as yeast will not activate well in cold water.)
3. Start mixing, then add oil. Mix well until all ingredients are blended.

4. Place on a lightly floured cutting board and knead well.

5. Place in a bowl in a warm place, cover slightly, and allow to rise for one hour.

6. After the hour, separate dough into two balls and allow to double again in separate covered bowls. This second process usually takes about one more hour, depending on the temperature.

7. When risen, stretch the dough to fit the pan.

Yield: 2

Michael's Favorite Pizza*

marinara sauce (see recipe, page 44)

2 cups grated mozzarella cheese

a hot or sweet Italian sausage sliced into ¼-inch rounds

1 cup sliced mushrooms

2 cloves minced garlic

½ teaspoon crushed red pepper

1. Make a batch of marinara sauce from my Penne Marinara (see page 44). Ladle enough sauce over the stretched-out dough and spread the sauce to make a thin layer.

2. Spread 1 cup of cheese to evenly cover the surface of the dough. Spread sausage, mushrooms, garlic, red pepper, and remaining cup of cheese. Use more cheese if you like more, less if you're not so crazy about cheese.

3. Bake in a 500-degree oven for 20–25 minutes.

---

*Pizza toppings can be a very personal thing. Although this is my son's favorite, you probably have your own. You can be as creative as you want to be. I like shrimp and goat cheese. My grandson Andy likes only cheese. Grilled veggies work deliciously . . . make some of my meatballs and slice them . . . see what I mean?

Part Three

Reminiscences

Chapter 7

What's the Worst
That Could Happen?

Every time life has presented me with what I thought sounded like a great opportunity, there's been someone nearby eager to advise me that it wasn't. What they're usually so ready to explain is that whatever I am so enthusiastic about isn't all it's cracked up to be, that there's danger lurking somewhere, and that taking a chance would place me in some kind of risk.

That's what taking a chance *is*, of course. It means taking a risk. It's acknowledging that whatever it is in life that you're aching to change is painful enough for you to risk being knocked on your keester. Maybe taking a chance won't get you something better than you already have, but it might open up a few new possibilities. At the very least, you'll get some fresh problems. As I was trying to claw my way up into the world of New York theater, my mother had a lot of chances to shake my optimism and replace it with her fear.

When I was twenty-one and newly married, I was chosen to be part of a regional theater company that had a six-week season in Ann Arbor, Michigan. I was ecstatic at this chance. Up till then, I'd been getting small parts in television and on the stage and taking a lot of classes, but this finally offered me the opportunity to work in a company of actors. Not only could I learn a tremendous amount about the craft of acting, but I'd be able to focus completely on theater without the distractions of work and family. It was hard work for very little money. To me, so stage-struck and so young, it seemed like the best vacation I could ever imagine. Unfortunately, I needed my mother's permission, because she also happened to be my boss. Imagine working for your mom! I couldn't quit because I'd get grounded.

I described this exciting opportunity to her, and, to look at her face, you would have thought that I was proposing to run away with the circus. My mother was old-fashioned and concerned about me being so far from home. She didn't think I was capable of taking care of myself, especially in an unfamiliar place surrounded by strangers. As if Michigan is stranger than New York! She scowled with worry, but the real feeling I got from that look was that I was insane.

"But you just got married!" she said.

"I've been married for three years," I reminded her.

"Exactly what does your husband have to say about this?"

"He's fine with it. He's happy for me."

She snorted.

"You go all the way to Ann Arbor with a bunch of actors! What if they don't pay you? You'll be stranded there."

"It's a very respectable company in an established theater," I said.

"Where will you live?"

"The theater company gets a discount at a rooming house near the playhouse."

"Rooming house! You're going all the way to Michigan to live in a rooming house? Do you know what kind of people live in rooming houses? The rooms will be full of disgusting old men. Deadbeats who can't hold down a job. Every time you walk down the hallway you'll hear them breathing and moving around behind the doors."

It was as if my mother was describing the latest horror movie: *Doris Doom, Part III—Rooming House Revenge*.

"I'm sure the theater company wouldn't put me in a terrible place. Besides, no matter where they put me, I'm sure I can handle it."

"How will you get there? How will you get back?"

"The company will pay for everything. It's part of the deal."

"Not when they run out of money, it isn't. You can't pay for something when you've got nothing. When the company has no money to meet its bills, you'll be stranded there and you won't be able to get home." My mother was now Nostradamus. She wasn't just predicting my failure, but that of the entire company. Next, the end of civilization.

I snorted back.

"What's the worst that could happen, Mom?"

"All right, go," she huffed. "But don't be surprised when you come running back to me when this all falls apart."

Here was a woman who had spent her whole life running back and forth in the narrow rut she had dug, from her job in Times Square to her apartment in the Bronx. What did she know about anything outside her claustrophobic little world? I rushed out to pack, knowing this was my chance to prove her wrong.

When I first got to Ann Arbor, the theater company put me up in a rooming house filled with men. I was the only woman there. Okay, so my mother was right about that. To go to the bathroom, I had to go down the hallway in the middle of the night with the dimmest light leading the way. This was one of the scariest experiences of my life. As I walked down the hallway, I *could* hear rustling around behind doors. What were they doing in there? Could their ears detect the difference between the footsteps of a woman and those of a man? Was my mother actually directing this film?

On the way back, some of the doors would open just a crack as I passed. This was frightening. Really frightening. By the time I got back to my room I was in a state of panic. I couldn't sleep. The loudest sound of that night came from behind my door. It was the sound of me pushing every moveable object in that room up against my door. I lasted only a few days in that place. By then I was sleep deprived and desperate. I asked some of the other actors where they were staying. They had found a place that was run by a kind elderly lady.

Okay, I reasoned, so my mother was right about one thing. The worst that could happen had already happened. Everything else will be fine.

I knew this job would be tough, but I loved it. I was living the life of the theater. We were doing six plays in six weeks. While we were performing one, we rehearsed the next. We worked from Saturday to Saturday without a break, and all the money we made we spent on food and housing, with whatever was left over reserved for the occasional drink.

I didn't care. You don't go into theater for the money. I was having the time of my life in this company of struggling actors, all in the same situation, all of us trying to prove our mothers wrong. We were an instantaneous family. We shared secrets about the best cheap restaurants, places to get your laundry done, and bars where the drinks were generous and cheap. We spent all day exposing the most vulnerable parts of ourselves in our rehearsals, and our nights laughing and commiserating about the performance. I would have lived in a tent. I would have paid the theater company for this experience.

After a Saturday night performance halfway into the run, a small group of dour people came backstage to address the cast.

"We're sorry to have to announce this, but we're bankrupt," said the president of the theater's board of directors. "We're canceling the rest of the run. We don't have money for the rental on the theater or even enough to pay you."

One of my fellow actors interrupted the president with the most important question.

"Is this going to take long?" he said, looking at his watch. "Because the bars close at one."

When the board of directors slunk off, we stood around dumbstruck backstage, trying to figure out how we were going to get out of town. Saturday was payday, and most of us had only a few cents in our pockets. I thought of that sweet lady who ran the boarding house and how she'd taken me in. I had explained to her that I didn't have enough money to pay her up front, and promised to do so as soon as I got my pay on Saturday. She said she trusted me. I had such an honest face. Little did she know I had my stage makeup on. How could I look her in the eye now? My mind was so frozen, I couldn't imagine how I was going to get out of this. All I could imagine was my mother saying "I told you so."

Some of the other actors hit on a plan similar to a prison escape. When we got back to the boarding house, I slunk past the owner and tiptoed up to my room, which was in the back of the house and far out of the landlady's earshot. Once there, I fashioned a rope ladder out of my blankets and sheets and tied the end of it to the radiator. I waited until two in the morning to make my move. I tossed the "ladder" out the window. Unfortunately it didn't reach all the way to the ground.

It was winter in Ann Arbor, and there was a fifteen-foot high snowdrift up against the side of the house. I tossed my suitcase out and shimmied down the rope, making a six-foot drop into the soft snow without injury. I grabbed my suitcase and scrambled to the sidewalk, waiting for the other escaping actors at the corner.

We hoofed it to the other boarding house, where one of the leading actors was staying, the only guy who had enough money to settle up his bill. We all crashed on the floor of his room. The next day we had to figure out our other problem: how to get home. None of us had enough money for bus fare back to New York. One of the other actors had heard that some of the big auto companies in Detroit had cars they needed to get to New York City. We could apply to drive one home, if we could just find a way to get to Detroit. After we pried the sleep out of our eyes, we assembled on the side of the interstate and hitched our way into Detroit.

We expected that the automobile company would take one look at this disheveled group of tossed-out actors clinging to their battered suitcases and decline to trust us with one of their expensive new cars. The rest of us hung back while the most well-dressed and respectable sounding one among us went off and got a car.

When he came driving up in a gleaming new Ford, honking the horn, the four of us hugged each other just at the sight of him. We pooled our nickels and quarters and bought a box of Hershey bars for the trip. With all the solemn precision of contestants on *Survivor*, we carefully rationed out an equal number of bars for each passengers. Three days of Hershey bars in a car full of down-on-their luck actors scamming their way back to New York after being tossed out of Ann Arbor. The side benefit of this disaster was that it put me off sweets for a month. If only it had been for life.

When I got back to New York I didn't tell my mother any of it. Hadn't she admonished me not to come running to her when things fell apart, as they were sure to do? That's what I said to myself then, but I also knew I didn't want to give her the satisfaction of being right. Nor did I want to have to endure weeks (probably years) of her reminding me how right she had been, every time I wanted to take a chance.

I knew she would never appreciate how great it felt to survive that embarrassing episode at the rooming house. How we laughed at our gumption and our pratfalls that night, as we fell asleep on our friend's floor. She wouldn't approve of the poses we struck on the roadside, attempting to encourage drivers to give us a lift to Detroit, or the songs we sang in the car to entertain us on the long ride. The only part I knew she would have understood is the exhilaration and relief I felt when we first glimpsed the skyline of New York, as we approached from New Jersey on our last leg home. It was the worst that could happen, and it wasn't all that bad. And I learned to make a ladder out of sheets!

In honor of the Hershey bars we ate on our trip home, here's a more elegant way to consume your chocolate calories.

Fallen Chocolate Cake

8 tablespoons unsalted butter, and more for ramekins

8 ounces semisweet chocolate, coarsely chopped

4 large eggs + 1 egg yolk

1 teaspoon vanilla

¼ teaspoon salt

½ cup sugar

2 tablespoons flour + more to dust the ramekins

whipped cream for serving (optional)

1. Adjust oven rack to center position and heat to 400 degrees. Generously butter and flour eight ramekins and place on a shallow jelly roll pan or baking sheet.
2. Heat chocolate in a microwave at 50-percent power for 2 minutes. Take out, stir and add butter. Microwave at 50 percent for another 2 minutes, stirring after 1 minute.
3. Beat eggs, yolk, vanilla, salt, and sugar in a standing mixer until volume triples and mixture is smooth and thick (about five minutes). If using a hand mixer, beat for 10 minutes.
4. Scrape mixture over melted chocolate and sprinkle flour over mixture. Gently fold until mixture is uniform in color.

5. Ladle or pour batter into ramekins. Cover lightly with plastic wrap, and refrigerate for 8 hours. Return to room temperature for a half hour before baking.

6. Bake until cakes have puffed above rims of ramekins, have a thin crust on top, and jiggle slightly in the center when shaken gently (12–13 minutes).

7. Run a paring knife around the inside edges and unmold onto serving plates. Cool for 1 minute. Serve confectioners sugar or cocoa powder over cakes to decorate. If you are feeling lazy or are pressed for time, just serve it in the ramekins you cooked it in and dust it with confectioners sugar.

Serves 8.

Chapter 8

I Owe It All to My Fans

Everybody wants to be appreciated for what they do. If you're a mother and you make a fantastic dinner for your family, you wish that they'd compliment you before bolting from the table and rushing off to the Internet, or the television, or the telephone. If you're the provider for the family, many times your efforts go unacknowledged, too. Rare is the day when the other members of the household spontaneously cheer your daily slog to the job that keeps the whole home operation going. You'd probably faint into a chair if one of your children took you aside and said: "Thank you for creating such a safe and secure environment for me to grow up in." You'd assume that the next thing out of her mouth would be: "And by the way, can I have twenty bucks?"

Each week I enter millions of people's homes, and as a result I get a lot of reinforcement. Not all of it comes across as all that positive, of course. Partly because of who I am, and partly because of the characters I've played, people are not in awe of me. They don't stand back when they see me and whisper to their friends behind a cupped hand the way fans probably do if they see Lauren Bacall or Johnny Carson. Nor do they try to act nonchalant, as if the sophisticated way to respond to the presence of a celebrity is to pretend that they themselves are celebrities and they're way too cool to get excited in the presence of one. I am everybody's mother, neighbor, and best friend.

This lack of separation is mostly fine with me. I don't travel with bodyguards, like Jennifer Aniston or Tom Cruise. I love it when I look up and see a fan coming toward me. They always greet me with looks of unconflicted joy on their faces, as if seeing me was pure delight. I should get such treatment from everyone in my life!

Of course, after that smile, sometimes things go downhill pretty quickly. Everybody, it seems, wants to give me a hug. And while I like hugs, I don't necessarily want to hug *everybody*. And there are days when I don't want to hug *anybody,* even George Clooney. These are days I should know not to walk out of the house, because surely those are the days when everyone who passes me by will give me one. People want to have their pictures taken with me to prove to their friends that they saw me. They get as close to me as possible. They usually are satisfied only if we go cheek to cheek with a nice hard squeeze to the rib cage to remember them by. This has not been too terrific for my osteoporosis.

Everyone should have such complaints, right? I love the fact that I make people laugh and that they see traits of their own mothers in me. I'm willing to endure the roughest cheeks and the most clumsy embraces, as long as I'm sure that the people who are hugging me know that it's actually Doris Roberts they have their arms locked around.

Recently, when I was presenting an award at the Tony's, New York theater's equivalent of the Oscars, a young reporter asked me if she could interview me for the radio. She asked me why it was that I liked the songs of Stephen Sondheim so much. Although I do love Sondheim, I thought it was a pretty strange question for a non-singing sitcom star. I asked her who she thought I was. When the reporter said "Barbara Cook" I was shocked. This reporter had no clue who I was.

Sometimes I get an insult embedded in the compliment from a fan. That same night at the Tony's, a man came up to compliment me about my work. "So you're pretty much fully retired now, right?" he said. Is it my job to educate him who I am? I didn't have the patience, so I just smiled and moved on. I'm glad there is another star this fan admires, and I accepted the compliment on her behalf.

A few years ago a woman came up to me when I was walking down Sunset Boulevard and asked: "Did we play bridge last Thursday?"

"No, we didn't," I assured her.

"Are you a friend of Thelma's?" she continued.

"No," I said.

"I *know* I know you," she said, looking at me very carefully.

"You know me because I'm an actress you see on television," I tried to explain.

"No, no, no, no, no," she insisted.

"No, no, no, no? Then I don't know who the hell I am," I said, and walked away.

When people recognize me as me it's not always the greatest either. One woman recognized me at Century City, a shopping center near my home in Los Angeles, and asked for my autograph while I was rushing past. I told her I had to go to the bathroom and she said that was okay with her. She trailed me into the bathroom and stood outside my stall to make sure she snagged me after I'd done my business. I've heard of celebrity stalkers, but never of celebrity bathroom stalking.

A few months back at that same mall a woman came dashing over with a welcoming smile on her face.

"You're Doris Roberts, aren't you?"

"Yes I am," I said, returning her beautiful smile.

She turned away from me toward a group of other middle-aged women who were standing thirty feet away looking over at us expectantly. She pointed at me with a big swoop of her arm and shook her head up and down to indicate "Yes!" Her friends nodded their heads yes, too, all smiles.

"I knew it was you! I told them, but they didn't believe me," she said as she handed me a pen and a scrap of paper to get my autograph. "They said it couldn't be you. When the stars go out, they dress up."

Okay, so I'm not Joan Crawford sweeping down the staircase in a chiffon gown and matching turban. But I didn't look *that* bad.

When I worked on the television show *Angie* with my friend Donna Pescow, I played—no surprises here—a mother named Marie. My daughter had married a very rich doctor, but we were from the wrong side of the tracks. His rich and snooty family looked down on ours, and most specifically on me. There was a lot of fish-out-of-water humor generated by this conflict. After one particular show aired, I got a letter from a young woman who was a new fan of the show.

"I hope this letter finds you, because it is important that you know what's happened to me," she wrote. She had found out that she had multiple sclerosis and had fallen into a deep depression. She shut herself off from the world in her bedroom with the blinds drawn. "I didn't want to talk to anybody or to be with anyone. I would eat alone and watch television. One night, I was watching you in a show called *Angie* and you were going to Atlantic City to gamble. I was watching you on that show and I started laughing. I heard my own voice laughing and I thought: 'What am I doing in this dark room by myself?' I came out of that room and I went back to school. I want you to know that you've changed my life."

I wrote her back that I wanted her to keep in touch with me. Her letter touched me greatly. I wrote her, saying I was so excited that she had gotten back into life and that I could play a part in that. Two years later she sent me a picture of herself in a cap and gown. She had returned to college and graduated magna cum laude.

More recently, I met a woman who wanted my autograph. She was very modest and asked me to excuse her for interrupting me, but my signature would mean a lot to her mother. After a long illness, her mother was dying in the hospital. "Monday night, when *Everybody Loves Raymond* is on, is the night she waits for all week," the woman said. "She waits to see you, because you always make her laugh."

As an artist, your job is to give voice and form to the emotions that all of us experience. You hope that by honing your craft you will be able to touch people in a way that soothes them, connects them to the human spirit, and alleviates some of the loneliness of everyday life. If you are good at what you do, you can make them feel more deeply than they allow themselves to feel. Or you can show them that some of the stuff we all take take so seriously is actually pretty funny, if you look at it another way.

The act of touching strangers so intimately is awesome, but I know I don't inspire awe. I'm happy that people feel so comfortable with me because, it's exactly the way I've always wanted to do my job: with humanity, the intimacy of the theater, and the reach of television. Helping distract someone from the pain of an isolating illness, or just a rotten day, is worth more than any paycheck to me. I love to hear all of you laugh.

I made this recipe on *Everybody Loves Raymond* and received a flood of requests for it.

Steak a la Pizzaoli

2 pounds boneless sirloin steaks about 2 inches thick

1 large can whole tomatoes

3 large cloves garlic, chopped

salt and pepper to taste

1 tablespoon oregano

2 tablespoons olive oil

1. Preheat oven to 350 degrees.
2. Trim the fat from the steaks and cut into ½-inch strips.
3. Place steak strips into a medium-size baking dish. Pour tomatoes over the meat. Add garlic, salt, pepper, and oregano. Stir.
4. Drizzle olive oil over the top, cover with foil, and bake for 1 hour. Uncover, stir, re-cover, and bake for another hour.
5. Serve over your favorite pasta.

Serves 4.

Chapter 9

Entrances and Exits

When my late husband, William Goyen, and I argued, one thing that exaggerated our disputes was our shared flair for the dramatic. He used to say that my entrances were great, but I made lousy exits.

This was quite a bruising criticism for a respected actress such as myself to hear, but it was true. When we were arguing, I'd just stalk out when I'd had enough or if I couldn't think of anything stinging to rebut him, unlike the women I played on stage, who had the benefit of professionals to write their lines. In memory of his astute observation, I'm going to share with you some of my low moments on the stage, those terrible faux pas and technical glitches that have stayed in my mind long after the curtain has gone down.

Nightmares Come True

Every actress I know has a recurring stage nightmare. Mine has two parts: First I can't find the door to get on to the stage. Then, once I get on, I'm doing my scene and the first ten rows of the audience stand up, wave their hands in disgust, and walk out.

"Please, please, wait! Let me do it again. I can do better. I can do better!" I plead with them.

One night, I was on stage in *The Last of the Red Hot Lovers* when my nightmare came true. I noticed the first ten rows of the audience were up on its feet and some of them were heading for the exits.

Oh my God, I thought. *I can't be that bad.*

My eyes followed the gaze of the audience. Across stage right from me was the biggest rat I'd ever seen, and he wasn't one of the cast.

I eyed the rat. The rat eyed me. With great stage decorum I blurted out: "Holy shit! It's a rat!"

The laughter rolled up from the audience, but the stage crew was wide-eyed. In fact, the stage manager was standing on his stool, frozen in panic. The rat wasn't frozen, he was terrified. I'm not sure if the audience's laughter or my scream scared him, but he exited stage left. We composed ourselves and continued with the play. When I came out for my curtain call, I don't believe the warm applause from the audience was for my performance as much as it was for my steely bravura at sharing a stage with a rat.

The Eyes of Kong

The audience shows its restlessness when a poor piece of theater is on the stage, but the actors are expected to cover theirs.

I was in a play in Boston called *The Secret Affairs of Mildred Wilde*, not one of the best plays I've ever done. It was constantly being re-written as we worked on it. Maureen Stapleton played Mildred, a woman who ran a little candy shop and lived in a small apartment behind it with her pet canary, Miss Pickford.

Mildred's life was very drab, and she filled her days with fantasies about movie stars who came to life around her in the shop. At the end of the first act, when Mildred was imagining herself as Fay Wray in *King Kong*, the huge hand of King Kong came out onstage and took Mildred off. As the play ended, the enormous head of King Kong loomed up over the rear of the stage with his big eyes staring.

We had been told by the producers that we were closing that night. But as we gathered for the curtain call, I heard the prop master talking to one of the other members of the stage crew.

"Don't take the eyes out of King Kong," he said.

"What does that mean?" I asked.

"We're not closing tonight, kid." he said.

So, as the relieved cast was taking its final curtain call in a state of euphoria, I grabbed the hand of fellow cast member Elizabeth Wilson on one side and that of Maureen Stapleton on the other and delivered the bad news in as odd a sentence as I've ever spoken.

"Don't get your hopes up," I said in a stage whisper over the applause. "They're not taking the eyes out of King Kong."

The next day, we found that Billy McIntire, the actor who had played the manifestation of Miss Pickford in a big yellow canary suit, had a substantially rewritten part. In the first version, he died in the first act, never to be seen again. In the new version, he miraculously came back to life in the second act, despite his wishes.

When the play came down that night, we went out to celebrate at a little honky-tonk bar. We kept giving Billy grog, and Billy was not much of a drinker. He got quite drunk, and it looked like he wasn't going to be able to make it back to his hotel under his own power. He wasn't staying at the hotel I was staying at, but instead at some really seedy hotel on the fringes of the neighborhood. I got him up to his room, took off his shoes, and opened the belt of his pants to allow him to sleep more comfortably.

"I don't know how to help you, honey, but when you wake up in the morning, you're not going to feel too good," I said and left for the elevator.

When the elevator door closed, I got a look at myself in the reflection of the faceplate that covered the floor buttons. I had all my stage makeup on and double-mink false eyelashes. The elevator went down one floor, and when the door opened there stood two Marines, one of them in his underwear, with a clenched fist raised up near his face. He took one look at me and started cursing me out. In his drunken state, he thought I was the hooker who had just robbed him.

He was in my face, swearing at me and threatening me. I don't know what told me to do this, but I remembered how as a little girl, if I didn't want to be someplace I'd hold my breath and make believe I'd disappeared. And that's exactly what I did. I held my breath and looked straight up. I wouldn't make eye contact with this guy. To this day, I think that if I had looked at him and said: "I'm not who you think I am," or opened my mouth to say any other thing, I would have gotten his fist right in my face. But I didn't. I just held my breath and stared at the ceiling of the elevator.

The next thing I knew, the doors opened. We reached the ground floor where there was a policeman who seemed very interested in my companion's choice of wardrobe. I've never let out my breath faster. I hightailed it back to the bar grateful nobody was following me to get their money back!

Get A Room

That wasn't the only time I was mistaken for a hooker. After all, if you leave the theater without taking the time to remove your face paint, people can be forgiven for misidentifying your job.

One night, when I got off work from *Bad Habits*, I had arranged to meet some friends at the theater hangout, Joe Allen's. I rushed out of the theater in full makeup and headed up Eighth Avenue, which at that time was a lot more seedy than it is these days. As I strode up the avenue, I was approached by a man.

"Twenty, fifty," he said.

I thought for a moment, trying to figure out which direction he should go to get to that address.

"I think if you head that way you'll find what you're looking for," I suggested. He just scowled. I'd never seen anybody so rude after getting directions from a total stranger.

When I got to Joe Allen's, I told the bartender about this conversation and asked him if 2050 Eighth Avenue was in fact farther away than I thought.

"Doris, that guy wasn't asking for directions," the amused bartender explained. "He was saying he'd pay twenty dollars for the room and fifty dollars for you."

Pigs-in-a-Blanket

Jealousy often figures in theater stories. And never more so with me than when I was in the play *Cheaters* by Michael Jacobs. My character was supposed to sit at the side of the stage during a big monologue of one of the stars and eat those little pigs-in-a-blanket from a tray every time she got nervous. One of the actresses was furious with me because I was getting a lot of laughs. Finally she could stand it no longer. She strode across the stage, grabbed the silver tray out of my hand, and flung it across the stage between Jack Weston and Lou Jacobi, missing both of them by maybe half an inch.

What she didn't know is that I had one more pig-in-a-blanket tucked in the palm of my hand.

I waited for the tray to fall and make that big clattering sound. Then I waited a few more beats for the impact of this violent gesture to resonate across the stage. After the long pause had played out and the silence expanded, I opened up my palm and deliberately ate my last pig-in-a-blanket. I showed her. With that one perfectly timed bit of business, I got the biggest laugh of the night.

She could have really hurt Jack and Lou with that childish stunt. As we were taking the curtain call, faces all smiles and hands intertwined, I whispered to her: "I'm bringing you up on charges."

When the curtain came down, I stormed off the stage to my

dressing room. A few minutes later, I heard her in the hallway pleading with me not to file charges against her with the union. The voice
sounded too far off, however. I opened my door and saw her on her
hands and knees in front of Lou's door. It was too delicious. I shut
the door and waited. Finally she realized she was begging at the
wrong door and crawled over on her knees to mine.

I let that be her punishment.

Yes, But It's a _Tasteful_ Nude Scene

A lot of actresses have problems with nude scenes. Many contracts
even specify that the actress will under no circumstances perform
without her clothes on. Others will negotiate, as long as they consider the context to justify it, and that the cinematography is taste-
ful—although in the end the actress doesn't have much control over
how the footage is used. My only problem with nude scenes is that
I've never been asked to do one. And at this point in my career, it
looks as though I won't get any invitations.

My friend Jimmy Coco was in a film called *Bye-Bye Monkey*, an
odd movie by an Italian director, that, despite the unusual script,
managed to attract a great cast, including Marcello Mastroianni.
One of the cast members was a young woman who had been asked to
play a nude scene. She objected to this so strongly that they had to
close down production for a few days while they sorted it out.
Finally, they talked the actress into it, and when I saw the film at the
screening I thought it had been handled in great taste.

After the screening, Jimmy, Elaine May, Bobby Drivas, and I
went out to dinner with the promise of a special screening of another
movie at Jimmy's house after the meal. Elaine was very rigid about
her diet. She insisted that her fish be cooked without salt. There
could be no salt in the spices, no salt on the grill, and no salt on the
plate. This was extremely important, she said, because salt was very
dangerous for her.

The waiter scurried to the kitchen, like a man on a mission to convey these very strict instructions to the cook. I could hear him out there repeating, word for word, that Elaine May must have no salt of any kind anywhere near her entrée.

I'd never heard Elaine be so restricted in her diet, so I was a bit concerned. I turned to her and asked what it was that salt did to her.

"Oh," she said. "It makes me puffy."

After the meal, we adjourned to Jimmy's, where he put on a porn film called *Seven Into Snowy*. What was he up to? I was a little uncomfortable sitting with three friends watching these sex scenes, but I could see from the mischievous smile on Jimmy's face that he had a plot underway. Elaine didn't appear to be uncomfortable at all, on the other hand. She was examining the film from the point of view of a director. "Why do you think they shot the scene from that angle?" she'd ask. A few minutes in, Jimmy squealed with delight when the shoe finally dropped and the real star of this little blue movie came on screen: yup, the girl who battled so hard over the nude scene in *Bye-Bye Monkey*.

Hard Day at The Office

I was honored to be cast in *The Office*, a play by Marie Irene Fornes directed by Broadway legend Jerome Robbins and starring Elaine May, Jack Weston, Tony LoBianco, Ruth White, and me. What I didn't realize was that Robbins was first and foremost a choreographer and he gave his cast a dancer's workout on the stage. He had me doing things that were so frightening, I don't know how I survived.

My character was an ultra-efficient office assistant whose only life was her job. I chose to wear my shoes on the wrong feet, which gave me the walk of a waddling duck. As the curtain rose on the first act, I waddle to my seat on an office chair with wheels at my desk down front stage left. My foot rested on a board built into the footwell. With a solid thrust on that board, I pushed myself all the way upstage to a filing cabinet. I opened the cabinet with my right hand and with my left hand took out a file. Then I thrust down stage right to another desk to stamp the file. Once stamped, I pushed clear across the stage back to my original position. This feat would be difficult enough on a level surface. Robbins chose to illustrate the main point of the play—corporate culture coming down on us all—by placing the stage on a hydraulic press. As the action evolved on stage, the office rose up before the audience. If I misfired on my thrust to the desk, I could end up twelve feet below in the orchestra pit.

When the curtain came down the audience booed. The curtain rose to reveal the actors and that audience booed even louder. Elaine May kept smiling and started to applaud, calling out: "Author! Author!"

I had braved hail and humiliation for my Broadway debut, a paltry three lines in William Saroyan's *The Time of Your Life* but three lines that were mine and mine alone. The cast was impressive with Franchot Tone, John Carradine, Myron McCormack, Harold Lang, and a very young Gloria Vanderbilt. Gloria was a big celebrity, a rich debutante who was willing to try anything, including acting. Her evenings out were chronicled in the gossip columns and we all knew her sequence of boyfriends. I used to say I knew almost as much about her love life as she did. Through working on this play I grew to know exactly as much as she did.

The dressing rooms at the City Center Theater were built one on top of the other in the tier. We of the smallest parts got the most inconvenient ones up at the top. I shared my dressing room with some of the other minor characters and Gloria was directly below us in a dressing room she shared with Carol Grace. We discovered that if we were extremely quiet we could eavesdrop on Gloria and Carol while we were putting our makeup on and we got an earful of romance and carryings-on that was quite delightful to us.

My scene was with Gloria. I was a town prostitute in the background of a scene when Gloria entered. When she exited I had the last line: "It's floozies like her that raise hell with our racket." The line got a tumultuous response from the audience—whistling and stomping—because of Gloria's notoriety.

At the opening night party, William Saroyan sought me out through the crowd. I was expecting great praise from him. Instead of that, he told me he was going to cut that line. I instantly grabbed the lapels of his jacket. "Please, please, don't cut that line," I pleaded. "Do you know what it has taken for me to get those lines?" He didn't cut them. But for a moment there I thought a third of my debut was disappearing.

Remaining in Character, No Matter What

Actresses have to work to give off the idea that they are big in stature. It's important to make a strong appearance. When I was cast in the part of a gypsy in a summer stock production *of The Skin of Our Teeth,* I wanted to really inhabit my role. I wore great strands of beads and my first putty nose. Looking back, I realize my performance was rather histrionic. Lot of hand motions! Oh, the deluge! During one of those scenery-chewing moments, I tossed the strands of beads around my neck and one of them fell across my nose. I shook my head and it was still on my nose, lodged deep in the putty, which was rapidly softening under the hot lights. I struggled to remove the beads and in the process, part of my nose came off. Yet I had to remain in character. I completed the scene, all the while maintaining the grand illusion that I was a mystical creature, even though my nose had just fallen off.

Here's a gourmet (aka fancy schmancy) version of those delicious Pigs in-a-Blanket.

Sausage in Puff Pastry with Honey-Mustard Dipping Sauce

6 andouille sausages, or your favorite Italian hot or sweet
   sausage

1 sheet puff pastry (available frozen in the grocery store)

1 cup whole-grain mustard

⅔ cup honey

1 shallot, minced

¼ cup chopped chives

salt and pepper to taste

½ cup vegetable oil

1. Arrange sausages on a cookie sheet and place into an oven
   that has been preheated to 350 degrees. Roast the sausages
   for about 20 minutes.
2. Remove from oven and let cool to room temperature. Slice
   sausages on a bias about ½ inch thick.
3. Roll out puff pastry and slice into lengths that will contain
   the sausage slices. Wrap sausage slice in puffed pastry and
   arrange on a cookie sheet. Bake until the pastry turns golden
   brown.
4. While the puffs are baking, combine mustard, honey, shallots, chives, salt and pepper in a bowl, whisk to blend; then
   drizzle in the oil, whisking constantly.
5. Arrange puffs onto a serving platter and offer the vinaigrette
   to dip on the side.

Makes 36 puffs.

———⌇———

Chapter 10

Uncle Willy

I think people who triumph over a tragic childhood survive because they found one adult who believed in them. While everyone else may be too self-absorbed or distracted to pay a child the kind of attention he or she deserves, an uncle, a grandmother, or a teacher can give that young person praise and a sense that they have something to contribute. The smallest kindness can have a miraculous effect: a kind word from a neighbor, praise from a coach, or from a librarian who steers the child to a series of interesting books. In my case, the believer was my Uncle Willy, the grown-up who taught me humor and gave me unconditional love.

I now think that part of the reason Willy and I became so close is that we were both discarded by the family. In my case, it seemed as though my arrival on earth was an imposition to a bunch of people who had other things they'd rather be doing than tending to a child. In Willy's case it was because he was deformed.

Uncle Willy had been born dead and brought back to life by the midwife who happened to be playwright Moss Hunt's mother. He had severe muscular atrophy. While he grew to a full six feet tall, he had a lot of problems with his left side. He didn't walk until he was nine and even then he walked with a limp. There were no special needs classes then, so he was unable to go to school. No one in my mother's family could afford to send him to a special school for the handicapped, so he just stayed home quite literally underfoot for the first part of his life.

I was born on his twentieth birthday, and from the moment I arrived in the house I was his pet. He was one of the most handsome men I've ever met. His hair was jet black and his eyes were china blue, with the irises rimmed in black. His inner beauty was far greater, however. He was one of the least bitter and most generous people in the world. He cared about my dreams, kept my confidences, and attended to my moods.

I kept myself company writing my own plays, and it didn't take much to get me started. When we studied the primitive tribes of Mexico and South America in elementary school, I wrote an opera from the viewpoint of an Inca warrior. My teacher appreciated my vivid imagination, and my first play (with songs and lyrics no less) was featured at a school assembly. We had a semester studying the religions of the world, and I became a young Jewish girl obsessed with Jesus. On my way home from school, I'd stop off at the local Catholic church and spend an hour in that sanctuary staring at the stations of the cross as depicted in the stained-glass windows. I didn't have a clue about the tradition of the stations of the cross. I'd look at the scenes of Christ's agony depicted frescos on the chunda walls, and I felt profound sympathy. I'd whisper that I hoped he felt better now, and told him to let me know if there was anything I could do. I could never share these experiences with anyone but Uncle Willy. I knew everyone else would make fun of me or ignore me.

My mother had recently bought the public stenography business she'd always worked for from her bosses, and we moved to an apartment in a working-class neighborhood on Eleventh Street between Second and Third Avenues. Even though my mother got a two-bedroom apartment, there still wasn't a bedroom for me. As always, my space was public space. The master bedroom was for her and my stepfather, and the second bedroom was for Uncle Willy. Even though I was a growing girl, eight years of age, my bed was the sofa in the living room. Hey, who's complaining? It was better than the kitchen or the dining room, and at least it wasn't the hallway.

Uncle Willy loved taking care of me. He would walk me to school in the morning—which I loved—and he'd also be there to pick me up. He made my breakfast, packed my lunch, and fed me dinner. In the morning, he spooned the cream off the top of the milk bottle into my glass. He also tended to me when I was sick. His left hand didn't get very good circulation. He'd place that hand across my head like a chilled towel when I had a fever.

When I had nightmares, I'd go to my mother's room for comfort, but she'd pretty much always tell me to get back to bed because she had to work in the morning. Uncle Willy, whose nickname for me was Bozo, would hear me making my way back to the couch. He'd call out: "Hey Bozo, come here. There's room at the foot of my bed." Those nights sprawled across the foot of Uncle Willy's bed gave me some of the most peaceful sleep I had as a child.

When I became old enough to walk home from school on my own, I had the children of Eleventh Street between Second and Third Avenues as my caretakers. This was the late 1930s, a time before daycare centers and structured after-school programs. Each day following school, a great gang of kids roamed the streets—and I mean gang in the best sense of the word. Sort of like Alfalfa, Spanky, and their pals. We were not a society of young criminals, but a group of kids mixed in ages, with the older kids proud of the fact that the little ones were their responsibility. When the weather was warm, we'd play endless games of ball, or we acted out elaborate fantasies. In the winter when it snowed, we'd build great big (to us) igloos, and spend hours pretending we were Eskimos huddling down to survive the winter. Yes, it did snow that much in New York before global warming.

Being part of this group of kids of every nationality—Russian, Irish, Polish, German and Italian—was the closest I came, as a child, to feeling I was safe, and part of that feeling was Uncle Willy. As I played on the street, he watched from the window. If any of the boys got too rough with me, Uncle Willy limped down to the street and gave them a piece of his mind. I was horribly embarrassed by his overprotection, but I also loved the fact that someone was watching over me.

When I reached the age of twelve, my mother decided it was time I had my own room, at last. So Uncle Willy went to live on his own. He found a first-floor room in a building just around the corner. Unfortunately, this move came about at the time when his disease was starting to accelerate, and he was losing control and strength. I visited him almost every day and saw how courageous he was in the face of his crippling illness. He fought hard to hold on to his independence. He fashioned a shaving kit out of a razor embedded in a block of wood. His gnarled hand could no longer hold the slender handle of a razor, but by attaching it to a block of wood, he could control it enough to shave using both hands.

From his seat at the window of his room, he became a fixture in the neighborhood—one of the people who held the community together. He kept my old children's books in his room, and the neighborhood kids would sit on the stoop next to his window to listen to him read. We were just a short distance from the Bowery. The Bowery bums, who didn't have two nickels to rub together, would bring Uncle Willy a Coke on a hot summer day as a thank-you for his kindness and conversation. He showed me how to look for the humor in everyday disasters and reversals. If your haircut came out funny, or your dress didn't look that good, he tried to move you away from the disappointment and on to the humor in the inevitability of dashed expectations. I know it was how he survived his physical deformities and meager circumstances. Everyone he met responded to just what I responded to: his deep humanity.

As his atrophy gradually ate away at his muscles, the tables were turned. I took care of *him*. As more and more of his capacities were eaten away, he needed someone to help him with his basic hygiene. I used to give him a sponge bath a few times a week and cut his hair. As I was older, I could finally hear *all* his stories, including the mystery of the very close woman friend of his, a woman who had come to the park with us often when I was a kid. She had loved him despite his mangled body, and she'd asked him to marry her. He refused, because he confessed that he was incapable of consummating the marriage. She remained a friend of his throughout his life.

At first, I wondered why his brother and sisters never came to visit him, but later I realized that they couldn't see his beauty or his humanity. They had always been embarrassed by the brother who couldn't walk, couldn't hold a job. They considered him an imposition. My late husband used to say: "If there's a poor creature on earth who is walking the street who is in some way formed abnormally, we shun them. We don't look at them. We take their light away from them." That's what the family had tried to do to Uncle Willy, but his light was much stronger than that.

When it became impossible for him to maneuver into the bathroom, which was up a flight of stairs, he decided to check himself into Roosevelt Hospital. He didn't consult a single member of the family for assistance; he arranged it all with city social services. I went to visit him there for two years. Toward the end of that time, his legs had grown completely numb. He burned one quite severely on the radiator in his room, because he was unable to feel the pain of the skin burning.

The doctors erred in giving him penicillin for the infection on his leg. He was allergic to the drug, and the complications of that reaction, plus the general weakened state of his body, was too much for him.

I was standing in my apartment on Fifteenth Street when my mother called to tell me that Uncle Willy had died. It was a moment of pure pain unlike any I had ever experienced. I had known anger, and betrayal, and abandonment, but never such a dizzying feeling of fundamental loss.

Uncle Willy taught me love. I wasn't clear about what love was before Willy. He showered me with the best kind of attention. There was nothing I could do that was wrong, and nothing could harm the love he had for me. He couldn't have been more loving if he were my own father. His devotion to me was extraordinary.

I thought, when he died, how important it was that he and I had found each other. I gave his life a purpose. If it hadn't been for his caring for me, he probably would have lived his life in my grandparents' home until they died. Then he'd probably have been shipped off to an institution by his embarrassed brother and sisters. Later, I appreciated fully how much purpose he gave to my life. Where would I have been, if he hadn't taught me that I was loved and could love? I can't imagine what I would've turned out to be—what kind of woman, what kind of actress—if I hadn't been shown true love by Uncle Willy. His influence helped to form the best parts of the woman I am today, and for that I am eternally grateful.

When I finally taught myself how to cook, this was one of the things I made for Uncle Willy that he liked the best.

Fettuccini Carbonara

1 pound fettuccini noodles

½ pound prosciutto, wedge (not sliced)

1 small onion

2 tablespoons butter

½ cup heavy cream

¼ cup romano cheese, grated

¼ cup Parmesan cheese, grated

1 sprig fresh parsley

1. Fill a 4-quart pot with 3 quarts water and bring to a boil.
2. Cook fettuccini until al dente, approximately 7 minutes.
3. Chop prosciutto into tiny pieces and dice onion.
4. In a 2-quart saucepan, melt butter and add prosciutto and onion. Cook until onion is clear.
5. Add heavy cream and two cheeses. Simmer for 10 minutes, being careful that the mixture does not burn.
6. When done, pour over pasta and toss. Sprinkle parsley and serve.

Serves 6.

Chapter 11

Outtakes

When I was eleven years old, I mustered up the courage to audition for a spot on Hearn's Amateur Hour, a talent show run by a huge New York City department store that, at that time, was a competitor to Macy's. My memorable (to me) appearance as Mrs. Potato in kindergarten had fueled my acting ambitions, which grew to a raging wildfire by the time I reached eleven. Part of it was resentment. My cute, more fortunate little cousin got dancing, and singing, and music lessons. I wanted to show all of them.

My Uncle Willy, who thought I was the most talented person in the entire world, was convinced I could earn a spot on Hearn's Amateur Hour. He listened to me sing *Winter Wonderland* dozens of times to prepare for my moment. The look on his face at each performance was one of pure rapture. If I was even half as good as what I saw reflected in his eyes, I was a shoo-in, I believed.

Still, we told no one, reasoning that it would be much more effective to trump my cousin with a *fait accompli,* than to let her know that I was going up for the audition and endure her doubting looks. Willy and I liked being conspirators against the family.

That Saturday, we took the bus down to Hearn's and walked into the chaotic audition room where people of all shapes and sizes were singing and juggling and dancing to warm up. It was like "open mike night" at the circus. I held Uncle Willy's hand tightly in mine, intimidated by the commotion, and too frightened to open my pipes among all those people. Finally, a woman with a clipboard called out: "Doris Roberts!" Uncle Willy gave my hand a squeeze and told me how beautiful I looked, then instructed me not to be nervous, just sing the song just like I'd sung it to him at home.

I stood way up on stage, a figure clenching her fists at her sides. I gathered in my breath and stared hard at Uncle Willy for support. He was smiling that same approving smile that had been my beacon. I focused on him as I cleared my throat and began.

What I had not realized (and what adoring Uncle Willy had ignored) was that I had a terrible lisp. I wetted down all the Ss and Ths in this very phonetic song. My version of it came out: *"Thsleigh bellsth ring. Are you listening? In the lane, sthnow is glisthening. A wonderful sthight. I'm happy tonight. Walking in a winter wonderland."*

Of course, I looked awfully cute to Uncle Willy. There are few things cuter than a plucky little girl belting out a song with all her heart, even though she's mangling it beyond repair. The judges somehow took a different point of view. I heard the bell, the gong, and the buzzer, as they scrambled to yank me off the stage. I thought they were going to file a lawsuit banning me from using the letter *s*.

I cried all the way home on the bus, with my head pressed into Uncle Willy's rib cage as he patted me and told me it didn't really matter. What really mattered was that I had tried. I sure didn't feel that way. And I was *so* thankful that we hadn't told my cousin.

A rational individual would have never gone into show business after an experience like that. Those of us who end up in the world of the theater think that sanity is highly overrated. And therapy and medication are highly underrated. You know the rest of my story. I pressed on, as have all my peers in this great business for a while.

I called this chapter "Outtakes" after those embarrassing

moments when you don't get the scene right and your efforts end up on the cutting room floor. I guess why audiences love outtakes so much is that we finally get to see the grand stars with their masks pulled away . . . much like seeing the banker get a pie in the face (or serve time for embezzlement).

When you see the stars in movie magazines, a team of stylists and lighting experts have arranged a perfect environment, where they appear flawless and beautifully composed. Or you see them strolling down the red carpet at an awards ceremony in an eight-thousand-dollar designer gown and a million bucks worth of jewels that *they got for free*, just because they are stars. As much as you envy them their poise, money, and beauty, part of you wants to see them trip over a loose thread in the hem of their pants or get tangled up in the train of their gown. You *know* that no one's life can be that perfect.

Doris Roberts Is Working!

When I was a young actress in New York, I auditioned for a *lot* of commercials. I was even cast in a few. There's a special knack to selling a product, and I seemed to have it. Perhaps the "special knack" is desperation. Some actors think that working in commercials is beneath them, and it shows when they go up for the part. They can't extol the virtues of the air freshener or floor wax with conviction, perhaps because they can't find a moment in their childhood to call upon that produces a genuine emotion for use on this brand of salad dressing. Maybe it's that they've never been that enthusiastic; maybe it's that they don't like salad dressing. This was not the case for me. I didn't care if I had to say that the floor wax was *also* a great salad dressing. I had bills to pay.

Although I regularly got commercial work at advertising agencies all over Manhattan, I was never able to break through at one of the biggest: J. Walter Thompson. I thought that the casting director had a sadistic obsession with humiliating me. If she just plain didn't like me, she could have instructed my agent not to send me to audition for her company's commercials. Yet, she'd call me in for audition after audition. She'd start shaking her head with disapproval almost before I'd completed my performance. It must have given her some kind of thrill. But her reaction only sharpened my determination. I vowed that some day I would get a commercial for J. Walter Thompson.

One day, the J. Walter Thompson casting director called my agent to offer me a part.

"Sorry, she's not available," my agent replied.

The casting director was speechless for a moment.

"What do you mean?" she asked

"Doris Roberts is working," he said.

"That can't be true. Doris Roberts is working?!" she said with a mixture of incredulity and suspicion.

Yes, Doris Roberts was working, and I've been working steadily ever since. For the last thirty years I haven't had to wax my own floors, and I prefer my dressing on the side.

Look Homeward, Someone

I was on my way to Montreal to film a television version of *Look Homeward, Angel* with a spectacular cast that included E. G. Marshall, Geraldine Page, Nancy Marchand, Timothy Bottoms, and Charles Durning. Our employer—David Susskind's production company—had printed up instructions on how to behave as we made our way through customs so our rather large group could get through quickly. The paper said we were to explain that we were coming to Canada to shoot a film and would be there for ten days, after which we would return to the United States.

Charles Durning, who at that time was undiscovered, had a small role. In television they classify it as an "under five," meaning he had five lines or less. Charles was at the head of the line. Behind him was Geraldine Page, wearing several hair pieces—falls, as they used to call them—that appeared as if they had not been brushed for several weeks. Timothy Bottoms was next, wearing a serape, his guitar and his long hair reflecting the fashions of young people in the mid-seventies. Then E. G. Marshall, myself, Nancy Marchand, and several members of the crew.

When Charles was asked the reason he was coming to Canada, he took out the little mimeographed slip of paper given to us by the production company and read: "I'm coming to Canada to film *Look Homeward, Angel.* We will be here for ten days filming. At the end of that, we will return to the United States." The agent asked to see the piece of paper and at that point Charlie rolled it into a small ball, put it into his mouth, and swallowed it.

The joke was on us because after that stunt, we were trapped in Canadian customs for hours while the inspectors did everything but body-cavity searches. Geraldine Page had her entire coiffure disassembled and combed through (which was very helpful to her overall look, actually). Timothy Bottoms was examined and so was his guitar and all his other belongings. My most enduring memory, however, is of E. G. He passed through customs quickly and spent the three hours pacing the waiting room cursing Charlie and bemoaning the fact that we couldn't get a drink.

Only for Variety

In 1975 I was in tryouts for a play called *The Opening,* written by the actor Charles Grodin, who had gathered an incredible cast: Alan Arkin, David Marguiles, Renee Taylor, Louise Lasser, and the comedian, Sandy Baron. The play didn't get enough backing, so we all moved on, me to a part in the Broadway production of *Bad Habits.* One evening, I was watching some six o'clock news on television when they announced that Sandy Baron was missing. He'd been in a touring production of *Lenny* and had not shown up for the performance. I was so upset. I'd really gotten to like Sandy in the weeks we worked on *The Opening*, and I was very concerned for his welfare.

I left that evening to go to the theater, and I saw Sandy hovering in the doorway of my apartment building. He looked terrible, as if he needed medical attention. At first I wondered how he had found my apartment, but then I remembered his telling me that he was a patient of a chiropractor who had an office on the ground floor of the building.

"Sandy, is there anything I can do for you?" I asked.

"Adopt me," he said, pulling his sport jacket even closer around him.

I didn't have a comeback for that. This is going to sound terrible, because it *was* terrible, but I looked at my watch and saw that I was already late for the theater, and I absolutely had to go. "Where are you staying?" I asked him.

"On the couch of my chiropractor's office," he said. Of course, sleeping on a couch is what causes people to go to the chiropractor in the first place.

"Can we have breakfast tomorrow?" I asked. "I'll figure out some way to help you then."

"Okay," he said.

The next morning, I got up very early (well, early for someone who works nights in the theater). I was up by 9:30, and on the phone. I got through the switchboard to the agent who handled Sandy.

"I've found Sandy Baron," I said. "He's sleeping on his chiropractor's couch, and he's in bad shape. He probably needs to be hospitalized."

There was a pause.

"We only handle Sandy Baron for variety," he said, and hung up.

This is the absolute worst agent story I've ever heard—and everyone in the business has a couple of doozies. When I hear actors crow at awards ceremonies about the "show business family" I can't help thinking of Sandy Baron.

She's like a Sister to Me

I was doing a summer tour of *Last of the Red Hot Lovers* in 1973 with Sid Caesar, and we'd come to Ohio for the last three weeks of our commitment. I got a call from my agent with the spectacular news that Norman Lear wanted me to appear in the hit situation comedy *Maude* as Bea Arthur's best friend. Bea in fact was a close friend, someone I'd known for years in the world of the New York theater. I guessed she might have even been the one who suggested me for the part, and anticipated what a great time we'd have working together.

Spectacular news and spectacular money, but the thrill only lasted for a moment. How was I going to get out of my summer commitment to *Last of the Red Hot Lovers* for the job on *Maude*? I couldn't find a replacement for me, so the producer of *Maude* agreed to wait the three weeks until the run of the show was over. The night the show closed, I got on a plane to Los Angeles.

Getting to Los Angeles from Ohio wasn't easy back then. There were no direct flights. I had to go to Chicago after my last performance and transfer to a plane to Los Angeles. I didn't get to L.A. until 11:30 in the morning, and the airline misplaced my luggage. The studio spared no expense for my arrival. They put me up at the improbably named Farmer's Daughter Motel, directly across the street from CBS studios at Fairfax and Melrose, so I wouldn't have to rent a car. No Four Seasons for this demi-diva. At the Farmer's Daughter, there was only one season—long, hot summer with a broken air conditioner.

I pretended I liked the idea. It was *good* to get in a walk before work. I *enjoyed* the smoggy air. Such a bracing change from New York City! Plus I loved all those interesting characters at the busstop. Apparently, "happy hour" comes early and often on the West Coast.

Despite my groggy looks and disheveled clothing, Bea gave me an opened-armed, sisterly embrace when I entered the sound stage. Then we stepped back for a moment and realized we were wearing the same outfit. We both were customers of a New York store named Bebe (but pronounced "Bibby") that catered to larger women.

"I've got it in blue," she said.

"I got it in purple," I said. "I got it in black."

"I got it in brown," she responded. We were like kids talking about the different crayons we had in our boxes.

We were doing this whole spontaneous routine, without embarrassment, about our outfits! I was so happy we would be working together.

The day went off flawlessly. Bea offered to drive me home after work. I told her to take a right out of the parking lot. What she told me during that drive made my head spin.

"They want you to be a regular on the show," Bea said.

"What?" I said.

"Oh yeah, that's why they waited for you to get out of your commitment in Ohio," Bea said. "I'm telling you, Doris, you'll make more money than you ever could dream of making on the Broadway stage. You'll be seen by millions of people every night. Would you be willing to give up New York?"

"Yeah, I guess so," I said. "Take a left into the parking lot. I think I could give up New York for this."

Bea looked up at the Farmer's Daughter Motel.

"Why the hell would they put you up some place like this?" she said.

The producers weren't telling Bea everything. That night, as I idly scanned the classifieds for a house to rent, I got a call from the show's producer.

"I'm glad I caught you in," he said.

"I wasn't sure where to go around here," I replied.

"I'll be right over," he said.

He confessed that there had been a terrible mistake, and he didn't mean the motel.

"You're a little Bea Arthur," he said. "The two of you are so alike, there's no conflict. We want you to be her best friend, but you're just like her. You're just littler than she is."

In the end, they hired Rue McClanahan, another friend of Bea's, but someone very different from both of us. It didn't matter. I was destined to work in television anyway. Bea just brought me to Los Angeles and opened the door. As soon as it was slammed shut, another door opened.

My Greatest Performance

When I got cast as Mildred Krebs, in *Remington Steele*, I'd just spent six months in bed suffering from a terrible inflammation of my sciatic nerve. For those of you who have never experienced sciatica, it's as though a nerve that stretches from your ankle to the base of your spine is on fire, a crippling pain that makes it very difficult to walk. In fact, I did my whole audition for *Remington Steele* in a back brace, and I was still wearing it for the physical you must take to satisfy the production company's insurers that you are fit to handle the work the part requires.

I sat in the examination room, worried nearly sick that the doctor would discover my back brace. If he did, most likely he wouldn't permit me to take the part. He raised his stethoscope as he came toward me. I shrunk back on the table with my shoulders hunched forward in alarm.

"It's okay," he said. "I'm not going to hurt you."

He took another step, and I inhaled sharply and crumpled more.

"Believe me, I never go where I'm not supposed to go," he said reassuringly.

"I know, doctor. It's just that I'm so shy," I said.

What a joke! I had been shy when I was a kid, but years of therapy and decades of performances on the stage and screen had eliminated that from my repertoire. I could have given *him* an exam. He believed me, though, and didn't conduct a full physical examination. This was one of my greatest acting jobs of all time. If he had discovered my back brace, I'd never have gotten the part. I felt as though I should have gotten an Emmy that afternoon. But my back hurt so much then, I wouldn't have been able to lift it anyway.

This recipe always gives me comfort, which anyone suffering an outtake in their real life needs at the end of the day.

Soul-Warming Real Mac & Cheese

6 tablespoons butter

1 tablespoon flour

salt and pepper

3 cups milk

1 pound macaroni, cooked according to package directions

1 cup crumbled goat cheese

1 cup grated cheddar cheese

1 cup diced brie

¼ cup bread crumbs

1. Melt butter in a heavy saucepan. Sprinkle in flour and stir until combined and almost a paste. Salt and pepper to taste.
2. Pour in milk and stir to combine. (Don't be scared, the butter and flour are *supposed* to lump up.) As the milk warms, the butter and flour mixture will combine well with it. Stir con-

stantly and gently until mixture thickens to a gravy-like consistency.

3. Meanwhile, toss cooked pasta with all three cheeses, mixing thoroughly; then pour "béchamel" over top and again mix thoroughly.

4. Place in a 13×9-inch baking dish. Sprinkle Parmesean cheese and bread crumbs on top and bake for 30–40 minutes, or until cheese melts and the top is a yummy, golden brown.

Serves 6.

Chapter 12

How to Be a Fan in Three Easy Lessons: Cary Grant, Federico Fellini, and Laurence Olivier

I believe every great actor starts out his or her life as a fan. I know I did. From the very first play my mother took me to on Broadway, I saw actors whose performances I couldn't forget, and who set me wondering if I could do as well myself. I worshipped Laurence Olivier when he starred in *Oedipus Rex,* and Cary Grant in all those Hitchcock movies. Later, I was one of those screaming bobbysoxers who swooned over Frank Sinatra. The pure emotion, the pain in his voice made me believe that he was singing directly to me. When I was a little older, I discovered Italian movies. I idolized Eleonora Duse, an Italian actress whose great humanity was demonstrated in *Cenere,* Italian for "Ashes," one of the most restrained and powerful performances I'd ever seen. Moments from Federico Fellini films appeared in my dreams.

One of the great perks of my job is that it gives me a better chance than the average person to meet my idols. Early in my career, I was flown out to California to audition for a part in the television show, *Alfred Hitchcock Presents,* which was filmed on the

Universal lot, before it was transmogrified into the theme park, Universal Studios. Walking around the place where so many of my favorite movies had been filmed had me as giddy as a girl on the first day of school.

The problem was that my sense of direction was off. This is not to say that it was very good to begin with. I was wandering around the lot, lost and having a hard time trying to find Hitchcock's office. All the big producers who were under contract to Universal had cottages on the lot that were identified by little brass plaques. It was late afternoon when I was searching among the buildings, and the sun glaring off the brass was making them very hard to read. As I squinted at one of the plaques, I saw a figure approaching out of the corner of my eye. I squinted in the glare to address him.

"Oh, oh, oh (giggle)! Oh my God!" I could not open my mouth to say any more than those word-mangling giggles. "Oh my God! Could you? (giggle, giggle) Could you? (giggle, giggle) Do you (giggle, giggle) know where Hitchcock is?"

Could there be a dumber question in the entire world to ask Cary Grant?

He smiled that glorious smile of his and trained his twinkling eyes on little me, as he pointed me in the right direction. I continued my idiotic giggles as I thanked him. As I made my way to the Hitchcock offices, I was relieved by the idea that I'd probably never see Cary Grant again.

The next day, I was sitting in the Universal commissary surrounded by some of the most popular stars of the time. At one table was Tony Curtis, and at another was Jack Warden having lunch with Burt Lancaster. I was eating with the director Alan Pakula, although I barely tasted my salad. This was it, the place I'd dreamed of being, among the people I wanted to have as my peers. I looked up from my salad and was mortified to see Cary Grant ambling toward my table with his signature semi-sideways gait. He *couldn't* be coming to my table. Surely he would turn away. Nope. He was coming over to say hello to Alan.

When he reached the table, I wanted to slip beneath it. Alan introduced me to Cary, who again bathed me in his gracious smile.

"Oh, we met yesterday," he said.

Damn, I couldn't believe he remembered. Well, I thought I'd die from embarrassment, especially because I still couldn't control my giggles. And it would have been a relief to die from embarrassment, the way Alan was glaring at me. They talked for a bit, and Cary went away.

None of the things I might have said to Cary Grant about the incredible experiences he gave me at the movies found their way to my lips when I was in the presence of the great star. I was so concerned what he thought of me, I didn't tell him how much he meant to me. Opportunity lost.

More than a decade later, fate threw me into the room with the great Italian director Federico Fellini, and I didn't make the same mistake.

One night, when I was in the cast of *Last of the Red Hot Lovers*, I was invited to a party for a New York film critic. The recent death of my good friend, the actress Ruth White, was very much on my mind that night. She had died unexpectedly. I mourned that, and I also regretted that I never told her how good an actress I thought she was. As I entered the party, I was pledging to myself that, from that moment on, I would make a point to tell everyone I admired how much they meant to me, because, the way life goes, I might never have that opportunity again. I hadn't seen Cary Grant since my fumbling introduction to him that afternoon in Los Angeles. Just as these thoughts were in my head, I looked across the room and saw Federico Fellini.

I had watched his film *I Vitellone*, about a writer leaving behind his boyhood village to seek his fortune in Rome so many times that I knew it scene by scene. Why be shy? That's the question of a true fan.

I made my way across the room, trying to figure out what I ought to say. Whatever I said, I wanted it to come from the heart. I simply introduced myself and told him how much I admired his work, particularly *I Vitellone*. "I will never forget the actor on the stage, surrounded by all strippers as he recited Shakespeare," I said. "I'll never forget the retarded man on the beach with the statue of the Madonna, and the way he cherished it, and how he held it, and how that was pure religion. It was this great faith between this simple man and this statue. I will never forget the main character leaving on that train. It was like you were pulling heartstrings, cutting to one friend's face, and then the train moving away, and then another friend's face."

He was so delighted that someone knew his work so well and felt so passionate about it that he asked his distributor to send me a copy of the film. I started to feel guilty that I had taken up so much of his time, and excused myself. Later on, someone introduced me to him again as an actress. Fellini was amazed that we had talked so long and I'd never mentioned that fact. "You are the most unpretentious actress I have never met," he said. "Not once did you ask me to be in any of my movies."

I wasn't standing in front of him as an ambitious actress. My admiration was so overwhelming that it wouldn't have occurred to me to try to get something out of our meeting. Merely standing near him was enough; I hadn't even asked for an autograph.

At least I didn't make a fool of myself, like I did with Laurence Olivier.

I had been in a 1980 television version of *The Diary of Anne Frank* with the actress Joan Plowright, who was married to Olivier. We had become such good friends that I was sorry when the filming ended. From time to time, when Joan came to Los Angeles, she would stay with me, and we always had great visits. Even after all Joan's visits, I was still surprised to receive the phone message of my life.

"This is Larry Olivier of London," my answering machine tape announced. Where else would he be from? Queens, Long Island? "And I'm coming to your country Thursday next, and I would like to take you to dinner Sunday. So, if that's all right with you, leave it on Dickie's answering machine, and his number is 654-2 oh no 653 oh, oh *shit*." He hung up.

Shit! The great Laurence Olivier had said "shit" on my answering machine.

My heart was racing. This was *the* Laurence Olivier, the one I had seen in *Oedipus Rex,* perhaps the most memorable of my many nights in a theater seat. How could he tease me like this? Maybe he wouldn't call back. What if he did? Thankfully, the tape suddenly started up again.

"Disregard the first message," Olivier said, and left the number.

That day, I was going to a luncheon at a friend's and I was already so nervous about meeting Laurence Olivier that I could talk of nothing else. I asked my friends: What should I do? Should I kiss the hem of his gown? Is there a ring that I can kiss? All they could say was: Be yourself.

Be yourself is probably the worst advice in the world. Do I *have* to be myself? Can't be someone else for once? Someone taller, prettier, thinner, and more articulate?

The big day arrived, and I tried to keep myself busy so I wouldn't completely freak out before I met him. I had lunch with some friends and the singer Marta Stephens, who, it turned out, was a friend of Lord Olivier's. She told me to give him her love, and a little later that day she dropped by a note for me to give to him when we met.

That night I waited outside La Scala in Beverly Hills. I wanted to be on time, so I got there early; but I didn't want to seem too eager and too anxious. At the stroke of eight, I entered the restaurant, where he was waiting at the bar. He threw his arms open to greet me and everyone in the place turned around to see who the hell I was.

"My dear," he said in that beautiful booming voice of his. "What an occasion!"

He threw his arms around me.

"Let's have a drink," he whispered in my ear and led me to the bar.

I thought I was going to fall off the stool, I was so overcome by his graciousness. I placed my hand on his wrist and warned him.

"I'm going to make a fool out of myself, but as the evening goes on I promise it will get better," I said.

He was in the middle of writing his autobiography, and I could see what an incredible book it would be. He had the basic ingredients: he'd lived a fascinating life, and he was a great storyteller. He'd tell me a story, and I'd ask if it was going to be in his book. Frequently he'd say it wasn't, and I'd be so disappointed. The truth was, he had so many memorable experiences in his incredible career, one book wasn't long enough for all of them.

We were like old friends. We shared a dessert and had drinks, along with all the stories. Near the end of the meal, I leaned over to reach in my purse.

"I have a note for you from a friend," I said.

He grabbed my wrist to stop me.

"No, no," he said. "Don't give it to me."

We talked about other things for a while, but my mind was still on that note from Marta. I had to ask again.

"Don't you even want to know who it is from?" I asked.

"No," he said again. "No."

"God, I hope I get to a point in my life where I don't even want to know who the note is from," I said incredulously. He didn't wonder that he might be missing something? I just couldn't believe it. He was at a point in his life where he felt comfortable enough to know that he was fine just as he was, and nothing the outside world could offer would change that. I still sort of don't believe it. I'm still not there yet, damn it.

Every time he came to town we got together. One year, when I was passing through London, he and Joan invited me to visit them at their home in the country. They sent a driver to pick me up, and I was very glad they did. To discourage intruders, they hadn't marked the entrance to their property, and had not paved the road leading to the house. I never would have found it on my own. When I got out of the car and surveyed their gloriously overgrown garden, I couldn't help but say: "I knew I was coming to Mandalay."

That afternoon, we stayed in the garden playing le boule, a game similar to bocce ball where you toss a small, heavy ball, trying to get it to go as close as you can to a master ball but not beyond. The garden in which we were playing was their Shakespeare garden, a place where every bush, tree, flower, and herb was one that had been mentioned in a Shakespearean play, just like the one in New York's Central Park, above the Delacorte Theater.

As we moved around the garden, Larry would stop at each plant and recite the relevant passage from Shakespeare. The first time he did it, I laughed and said how charming he was, but I couldn't hold on to the false Doris for long. Finally, I had to confess.

"Larry, you're barking up the wrong tree," I said. "I hardly know anything about Shakespeare."

I had finally reached my ultimate goal as a fan: I *was* myself, and he was just fine with me being me. I was right. I *had* made a fool of myself—as most fans do, and as *I* had done more times than I could count—but it did get better.

I'm still a fan. I still have the answering machine tape.

This recipe is elegant, like Olivier, and has a bit of ham.

Eggs Benedict

¼ cup white vinegar

12 eggs

1 pound of ham, sliced, (deli ham is fine)

6 English muffins, split in two

2 tablespoons of butter

Hollandaise Sauce (recipe follows)

2 tablespoons finely chopped fresh tarragon

1. Bring a large sauce pan filled with water and the vinegar to a boil. Reduce heat to a simmer.
2. Crack eggs into a bowl, so as to be able to fish out any stray shells easily, and one by one, plop eggs into the simmering water.
3. Create a water "tornado" encircling the egg by stirring around it. When the egg whites firm up against the yolk, plop, another egg.
4. Remove eggs with a slotted spoon when the whites become firm, and place on some laid-out paper towels to absorb excess water.
5. Meanwhile, stack the ham slices on top of each other and trim them to roughly the same size as the English muffin.
6. Melt 1 tablespoon of butter in sauté pan. Gently fry ham until warm and just starting to color. (Use remaining tablespoon of butter if the pan becomes dry.)

7. Toast English muffins. Top each muffin half with a couple slices of ham circles, then an egg, then slather with Hollandaise Sauce. Sprinkle a pinch of tarragon atop each egg to garnish.

Serves 6.

Hollandaise Sauce

(You'll need a double boiler)

1 stick unsalted butter

2 egg yolks

the strained juice of half of 1 lemon

1 teaspoon salt

pinch of cayenne pepper (don't be shy—and don't use your
    bare fingers, either!)

1. Melt butter in saucepan. Remove from heat and let stand for a few minutes.
2. Skim off the white, foamy top, leaving you with "clarified butter," or "drawn butter." Set aside.
3. Prepare your double boiler by bringing a bit of water to a simmer in a saucepan.
4. In a stainless steel or heavy ceramic bowl, whisk egg yolks until they are a much paler shade of yellow, and airier in consistency.
5. Place the bowl over the saucepan and whisk like mad. (You want the yolks to cook without scrambling. If you see that they are starting to scramble, remove bowl from heat and whisk like crazy until they have cooled a bit.) After whisking over the water for 3–4 minutes, remove from heat and continue to whisk until they have cooled.

6. Now, turn the flame off, return the bowl to the saucepan, and drizzle in the clarified butter, whisking constantly.
7. When butter has emulsified, whisk in lemon juice, salt, and pepper. If the concoction is too thick, squeeze in more lemon juice, or add warm water for a subtler sauce.

Part Four

Advice

Chapter 13

It's Okay to Look Back, Just Don't Stare

My mother always had a hard time complimenting me about anything, but particularly about my acting. Why is it always the thing you care about most that others have the toughest time acknowledging? The night my mother came to see me in the Edward Albee play *The Death of Bessie Smith,* a play in which I had the role of the nurse, is a perfect example.

It was opening night when I gave what I considered to be a knockout performance. There was a scene at the end of the second act when I had to scream. *Really* scream. I'm no creampuff, but each night after that scene I practically passed out. I think back to her greeting me backstage after the final curtain.

"Doris!" she beamed. "Your teeth are beautiful!"

I realize saying my teeth are beautiful is, in fact, a compliment (and probably a great toothpaste commercial). My mother was genuine and specific. She'd had a nice opportunity to evaluate the quality of my brushing and flossing during that gut-wrenching scream. Call me greedy if you will, but considering how much that performance took out of me that night and every night, I was expecting something more than a few kind words to pass on to my dental hygienist.

When I looked back at that opening night, I'd get *angry*. Why couldn't my mother compliment me? Reaching back into the memory doesn't really answer that question. It only showed me again that she did not. So I had to dig deeper and replay another memory.

I was opening in *The Last of the Red Hot Lovers* in Boston, and I flew my mother up from New York to attend the performance. I treated her like a queen. I had a limousine pick her up at the airport and I put her up in a big suite at the Ritz. I made sure to brush and floss. After the performance, she came backstage. The applause had come in a thunderous wave at the final curtain, but I was really more interested in what my mother would say. I stood backstage like an eager child waiting for my mommy to tell me what a good girl I was. I watched as she complimented everyone on their performances. She singled out various members of the stage crew. She even found a way to praise my understudy, who hadn't gone on stage (and hadn't fought plaque as diligently as I had). Everyone but me.

When we got back to her hotel, we went up to her suite. She was surprised when she came out of the bathroom in her robe and found I'd ordered us a pot of coffee from room service, even though it was close to midnight.

"You're not going to bed," I told her.

"Of course I'm going to bed. I'm exhausted," she said.

"You're not going to bed until you tell me how good I was," I demanded.

"Don't be silly," she said.

"You told everyone in the show how brilliant they were. Why can't you tell me?"

I busied myself pouring two cups of coffee. In my memory of this, the silence lasts a few minutes, while she squirms in the easy chair unable to look me in the eye. This is the most satisfying part of the memory, and probably the least accurate. I know in life, in real time with my mother, that it probably only took a few seconds before her discomfort level got so high she had to fill it.

"Well, you know I can't," she said. "I don't want people to think I'm prejudiced."

In the first scene I'm the victim. In the second scene I'm the hero. In neither scene do I get an answer to my question.

When I'd review how I got to be who I am, it usually took place on a day when I wasn't feeling too happy. The look back into the past was not so much a search for answers as an attempt to find someone else, preferably someone long dead and gone, I could blame for my bad mood. Maybe a relative who left me nothing but an excuse in her will. This is why I say it's okay to look back, just don't stare.

It's okay to look back and see what you did then, to possibly give you an insight into what you need to change today. Or, think back to a funny story that gives you comfort. But if you spend your precious time in the present, dumbfounded by what you see in the past, you have no chance of changing. None at all. Staring back at your past makes you stuck in both places simultaneously. It's stagnating, and it chokes you. You are ignoring the full life that you have today, wasting the energy you could use to appreciate what you have in front of you.

I'd get going on one of these memories, and I'd place myself in that long-ago room with all the appropriate family members. Very quickly I'd get so immersed in all the old emotions—where I played either victim or hero, but rarely anything in between—that it was like living that scene again.

Almost everyone has a few turning-point stories from childhood, the ones that they tell over and over again. These are the stories that you need to shake up, if you are going to make peace with what happened in your past and enjoy what's happening today.

I resented my mother's attitude for years, until the day I told my stories to an analyst. At that point, my mother had been dead for many years yet we were still arguing. When I was finished I asked him the same question I'd been attempting to ask myself for years.

"Why wouldn't my mother tell me how wonderful I was as an actress? Why couldn't she tell me that?"

"I don't know," he said simply. "Close your eyes and ask her."

"*Ask her?*" I resisted. I'm paying him a hundred and fifty bucks an hour to talk to dead people?! For these kinds of prices, I'd get a better deal calling the psychic hotline for the answer. Anyway, I already had my answer from her that night in Boston.

"Give it a try," he insisted. "Think of it as an acting exercise."

I closed my eyes and said the question out loud. Then I spoke as if I were my mother.

"How could I tell you how good you were, when I could never tell myself?" I said, as her. "I was embarrassed that your father wasn't there. I was embarrassed that I was a divorced woman."

Somehow, I knew all of that. It was all very close to the surface, as my session with the analyst demonstrated. But it wasn't visible, no matter how hard I stared. When I looked back without trying to prove myself right or wrong, I freed myself and my mother.

Lately, when I look back on the past, I can see my mother in a bigger context—the context of her struggles and her sacrifices. I can understand that, in her own way, she expressed love for me, even if it didn't always come in the form I wanted. I am happy with the person I am today. I recognize her importance and I now know that she did the best that she could. I can finally look back, but I don't stare.

Coffee with Liqueur

Coffee with liqueur is for a night when you have
to wait a long time to get the answer you want.
Make sure to brush after, so your teeth
"look beautiful."

Make a pot of strong, black coffee pour the coffee into big mugs, and add a shot of your favorite liqueur, e.g., Grand Marnier, Frangelico, Amaretto . . . and let the evening take its course.

Chapter 14

Put Down the Spears

I am a woman whose shoulders are still a little sloped from the forty-pound chip I used to carry on them in my youth. I was a mousy little thing with a vicious bite. I used to grumble under my breath: "You don't think I can do it? Just watch me." That chip on my shoulder made me slower, grumpier, and less fluid in my responses. The good part was how tough and resilient it made me. The bad part was everything else.

I think some of the greatest harm we cause ourselves comes from holding on to defenses that served us well in the past, but are no longer necessary in our present-day lives. It's the personal equivalent of still preparing to fight the last war. I made much faster progress in my career and in my personal life the day I learned how to put down my spears.

The world can be a very hostile place, and you can't rely on other people looking out for your interests, or even considering them much of the time. With that as a given, people tend to walk clutching imaginary weapons in their hands—spears, or knives, or guns— whatever form of defense suits them. We are so afraid we are going to be hurt, someone's going to take advantage of us or take away things that belong to us, that many of us move through the world always on the defensive.

We listen to each conversation, trying to hear a hint that the other person is putting us down. It affects our driving, our dealings, with store clerks, and the way we walk down the street. Is that guy trying to cut me off? I better give him the finger just in case. Is that clerk ignoring me because she doesn't like what I'm going to buy? That woman looking at the store windows in front of me, she doesn't even notice I'm trying to get around her. Sometimes you could just scream.

My imaginary weapon used to be a spear. A knife hanging from my belt loop, or a gun concealed in a holster, just didn't appeal to me. A spear is obvious. In my mind, my spear was six feet tall or taller, towering over my tiny body. With a spear, people know that you are armed, and perhaps they'll decide they'd rather not pick a fight with you. That's the point, as far as I'm concerned.

When I worked on *Remington Steele,* on which I played Remington's (Pierce Brosnan's) secretary, Mildred Krebs, the writers once came up with a wonderful script set in a circus with a comic relief story line of Mildred going undercover as a gypsy fortune teller. It was a chance for me to shine, and I was extremely proud of the work I did. I looked forward to seeing the dailies, the rough footage of the episode that the director reviews before advising the film editor how he'd like it to be cut. My heart sank when I looked at them. My acting was fine, but the lighting director had neglected to light me properly. Without the proper lighting, my skin looked a sickly gray, and my eyes did not sparkle. At a glance, I looked so bad I wondered if I'd contracted a terminal illness, which was not the look I was going for.

My first response was, haven't they seen my spear? Do they know how heavily armed I am? Maybe I should go after someone—or maybe several of them—depending on how much stamina I could muster. First, I thought they didn't respect me or care enough about me to do a good job, which led me to self-doubt. It was downhill from there to paranoia. This was clearly a plot, a deliberate attempt to sabotage me. While I was at it, I tossed in sorrow and self-pity. Why was this happening to me? When was I going to get the treatment I deserved? I was enraged. Somebody was going to feel the tip of my spear. I had it well-sharpened.

The first person I came across that evening happened to be one of the lighting crew. He was not the person in charge, but rather someone who followed orders. There was no point in getting mad at him. Instead of screaming at him, I asked him if he had any idea why they had lit me so poorly.

"Well, you know, honey, I told them to come around and light you, but that takes time, and time costs money," he said. "You should talk to the cinematographer."

Fortunately the cinematographer—a huge six-foot-six man named Kenny—wasn't around. While I was contemplating skewering him, I had time to think.

My usual response when someone from the crew asked me what I thought of the dailies would have been: "They suck! I hate them! I can't believe how cheap they are." If I started off with that reaction, I probably wouldn't win the lighting director's cooperation for the rest of the run of the show. In this case, I knew I could catch more flies with honey than with a spear.

Later that day Kenny was on the set. He'd heard how upset I was from the gossip network, which has always had greater bandwith and far more speed than any Internet connection. Fortunately, by the time we spoke, I'd decided to leave the spear in my trailer.

"I understand you didn't like the dailies, kid," Kenny said.

"Kenny, they wrote a wonderful script for me, and I'm awfully good in it, but I look so bad that no one can laugh at me. I look ill. I look sick. And now I am heartsick." I said.

His face and his posture softened. He put his arms around me and said: "Honey, that'll never happen again." And it never did.

Had I approached Kenny carrying my spear, we'd never have ended our scene with a hug. Instead, I just told him my feelings and they lit me like I was Garbo for the next four years.

You might think that if you are not clutching your spears constantly, you are undefended. We are programmed to believe that we have to stand up for ourselves, and that standing up for yourself means confrontation. You could pick those spears up so fast that the wind would blow. They're always close by, but very rarely necessary. Like lawsuits.

I believe that, in conflict, it is just as courageous, perhaps more so, to show your vulnerability and your need, and use that as the starting point for a discussion. When you allow people to feel your feelings you allow them to see your humanity, and you open the door for them to be generous and offer up some of theirs. There's a relationship, a give-and-take. You still might find yourself in a confrontation, but it will be clear to both of you that you're not dealing with an enemy. Kenny and I had a common interest: we both wanted the show to look as good as it possibly could. If you search for the point of connection, instead of the point of conflict, it is easier to find some common ground, and maybe even a solution.

The problem with carrying a spear is not just that you might be too quick to use it, or reach for it in the wrong situation. The real problem is what it does to your body to be clutching your weapon all the time. I know from personal experience that when you're toting a spear the muscles throughout your body are flexed, your chest is constricted, and your heart is beating rapidly. You've got on a heavy suit of armor, and it's all tiring.

When you're clutching a spear, people don't see you. They only see your anger. If you want life to surprise you, you've got to be open to it rather than defending against it.

It's hard to break patterns that you've had for many years, but it's possible. I find that when I'm dealing with people on the set, or about to go into a situation that could become a confrontation, I say to myself, "Let it go. Let it go." And it does, it goes. That doesn't mean caving in and putting up with what makes you nuts. Just say, for right now I'm going to let it go. Do this and you'll find you'll very rarely need to use your spear.

Use your spear to skewer this recipe instead.

Beef Kabob

One 2-pound flank steak cut into 1–1 ½-inch cubes

1 cup soy sauce

1 cup Worcestershire Sauce

1 cup red wine

½ cup honey

3 cloves garlic, minced

2 green bell peppers quartered, seeded, cut into 1–1½ inch
     pieces totalling 24

onions, quartered and broken into 24 sections

24 cherry tomatoes

12 wooden skewers

1. In a large bowl or zip lock bag, combine first six ingredients, mix well, and refrigerate for at least 3 and up to 24 hours. The longer the better.
2. Meanwhile, soak the skewers in water.
3. To assemble the kabobs, start with one piece of the meat on a skewer, then one piece of pepper, then onion, and last, a tomato. Repeat that order. Repeat on remaining skewers.
4. Grill 2–3 minutes per side.

Makes 12 skewers.

Chapter 15

Lean In and Talk Softly

My dear friend, the wonderfully talented actor Jimmy Coco, once taught me how to get whatever I wanted in a hotel, restaurant, or place of service. He explained that you go to the head person, lean into their desk, and do not move from that position. Don't pull back. Just lean in and, in a very quiet voice, simply tell him what you want. It's a lesson that I think also applies to disputes in life.

When Jimmy explained this technique, I thought he was joking. How was that going to help? My idea for getting what I wanted out of people who supposed to serve me was to act outraged: you explain how your expectations haven't been fulfilled, and that if you don't get satisfaction you'll ask to speak to the person's superior—and then the next superior, all the way up the chain of command.

Each time you move further up the chain, your voice has to get louder, in an attempt to intimidate and to convey your increasing righteous outrage. By the time you get to the manager, you're screaming. The only problem with this is, by the time you get to someone who can help you, your blood pressure is so high you could blow a gasket. Instead of a waiter, now you need a doctor, and in some extreme cases, a lawyer. How can you enjoy your victory from a hospital bed? It took me many years to discover that Jimmy was right. In fact, I didn't really appreciate it until I took a trip to Italy with my family a few years ago.

A few years ago, the cast of *Raymond* filmed a couple of episodes in Italy. We were scheduled to be away from home for three weeks, with a few weeks off after we finished our work there. Most of us took this opportunity to see a little more of Italy. I'd been there many times over the years, but always with my husband. Everywhere I looked there was something exquisite to see: paintings, sculpture, architecture. From that moment on, I loved going to museums and traveling to Europe. This time I wanted to share it with my family. Michael's father was Italian, so I thought it would be nice for him, his wife Jane, and my grandkids to see his father's native land. We spent two weeks touring all over the country.

An essential stop on any tour of Italy is a few days in Venice. I had been there several times before and stayed at the Hotel Cipriani, a first-rate luxury hotel on the tip of Guidecca Island, five minutes by gondola from St. Mark's Square, the heart of the city. I was happy to be able to treat my family to a stay in this remarkable hotel. It's no monotonous corporate hotel or cookie-cutter tourist trap. Each room is decorated in a grand and gilded fashion. In the middle of a crowded island, where real estate comes very dear, the Cipriani has extensive gardens and an Olympic-size swimming pool.

The hotel's swimming pool was what attracted me most of all when I was arranging the trip. Adults might be content viewing churches and historic ruins, and having a glass of wine to cool down, but the kids would need some place to blow off steam.

I rented us a suite of rooms with a terrace that overlooked the lagoon. The views and the tranquility of the place were absolutely extraordinary. When we first arrived, the kids instantly wanted to jump in the pool, so I took them for a swim. As soon as their feet hit the water, one of the very prim and proper pool managers insisted they leave. It turned out that at the Cipriani, children are not allowed in the pool between noon and 6:00 P.M. This was strict hotel policy.

I looked at the sad faces of my grandchildren and realized something had to be done. If I tried to keep them in the room, neither the room nor I would survive. The pool manager did not have enough power to overturn the policy, however. I got the kids out of the pool, wrapped them in hotel towels, and told them to wait for me on the lounge chairs. Then I headed straight to the hotel manager.

"Signor, do I look like an insane woman?" I asked. "Why would I order the presidential suite if my grandchildren could not swim in the pool? I would have booked rooms at the Lido."

"I'm sorry, madam, but this is hotel policy," he said.

"No one told me about this policy. I would never have booked the rooms if I'd known," I said. My emotions were a stew of guilt, embarrassment, and rage, as I imagined a difficult three days at the Cipriani where our entire schedule would have to be re-arranged to accommodate the limited hours the kids could use the pool. After all, noon to six is precisely the time they'd need to cool off.

Something so minor looks very big when cranky children are involved. I'd imagined this place to be an oasis in our trip, but it just had become the opposite. I was frustrated by the stupid policy, upset that I hadn't planned better. Although I was anticipating disaster, I knew that I couldn't allow any of these emotions into my voice.

Then I leaned in and spoke very softly. "My grandchildren will swim in the pool. If they are too noisy, you may throw them out, but they will swim in your pool today and for the rest of our stay."

"Of course, madam," he said.

When you lean in and talk softly, you shake up the conflict. In fact, I think you kill the conflict outright because you mix up the messages: the soft voice and gentle demeanor with the firm communication. It was almost as if I was taking the manager into my confidence and asking for his assistance, rather than issuing a demand. Like a charming bank robber to whom they happily hand over the money. I was using neither the stereotyped male or the female tech-niques. I didn't pound my fist on the reception desk and insist to be treated with deference, nor did I look lost and dismayed to get sym-pathy. So, all of us got what we wanted. He was able to be gracious without feeling as if he'd been bullied, and my kids were able to swim in the pool in the heat of a humid Venetian afternoon.

It worked out pretty well for the hotel, too. Later that day, one of the hotel guests lost her diamond and pearl necklace. She suspected it had fallen off while swimming and was lying at the bottom of the pool. Only in Italy does a woman go swimming in a diamond and pearl necklace! Geez, why didn't she swim in high heels, too? The other guests had had a lot of wine with lunch and were sleeping in the lounge chairs at the sides of the pool. None of them was in any shape to help this distressed woman. In fact, my grandchildren were the only people who *could* come to her aid.

Kelsey, Andy, and Devon had a grand time making a game of try-ing to find the necklace, much like the game we play at home in the pool where we throw coins in and they wiggle down like little gup-pies to retrieve the nickels, dimes, and quarters. Of course, this pool was bigger, and the game was insured by Lloyds of London.

They swam with gusto, and swept the pool bottom inch by inch until they found it. The woman was overjoyed, and the kids were given a reward of 50,000 lire. They were ecstatic. The manager was thrilled that the kids were able to assist in the rescue and recovery of her precious jewels. Not one of the guests complained about the behavior of my grandchildren, who were able to use the pool for the length of our stay.

All of this because I leaned in, talked softly, and didn't back down.

In memory of our trip to Italy, here's a hearty cheesecake my grand-children love.

Sicilian Ricotta Cheesecake
(50,000 Lire a slice)

2 pounds ricotta cheese

⅔ cup white sugar

⅓ cup all-purpose flour

6 eggs

2 teaspoons vanilla extract

¼ teaspoon ground cinnamon

2 teaspoons orange zest

⅛ teaspoon salt

1. Preheat oven to 300 degrees. Set rack in the middle of the oven.
2. Butter and flour a 9-inch spring-form pan, and tap out excess flour.
3. Place the ricotta in a large mixing bowl and stir it as smooth as possible with a rubber spatula.
4. Stir the sugar and flour, together, thoroughly into the ricotta.
5. Stir in the eggs one at a time.
6. Blend in the vanilla, cinnamon, orange zest, and salt.
7. Pour batter into the prepared pan and bake in the center of the oven for about 1¼ to 1½ hours, until a light golden color. (Make sure the center is fairly firm and the point of a sharp knife inserted in the center comes out clean.) Cool on a wire rack. It will sink slightly as it cools. Once cooled, cover and chill till serving time.

Serves 8.

Part Five

Travels

Chapter 16

In Africa, Everybody Is Somebody's Lunch

Everyone loves to talk about the competitive nature of our society, the dog-eat-dog world we all live in, where only the strong survive. Sometimes the brutal aspects of life can seem a little abstract. We do live in a competitive world, but none of us is getting literally gobbled up by those who envy us. Day to day, when your job is secure and you're moving through the world following your regular routine, you don't exactly feel the predators nipping at your heels. That is, unless you are either driving in Los Angeles or on safari in Africa. Either way, you should have a guide who speaks the language—and a hunting rifle.

About fifteen years ago, I left behind the world of Los Angeles drivers and traveled with a few friends to Africa for a photographic safari. The idea of a photographic safari has always had a romantic appeal to me. I thought of myself at a respectful distance from the great animals, with my trusty twenty-dollar camera at the ready to record my encounters with the creatures of legend—kind of like the fans who come to Los Angeles hoping to catch a glimpse of the stars in their natural habitat. Although I didn't imagine throwing my arm around a rhino and telling him how much I appreciate his work. I wanted the guides and the guards to keep us at a safe distance and make sure that that distance was maintained at all times. The animals, I found, followed a different set of rules.

The trip began well enough, with our journey to The Ark, a three-story hotel in the Kenyan region of Masai Mara. This territory of the legendary warrior tribe, the Masai, is also home to all five of the great African mammals—the rhino, the water buffalo, the lion, the elephant, and the leopard. The hotel overlooks a river where the animals come at night to drink. Sort of like the Oak Bar of the jungle.

The first floor of the building was at the level of the riverbank, with small openings bored in the concrete where visitors could position their cameras for a close-up photograph of the animals as they wallowed. Not the "depressed by my career" type of wallowing that they do in Hollywood. More of the "it's hot, there's flies, and I wish I had thumbs" type of wallowing.

The second floor was the dining room, which had huge, one-way plate glass windows, so diners could observe the animals as both nourished themselves. That dining room was like a cathedral, it was so quiet. Our four-star meal seemed simple when compared to their stalk, kill, and devour special of the day. And, as safe as I felt, if it weren't for that plate glass, I'm sure they would have been eating California Cuisine. We all ate our meals whispering, lest we scare the animals away. In fact, the real question was: who was in the cage?

When we went to our rooms on the third floor that night, the staff informed us that, if any of the great five arrived at the riverbed for nocturnal refreshment, a bell would go off. If we wanted to, we could slip into our bathrobes and go down to the second floor for a peek at the animals. Around two in the morning, the bell went off and I grabbed my robe, padding like a little mouse down the stairs with the others on our tour. We were incredibly excited to see a rhino going for a late-night swim in the cool water. Rhinos are the most difficult to glimpse, as so many of them have been killed by poachers. Our visitor was so close, we felt as though we could reach out and touch him.

On the way back up the stairs I came across my companions, Rosetta and Sam, showered, fully dressed, and Sam had shaved. Like new arrivals at the zoo, they were confused in their cage, and when the bell went off they thought it meant breakfast. The entire time the rhino was grooming himself, they were doing the same. When I told them that we'd just spent half an hour watching the rhino through the one-way windows on the second floor, they jogged down to the concrete portholes with their cameras in hand. All they got a glimpse of was the rhino's rear as he made his way off in search of a better midnight nibble. Clearly if you snooze, all you get is rhino tail.

The next day the safari part began in earnest. We were bouncing over the savannah in a Land Rover whose canvas top had been pulled back so we could stand up and take photographs of the animals. We came to a stop in a place where five cheetahs were sunning themselves in the grass. As the cameras clicked away, one of the cheetahs roused and took a long look at us. We were thrilled to think he found us as fascinating as we found him, as if this was an intellectual and cultural exchange, rather than his contemplation of a car full of exotic delicacies. Our admiration of him froze in place when he jumped onto the hood of the Land Rover.

I was standing up in the front passenger seat and found my proximity to the cat very exciting. So exciting, I almost wet my pants. I remained brave, however, because I didn't have much choice. If I fled the Land Rover, I would clearly be lunch. I should take his picture, I thought. How often in life do you get face-to-face with a cheetah? Unless you live next to Siegfried and Roy. I tried to get the cheetah to look me in the eye for a full-face photograph with my silly little twenty-dollar camera. "Here kitty, kitty, kitty," I sang out. "Here kitty, kitty, kitty."

The kitty evidently liked my little song, because he pounced within four inches of my face.

Sam, who was standing next to me, was assessing the Land Rover to determine which door would be the best to throw me out of, when the cheetah got really angry. This is the jungle, and the weak and the stupid are left by the side of the road. Clearly, Sam thought I was both. Everyone in the car was letting out tiny peeps of extreme anxiety. Surely these peeps communicated vulnerability across the species. And the wet pants didn't help, either. The cheetah lowered his gaze and looked deep into my eyes.

The driver gave me his cap and instructed me to wave it at my new best friend to scare him away. I looked at him like he was the one who should be left behind. Wave at this cat! Isn't that like waving a red flag at a bull? Besides, he'd told us in his narration of the physical attributes, preferences, and habitat of cats, that while they looked so sweet and playful sunning themselves, they don't have retractable claws. If he took a swipe at the cap, I'd be shredded with it.

Stalemate—as the cat assessed my nutritional content and I contemplated the state of my will. The driver turned on the motor, reasoning that if he moved the car just the right way the cat would fall off. Of course, if he moved the car the wrong way, the cat would end up in my lap. He quietly moved the car just a little bit, and the cat jumped off the hood of the car and went to join his buddies. We drove away slowly—agonizingly slowly—so as not to remind the gang of five that prey was getting away and encourage pursuit. There we were, lunch for five in the Land Rover. Meals on wheels.

When you're the lunch special on the menu in Africa, we found out, you usually don't know it. At another point in this journey in the Land Rover, we watched five lionesses stalking a gazelle. What a silly, self-absorbed teenager this gazelle was. She was jumping and prancing around for a male gazelle, unaware that in the bush behind her the lionesses were making their deliberate approach. They moved slowly and silently. First one would advance a few feet. Then another would take the lead, advancing a few feet over the position of her partner. Their stalking took close to two hours. When they all five were within striking distance, they sent out some imperceptible signal and all pounced at once. Lunch is served. We'll wrestle over the check later.

We were on our way to a group of mountains called the Matthews Range, in Sambura country, and were to be the first people ever to use this new camp. As we entered the camp, we went directly to the bar, thirsty for a few cocktails that could help soften the anxiety of our many brushes with death that day. We walked into the bar, and lying across the length of it was a huge green mambo snake, one of the most deadly snakes in the world, who very quickly answered the question of: what's your poison? You know, I think I have a flask in my suitcase that will do me just fine for now. We scurried out faster than wildebeests in a stampede.

The tents slept two people and were organized to provide as much of an assurance of safety as possible; but there were no guarantees. Inside, the tent had two little cots at one end and a basin to wash your hands in at the other. When you left the tent you unzipped it and were supposed to quickly turn and zip it back up so as not to let in the bugs, or the lunch crowd. About five feet away was another smaller tent with your shower and toilet. The whole arrangement was watched over by a Sambura warrior with a spear who stood sentry at the side of the tent. A Sambura warrior with a spear? I would have been much happier if he'd been a Marine with an automatic weapon.

Since I was in Africa and was facing death at every turn as part of my vacation package, I had a few glasses of wine that night in the hope that I could get to sleep. As I lay pretending in my cot, the pressure to use the facilities built within my body. I was like an eleven-year-old kid at sleep-away camp, but it wasn't the bears I was scared would get me. It was the cheetahs and the cobras. Not to mention that its intimidating to pee in front of a man with a spear. Outside in the African night I could hear the animals bellowing and growling and chowing down. How was that warrior, even if he was a spear-carrying Sambura, going to stand up against a hungry lioness? I unzipped the tent zipper just a few inches to look at the distance between me and the toilet. Yup. About half a mile away.

I zipped myself back in, and I looked around the tent for an alternative. The choices were limited to the floor, or faking a "summer camp accident." My eyes fell on the washbasin. *Ah*. It was large enough, it was made out of tin, and the shape of it was like an echo chamber. I danced around it for a while, trying to convince my body that I only had to wait a few more hours. Who was I kidding? I waded up Kleenex and stuffed it in the bottom of the basin to muffle the sound. Despite that, I know I sounded like an elephant peeing on a tin roof.

The next day, we took off for an early-morning hot air balloon ride. We flew silently over a river filled with hippos and saw herds of galloping giraffe. As we took in the rolling hills, we observed pride after pride of lions galloping across the tall grass in the same direction we were flying. I heard the sound of a bird's wings flapping very close to the balloon and turned around to see an enormous bird with a huge snake in his mouth. Maybe our bar snake had become part of someone else's happy hour.

The tour company had arranged for us to have a champagne breakfast when we landed in the middle of the Masai plain. Talk about luxury!

As we enjoyed our morning meal, we reviewed the lions' route. Suddenly we realized that, given the speed and direction they were traveling and the speed and direction of the winds that pushed our balloon, the lions would be at our breakfast site in about a half an hour. If we didn't get on our way, we'd be chicken in a basket.

The next stop was the home of Betty Leslie-Melville, the woman who was responsible for saving the Rothschild giraffe from extinction. We stayed at her wonderful house outside Nairobi, where giraffes put their heads through the open sections in the windows in the morning so you can feed them. My friends took a wonderful picture of me feeding a giraffe. I look like a little kid, I was so excited by what I was doing. I was also excited that, for the first time on the trip, I was no longer on the menu.

This is the lunch the animals missed.

Chicken in a Basket

1 whole roasting chicken
1 whole lemon
1 whole small orange
45 cloves garlic
a few thyme branches
a few thin pats of butter
salt and pepper

1. Clean chicken by removing innards and excess fat and discard. Place chicken breast-side-up onto a rack resting in a roasting pan.
2. Tuck the wings behind the shoulders so they do not burn.
3. Slice half of the lemon and half of the orange as thin as you can manage.
4. With your fingers, create a space between the skin and the breast.
5. Line the space with the lemon and orange slices and lay thyme branches between the fruit and the skin.

6. Juice the remaining halves of the orange and lemon. Stuff the inside cavity with the juiced pulp and rind and a couple of cloves of garlic.
7. Rub the outside skin with butter. Salt and pepper the entire bird, inside and out.
8. Line the bottom of the pan with about ¼ inch of water.
9. Put it in the oven at 325 degrees for 20 minutes per pound, basting with the juice of the lemon and orange occasionally.

Basket of Fries

1–1 ½ small-to-medium potatoes per person
canola oil
olive oil
1 teaspoon Herbes de Provence
salt

1. Cut potatoes into sticks of desired length and thickness and put cut potatoes into cold water.
2. In a high-sided frying pan, pour ½ inch of canola and ¼ inch of olive oil and sprinkle Herbes de Provence into oil.
3. Heat oil to 325 degrees (use a thermometer, or heat until a drop of water sizzles) but before it reaches the smoking point.
4. Drain potatoes as thoroughly as you can, as the excess water will pop in the oil. Add potatoes to hot oil so that potatoes are covered. You may have to work in batches to accomplish this.
5. When potatoes are the color brown you like, remove with a slotted spoon onto paper towels to drain. Salt the potatoes on the paper towels. Transfer to platter and serve alongside chicken.

Serves 4–6, depending on how hungry you are.

Chapter 17

Please, Allah, Not the Fat Ones!

In the years since my husband Bill passed away I've gone on some memorable three-week vacations with friends of mine: Africa, China twice, Australia, and the Middle East. In the course of these wanderings, I've picked up a number of travel tips for women, little things that I want to pass on to you.

Plan for Spontaneity. The most incredible itinerary and best educational experience was a Middle East trip I took with curators from New York's Metropolitan Museum of Art, a trip I didn't plan to go on. My good friend Joan LaCaille's brother, Brad, is one of the museum curators, and sometimes leads tours through regions of the world that are rich in art treasures.

We were visiting Brad's family one day, when his wife told us that as soon as he got back from Russia he was going to guide a Metropolitan Museum cruise through the Middle East: to Jordan, Syria, and Turkey. There were still two slots open for travelers. I turned to Joan and said: "We're going." Joan thought I was insane. How could we get ready so quickly? Wouldn't we need special shots, visas, and clothing? Would it be possible to get out of our other commitments on such short notice? This was just crazy.

Fortunately, Joan is crazy in the same way I am. That's what makes us such compatible travel companions. We had both longed to see the ancient Jordanian trading post, Petra, and this was our chance. It was Thursday when we found out. When Saturday rolled around, we were in the airport waiting for our flight to take off for Amman, Jordan. It was the trip of a lifetime, and if we'd waited, we would have missed it.

Anticipate Boredom. Joan and I were cruise-ship veterans, and we knew that meals would be a chore if we were seated at a table with couples whose conversation bored us, or who found our sense of humor a little too much to take. We stood with our group in the airport, sizing up our companions and trying to pick a pair to team up with for the journey. It was like a reality show—*Survivor: Cruise Ship Dinner Table.* We had to form a tribe quickly.

We examined clothing, body language, and the look in the eye. It's easy to spot somebody who's too uptight and had their toilet training earlier than they should have. Our eyes fell on Dr. Clem, a large man with a long, loose look about him, and Donald, whose eyes glinted with a spark of mischief and humor. Neither one had a wife! We approached them and asked if we could form a mealtime alliance. It turned out to be the smartest move of the trip. Dr. Clem and Donald were a lot of fun, and we spent all our time together during this trip, both mealtimes and touring. We are all still friends to this day.

Don't Be Afraid to Ask for Directions. On the way to Jordan, part of the tour was to trace the route that Moses took when he spent forty years leading the Jews out of Egypt to The Promised Land. Most of us think Moses is Charlton Heston in *The Ten Commandments,* a movie that went on for about forty years. In it, Moses is very distractible. Once he and his pals sprint across the floor of the Red Sea, he's got to go all the way up to the top of Mt. Sinai and get his marching orders from a burning bush, of all things. Couldn't God have burned the bush a little closer to home?

Then he's got to lug those heavy Ten Commandments down the mountain to his followers. This, in the days before chiropractors. God, use parchment next time, please. Once he's finally down there, no one wants to listen to him. They're too busy with the golden calf. With all this going on, you can see why it took him forty years to finally get home.

It took us about ten minutes to find The Promised Land. It's on a promontory. I looked over Jordan, which was the river right underneath my feet, and I began to sing: "*I looked over Jordan, and what did I see?/Coming for to carry me home?*" And what did I see? Jerusalem! Clearly, Jewish men have no sense of direction. And like all men, they must have been too proud to ask.

Bargain, It's Expected, and People Are Insulted When You Don't. We reached the legendary trading post of Petra, the ancient precursor of the New Jersey Turnpike (where to my amazement, there wasn't one Starbucks). The formerly nomadic Jordanian tribe of the Nabateans found this passage between the mountains on the Silk Road and built a city there, so they could charge every single camel that passed through. The Nabateans were a huge tribe of Michelangelos. Michelangelo said that, when he was about to sculpt, he took a block of marble and cut away everything that wasn't the figure he was sculpting. The Nabateans did this to the stone cliffs from which they carved a city.

The entire city of Petra was crafted by chiseling away at the rose quartz cliffs around it. It's a city carved out of luminous pink rock that glows as the sun passes across the horizon. We descended through a 4,000-foot-long, narrow gorge called a "siq," formed by a prehistoric earthquake. Earthquakes don't make for the most vehicle-friendly passageways. The width of the gorge varied six feet to fifty-five feet. It was hard to keep focused on the road. All around us, the burnt orange sandstone cliffs rose higher as we made our way to the city at the bottom of what once was an ocean floor.

Suddenly, the gorge opened into the main square of the city,

aglow with pink veins of copper and magnesium. Directly before us
was a hundred-and-thirty-foot-tall monument called El-Dhazneh—
or the Pharoah's Treasury—with six huge columns topped by an urn.
It is supposed to have taken a hundred years to chisel this incredible monument out of the rock. It wasn't even covered with graffiti,
pigeon droppings, or gum.

The Nabateans weren't just happy little monument builders and
toll collectors. The archaeological digs conducted in the last hundred years have unearthed a very advanced civilization. They built a
sophisticated plumbing system, paved their city streets, and built an
amphitheater that could seat eight thousand. Now that's my kind of
audience.

As we tromped around Petra, we got tired and stopped for some
tea. At the back of the café was an extremely large man, about as big
around as my dining room table. My dining room table with all the
leaves in set for Thanksgiving dinner. He was a Bedouin chieftain
whose face lit up when he saw me. It turned out that *Remington
Steele* played three times a week on Jordanian television, and the
chief was a big fan of the show. About as *big* a fan as you could get.
He motioned for me to come over and I obliged. I was afraid of what
would happen to the furniture if he tried to stand up. Through an
interpreter, he offered fifteen camels for me.

I stood in amazement. Who was he going to give the camels to?
But I knew this was the Middle East, and it was okay to bargain.

"Make it thirty and you've got a deal," I said.

Apparently thirty camels is too high a price for an old broad,
even one who's seen on TV!

Always Wear Comfortable Shoes, Always. The tour of Petra's eight
square kilometers took the entire day and ended up at the bottom of
a very steep hill, with a long climb back to the tour bus. Dr. Clem
and I were dragging after a full day of walking, and, as we headed for
the opening in the gorge that is the exit point for the city, we saw a

tiny Arab man with a cart pulled by a small horse. We both got the same idea.

"Should I bargain with him to take us back to the bus?" Dr. Clem asked.

"Oh please," I said, staggering with the heat. "I can't make another step, I'm so exhausted."

He bargained with the Arab until he indicated we could get into the cart. Dr. Clem was a very large man, and I'm no lightweight. It was hard for both of us to squish in, but with a little shimmying we got both of our big fannies into the small space and waited for our ride to begin. The horse took a tentative step and stopped. He tried a step with the other front foot, but strained under the effort. Slowly, he turned his head around, and, from the look of pain in his face, one could imagine his thoughts: "Please, Allah, not the *fat* ones!"

Suddenly, we were bathed in a horribly foul odor. I didn't know the good doctor well enough to ask him if he had been the one who had passed wind. Then I looked up at our beleaguered steed. He'd raised his tail at us. That horse was farting in our faces! He was trying to get us out of the cart.

The owner came running our way, screaming at us to get out of the cart. "No, no, no!" he screamed. "You get out. You will kill my horse!"

At least we had each other for comfort. Plus—thank God—comfortable shoes for the very long, very steep trek back to the bus.

This delicious Middle Eastern chicken recipe always reminds me of this journey.

Middle Eastern Chicken

2 cups plain yogurt

1 large clove garlic, minced

1 handful chopped fresh mint

1 tablespoon oregano

1 handful chopped parsley

salt and pepper to taste

1 whole chicken, cut into quarters

1 cup crumbled feta cheese

1. Combine first six ingredients in a bowl.
2. Place chicken in large bowl and pour marinade, reserving 2 tablespoons over chicken. Toss to coat. Let chicken marinate for 1 hour but no longer. Otherwise the chicken begins to cook in the acidic marinade, which is not what you want!
3. Arrange chicken in an oven-proof dish and bake for 30–40 minutes. Baste with reserved marinade halfway through.
4. Sprinkle crumbled feta on top of chicken 2–3 minutes before removing from the oven.

Serves 4–6.

Chapter 18

The Last Voyage of
The France

"The most beautiful woman in the world wants to take you to France," read the enticing advertisement in *The New York Times* for the ocean liner *The France*, in the summer of 1974. Just looking at the picture of it in the newspaper gave me a thrill. It was an enormous, elegant ship, one of the last of the thousand-foot ocean liners with a reputation for elegance and the best of service. My second husband Bill Goyen's book, *Arcadio*, was being published that July, and we were looking for a way to celebrate. We booked passage for ourselves and Michael on this legendary vessel that summer without catching even a whiff of the chaos that awaited us on board.

The France rose majestically alongside Pier 94 on the Hudson River like a sweeping figure in an art deco illustration. Its narrow hull swooped grandly to a wide deck. The hull was painted midnight black, and huge clouds of steam poured from its smokestacks. As Bill, Michael, and I made our way up the passenger gangplank, we felt so small, like little bugs, compared to the majesty of the ship.

There was hubbub on the pier, as hundreds of well-dressed families and their friends surrendered their possessions to the porters trucking dollies stacked with beautiful luggage into the hold of the ship.

The France was so big that families were able to ship their cars in its hold, drive them around Europe, and ship them back. I saw whole households of furniture being carted up the gangplank for the families who were starting a life in France at the end of this journey. Just by looking at them, you could see they were a different class of people, able to afford a more leisurely pace of life. They didn't hop on a jet and land in France. They had the time and the money to travel in style.

We settled in our stateroom, a room big enough for three, which featured one of the ship's big portholes as our window, and our guests began to arrive. Bill's publisher was among the many who sent us champagne for our bon voyage party, and the room was crowded with writers and theater people toasting Bill. When the gong sounded, we walked everybody to the gangway, crowding around the railing with the rest of the passengers to wave good-bye to our friends and New York City. As *The France* pulled away from the dock, we tossed handfuls of brightly colored streamers off the side, like silent fireworks against the darkness of the hull. The sight of New York behind us, as we glided down the Hudson along the westside of Manhattan, passing the skyline and the Statue of Liberty, and easing out into the Atlantic, is a memory that still thrills me.

As we relaxed on the deck chairs that afternoon, I couldn't help but compare this voyage to my last sail across the ocean. Fifteen years earlier, my first husband and I had arranged free passage for ourselves and Michael on a Greek freighter docked in Canada that was headed for Europe. I say Europe, because our specific destination was unclear. The ship was full of grain for which there wasn't yet a buyer. The captain was instructed to head east, and by the time the ship neared Europe, its owners would know whether the highest bidder was in Glasgow, Scotland, Kiel, Germany, or Genoa, Italy.

We'd driven our little car up to Canada, uncertain where we'd begin our European vacation.

That trip was supposed to save my marriage, but instead it ended up busting it apart. This trip on *The France* couldn't have been more different. I was a successful actress, in love with my husband, taking a transatlantic cruise on the world's most elegant ship. I sat in a deck chair savoring the champagne and life's ability to surprise you.

I'd worried that Michael might be bored on a six-day journey. Most of the people who could afford passage on a ship of this quality were well-off, middle-aged adults, or even older. Would Michael be able to find anyone his own age to talk to? We were incredibly fortunate that the cruise line had offered student discounts, and the ship had dozens of college-age kids on their way to spend a year in a European college, or so they told their parents. The time Michael spent unpacking his suitcase that first afternoon was the longest period of time I spent with him the entire way across.

We'd heard about the ship's Chambord dining room, which *The New York Times* food critic Craig Claiborne had called "the finest French restaurant in the world." Whoever designed it understood the theatrical aspects of dining in the grand style. The room had a domed, blue ceiling sprinkled with tiny lights that looked like stars in a twilight sky.

To enter the room, you walked down a grand, sweeping staircase. Each time we arrived for a meal, I paused at the top of the stairs. Men swore the women hesitated there because they wanted to make an entrance. That wasn't really true in my case. I hesitated because I was drinking it all in: the etched glass, the great chandeliers, heavy silverware, fine china, and fresh flowers on the heavy, starched damask table clothes. Okay, so maybe I didn't mind all eyes turning to me either—I'm an actress, you know.

The France was a floating city of eleven decks, three nightclubs, and a movie theater that could seat six hundred and forty people.

Guests could work off the richness of the incredible meals at either of the two gyms or pools. One pool was at the back of the ship, and it was enclosed, because, a lot of the time during the crossing, the weather made it impossible to swim outdoors. There was also an elegant French pool, illuminated by a chandelier, inside the ship, exclusively for the first-class passengers. If you didn't like exercise, there were plenty of other ways to pass the time—in the library, the music room, or one of the many, many bars.

Michael amused himself wandering around the ship when he wasn't chasing girls. He found his way into the engine room and got to see its inner workings. He threaded his way through the passageways until he found the kitchen, the source of a lot of pleasure and mystery on this ship. We'd heard that the twenty-two separate kitchen departments employed one hundred and eighty cooks. This had to be a pretty big operation. I think what Michael was really interested in was finding the source of the incredibly flaky croissants that were baked fresh every morning. We both swear we've never had better.

Four days into the journey, the crew started to rumble. It had been a very bad year for cruise ships, which had suffered a huge blow when the 1973 oil embargo more than doubled fuel prices. Fewer and fewer people could take the time to make an ocean crossing, and *The France*, which was subsidized by the French government, was sailing rocky political seas because it was losing a lot money. The crew got word while we were on board that this was the ship's last journey. When we docked at Le Havre, this gigantic crew of people, who had spent all their working lives on the grand ship, would be out of jobs, and their way of life would end. For some of them it would be a tragedy for the whole family, as generations of families had worked on these ships.

I felt sympathy for them, and sorrow that we were the last people who would have the incredible experience of sailing on this ship. I did the only thing an American does under the circumstances: I started circulating a petition asking the French government not to decommission the ship. People signed it readily, but I knew it was a futile gesture. I think the crew appreciated it, though.

That last night, as we approached French territorial waters, the crew rushed us through dinner. Through Michael and Bill's command of French, we pieced together that once the ship got into French waters, the crew was going to go on strike. As this was a ship, a strike was a mutiny, thus requiring the intervention of the French state police. The crew was nervous about the French secret service, who had a rough reputation, but they were firm about the strike. The minute *The France* entered French waters, the crew disappeared, the orchestra packed up their instruments, and the confused passengers were left to fend for themselves. Unlike *The Titanic*, this ship wasn't going anywhere.

The crew had positioned *The France* across the entrance to the Le Havre harbor, so that no other ships could enter. Then they shut down the boilers. It was frightening to be captive on the massive, silent ship, now that it was without power. Once the boilers are shut down, we heard, it takes two days to get them started again. Fear started to set in among the passengers.

There was absolute chaos on the ship, which went rapidly to hell. Trash started to pile up. People walked their dogs on deck, and no one bothered to clean up the mess. As the evening wore on, the hungry guests started to get a little crazy.

Michael's exploration of the ship's inner workings started to pay off. I bumped into him in the hallway and was surprised to see him carrying bread and an armful of table wine. Where did he get that? He took me down the service elevator and led me through a maze of passageways, then opened the door to one of the kitchens. Inside was the remainder of the days' croissants and a stash of fresh fruit. I'd retrieved one of our bon voyage presents—a bottle of fine champagne—and we uncovered an ice bucket and some champagne flutes. Even though we were in the middle of a mutiny, I still managed to find Dom Perignon and a nice brie.

Michael led me to one of the dumbwaiters, the little elevators no bigger than four-feet-by-four-feet that are used to vertically transport food into the bars and the dining rooms. He loaded me into the elevator with my arms laden with champagne, fruit, and croissants. He shut the door and dashed upstairs to be there when I arrived.

I made one of the most spectacular entrances of my life. Michael opened the dumbwaiter door with a flourish, to reveal me, crammed into this tiny space with a bucket of champagne and all the rest of the supplies for a party. The starving passengers burst into applause and rushed to extract me from the dumbwaiter. People produced musical instruments they'd brought along on the trip and formed an impromptu band. Although our provisions were pretty meager compared to the endless feasts earlier in the trip, I remember this as one of the best parties I've ever attended. The first song I remember them playing was, ironically, "We're In The Money." I was up and down in the dumbwaiter all night, getting whatever I could grab from the abandoned kitchen.

Our celebration came to a rough end when the sun rose and we faced our predicament. The harbor was crowded with small boats filled with reporters trying to get the story, boats full of French police, military, cruise line officials, and labor negotiators trying to board. The noise was deafening, as each group hollered in French through bullhorns. On the ocean side was a trapped mass of boats that had been blocked from entering the harbor.

We had been told to leave our luggage out in front of our doors on the previous night, so it would be easy to gather up when we docked in France. Around midday, the French struck a compromise with the crew that allowed the passengers to leave. A Swedish ferry boat pulled alongside *The France*, and some of the crew helped us get ourselves and our luggage off the ship. It was nothing like the grand way we had boarded the ship in New York. The hostile crew stood at the railing, tossing luggage onto the deck of the small ferry. A lot of it ended up in the water. My family fortunately had packed lightly, comparatively speaking. We carried our own luggage onto the ferry. I have no idea what happened to the poor souls whose cars and furniture were in the hold. *The France* ended up stuck in the harbor for two weeks before the strike was resolved.

I'll never forget my last sight of *The France,* as our overpacked ferry pulled away toward Le Havre. In every porthole up and down the side of the ship were the faces of the crew members. They'd opened the portholes and were waving to us while singing a mournful *Auld Lang Syne.* Some of these people had spent most of their lives on this ship, and the welfare of their families in Le Havre depended on their jobs. It was so sad. Not just the end of an era for them, but the end of a special kind of life of luxury we'll probably never see again.

For a classic French ocean liner, here's a favorite classic French recipe.

Classic Chicken and Mushroom Crepes

¾-stick butter

1 large shallot, chopped

1 pound white mushrooms, cleaned and sliced

1 healthy pinch of fresh thyme

¼ cup white wine

1 quart, plus 2 cups, heavy cream

6 boneless, skinless chicken breast halves, cut into 1½-inch
    chunks

1. Melt butter in a saucepan and add shallots.
2. When shallots are translucent, add mushrooms and thyme and sauté for 5 minutes.
3. Add wine and let evaporate.
4. Add the cream; adjust the flame to low, stir, cover, and let reduce, stirring occasionally. The cream will reduce and the sauce will thicken. This takes a while, but it is worth the effort.
5. As the sauce reduces, heat enough oil in a sauté pan to coat the pan. Just before the oil smokes, or when a drop of water sizzles, add chicken in one layer and sear all sides. It is not necessary to cook the chicken through.
6. Work in batches and transfer chicken to cream sauce. Let cook for another hour or so. The chicken needs that time in the saucepan though it will cook through in about 5 minutes, because long slow cooking enables it to absorb the sauce and become extremely tender.

Crepes

2 eggs

1 cup water

1 cup flour

1. Mix eggs and water in bowl.
2. Fold in flour and mix until smooth.
3. Grease a small fry pan and heat over a medium-high flame.
4. Ladle ⅓ cup of batter (for each crepe) onto the pan and cook. Do not flip.
5. Spoon some of the chicken and mushroom sauce onto half of the crepe. Fold the other side over and slide onto a plate. Spoon some sauce over the crepe, and get ready to die happy.

Serves 6 (two crepes each).

Part Six

Losses

Chapter 19

You've Got to
Turn It Around, Kid

No section on loss would be an honest reflection of what I miss in my life, if I didn't write about my dear friend James Coco: a beautiful man, an incredibly gifted comic, and the kind of friend with whom I never had a fight. Jimmy and I gave each other nothing but laughter and support, and most of the time they were mixed together. I was supported by his ability to see the comic in my most tragic situations. A lot of our laughter came from our shared struggle with our weight.

I met Jimmy when we auditioned for a toilet paper commercial. The casting people asked us to read together as a married couple. They were right, we were a couple—soul mates, in fact. We found each other tremendously amusing. Every line reading that one of us did sent the other one into fits of laughter. We were laughing so hard, we never quite got our lines right. We didn't get the commercial, but we did start a lifelong friendship.

We bonded over the fact that we were both on the same diet: the Scarsdale Diet, a grim and meager bill of fare that forced you to consume very tiny, precisely timed shreds of food. When the instigator of this diet, Dr. Herman Tarnower, was murdered by his girlfriend of many years one Thursday night, Jimmy was the first with a theory of the true motivation behind this cruel act. "It was Thursday night," he said. "Thursday night: spinach and a hardboiled egg. I've thought of killing him myself."

When things got really tough, Jimmy was always a sympathetic ear and a sympathetic eating partner. During the darkest days of my husband Bill's alcoholism, Jimmy was the one I'd lean on. His favorite saying was: "Turn it around kid, turn it around. It's rough right now, but it's not going to be rough forever, so turn it around, turn it around." His pathway out of depression was one I appreciated: food. Tons of it. The sadder we were, the more we ate.

We'd go out to eat, and he'd order more food than anyone could possibly devour, particularly in a Chinese restaurant. Dish after dish. As soon as you felt like you were groaning under the weight of your own overconsumption, the waiter would arrive bearing two more platters. If I scolded him for ordering too much food, he'd say that he just wanted me to taste it. "Put it in your mouth and taste it," he'd always say. "If you like it, swallow it. If you don't, spit it out." As if spitting any food out was possible with two lifelong overeaters! In my entire life, I've never thrown up. Why would I give any food back?

One year we decided the problem was bigger than our capacity for self-control. After all, we had spent most of the year proclaiming to the world that we were on diets, but had ended up *gaining* weight. This brought us to the conclusion that the issues involved must be emotional in nature. We had heard of a new program, a residential treatment facility for weight loss at Duke University in North Carolina. Betty Ford for fatties, where they confined you in a place free from your drug of choice and forced you to confront the real issues that were making you eat. The program was very expensive but, as any of you who have plunked down thousands of dollars on a weight-loss campaign know, the idea is that this time it's going to work. If it solves the problem that's been troubling you for decades, it's money well spent. And the faster you lose the money, the faster you lose the weight.

We flew down to North Carolina eager to have our Last Supper in a first-rate Southern restaurant. In honor of our coming period of self-sacrifice, our surrender to a program that was going to make us uninterested in excessive foods for the rest of our lives, we ate like pigs. We had heaps of fried chicken, towers of biscuits with gravy, mashed potatoes with gravy, gravy with gravy, mint julep after mint julep, and profiteroles, plus pecan pie with ice cream. I remember more about that meal than I do of any meals I had during the several weeks I spent at Duke. Despite the rigors of the program as it was then conducted, we looked forward to this every year, and even persuaded some of our friends to book space the same weeks we were there. Why suffer alone? We always lost the weight we were trying to get rid of, but we once figured out we were paying about a thousand dollars a pound.

The "lockdown" would begin the day after our feast. The program may be different now, but when we were there they had huge waitresses, people who really needed to be enrolled in the program themselves. We lined up cafeteria-style before Shamu and her sisters to choose our meals from the available low-fat, no-sugar, no-taste foods. They limited us to 750 calories a day. 750 calories is a slice of chocolate cake. When mealtime came, I'd ask for a quarter of a peach and an eighth of a cup of cottage cheese and the waitress would advise me that that I was ordering too much food. Everyone had his or her survival techniques. I saw one of the other patients reach over the counter when the waitresses had their backs turned and pocket a handful of chicken breast.

We'd stay for weeks at a time, hunting the countryside for antiques and staying up late playing cards. As the program wore us down and we became used to the tiny portions of food, we became more and more obsessed with television commercials that featured everything delicious we were missing. We muted the programs, but put the volume up for the food commercials. In between fast-food commercials one night came a commercial for Alpo. When the close-up came, Jimmy and I were transfixed by the glistening sight of the dog's meat in the shiny bowl. "You know, with lemon, capers, and mayonnaise, I could make a pretty good appetizer out of that," I said.

The program also required us to go to behavior modification sessions and weight-loss group therapy, which ended up being a lot of fun with Jimmy. He had a way of turning the most tragic story into a joke, not by ridiculing the person who confessed to some humiliating lapse, but by turning it on himself. His trick to turning it around was to always look for the point of connection with people, and tie the humor to the long view of life.

Most of the other patients at the clinic were far more obese than we were. Several of the women had arms that were as big around as my body. The diet was so restrictive, many people devised ingenious ways to get around it. One woman sent herself Candygrams each week. One year, a guy who had been there for seven months finally reached the breaking point during our stay. He checked out and went to Las Vegas where he rented a huge suite at one of the casinos. He ordered himself a bottle of scotch, seventy-five bucks worth of spareribs, and a hooker. The next morning, he woke up and the scotch was gone, the hooker was gone, and on the floor were all these bones. He thought he'd eaten her.

Eventually Jimmy did lose weight, but not on a diet I'd recommend. He became addicted to cocaine, and when I saw him at the height of his problem I became very concerned. After a disturbing evening I spent with him, I woke up and realized I was going to have to say good-bye to my best friend. I was losing him to drugs. I mentioned this to our mutual friend, Roddy McDowell, over dinner that night and he recommended an intervention.

An intervention is when people who really care about you come to your house unannounced to confront you about your addiction. You have to bring with you something you've written that explains your concerns about what this behavior is doing to your friend's career and relationships. The reason you have it written out is that many times the person you're intervening for isn't too pleased about it and throws all of you out. You can leave the paper behind and hope that after the group has gone he will realize the concern and affection that brought you to take this dramatic step, and that will inspire him to read your bit. And maybe that will turn him around.

Roddy got me in touch with a wonderful doctor who led interventions, and we set the event for eleven o'clock on a Saturday. Three of Jimmy's friends arranged to fly out from New York for it, and I agreed to pick them up at the airport early Saturday morning. In all, eleven of us were planning to arrive at his apartment close to midday.

On the Friday night before the intervention, the phone rang. It was Jimmy.

"Guess what? I got a movie. It starts on Monday," he said.

"Oh, how marvelous," I said. "Oh, my God. Who's at my door? Who's at my door at this hour? Hold on. I'll call you back."

I had to call everyone in New York and tell them not to come because Jimmy was starting work on Monday. You needed to be sure that your loved one had twenty-eight consecutive days free after the intervention for this to work. The goal was to get your friend to check directly into a month-long treatment program. After my frantic round of cancellation calls, I phoned him back.

"So tell me about this movie," I said. "I'm so happy for you. Tell me all about it."

"Well, I start on Monday and I work for a week and then I have a month off," he said.

"Oh, who the hell is at my door again?" I said. "I'll call you right back."

I called everyone in New York and said they should rebook their flights for the following Saturday.

When we all arrived at his door the next Saturday he looked so confused.

"What is this?" he said. "Is it my birthday?"

It worked, though. He didn't kick us out, but instead listened carefully to our anguish and our tears. At the end of our speeches, he took what would have been $3,000 worth of cocaine and dumped it in a coffee cup and said "I'm ready to go." The playwright Terrance McNally and I brought him to the treatment program. Jimmy asked me if I would come there every day and sit with him through the twelve-step meetings.

"I don't understand this," I said. "You snort, and I have to go to AA meetings?"

Of course I agreed, and it seemed to be working. One of the program's requirements was that participants have a complete physical to identify any maladies or imbalances that might be contributing to the addiction. Jimmy welcomed this. He'd been having a lot of trouble with his voice. He must have known that there was a serious problem there, because he asked if I'd be with him for the examination. On the day of the test he was trying his best to postpone it but he couldn't stop the collective will of the staff and his best friend.

I was there when the doctor came to give him the results. We knew from the doctor's attitude when he walked in the door that the news was not good. Jimmy had inoperable cancer of the esophagus, the doctor said, and suggested a referral to one of the hospital's top oncologists.

Jimmy turned to me and said I should get him directly to his pusher. I told him I'd get him anything he wanted. As we held each other, the kids from the program kept stopping by the room to tell him it was time for the meeting. We went to the meeting and the subject matter was expectations. The woman who was running the meeting gave Jimmy the microphone.

"Expectations? Expectations," he said with an ironic laugh. "Well, let me tell you about my expectation. I've just been told I have inoperable cancer."

That room just surrounded him with love. Surrounded him. Then he decided to turn it around.

"Okay, I'm going to go up to Vegas and I'm going to be back on Saturday," he said, although promising to stay away from spareribs. "I'm going to New York for treatment. I'm not going to get it here. I want to be near my family."

In New York he saw a doctor who said he could try to reduce the size of the tumor through radiation. If they could reduce the size of it maybe they could operate, he told me. I'd always seen him as buoyant, but comics are great at covering up their true feelings. I never knew he had such a capacity for resilience. He'd beaten his addiction at the eleventh hour and he was still in there fighting to live.

I was in the Bahamas to do *The Regis Philbin Show* when he was undergoing treatment. He tracked me down there late one night to tell me how well it was going. I was overjoyed to hear the fight in his voice. He closed the conversation with something I cling to to this day.

"I've got to tell you, you and I have been lovers all these years, we just never made love," he said. "I love you, Doris."

When someone in his condition makes the effort to track you down to tell you something like that you feel two things. You feel blessed to have heard it and sad, because you know he is saying good-bye. In fact, Jimmy died the next night. He had a massive heart attack, and I like to think that it got him out of the pain, and the fear, and the struggle. My beloved friend. Even as he was dying, he was helping me turn it around. And to this day, I'm still turning it around.

For a meal in memory of Jimmy, go to a Chinese restaurant and order four or five dishes more than you can really eat.

Chapter 20

I Want a Man
Dipped in Chocolate

I've been on dozens of diets, and I can safely say that none of them has worked, at least not for long. Despite the fact that the diet gurus tell you it's not a diet, it's "an eating program—one that will inspire you to make permanent changes in the way you regard food," none of them address the central problem: we love to eat. I suspect that people with my sluggish metabolism, who are thin, just don't like food that much. Or maybe they don't have recipes like mine.

I learned to cook on my own, and my first husband Michael, patiently endured my many barely edible errors. I did learn, finally, and was able to express my love for him—even at times when we weren't getting along that well—by continuing to cook him wonderful meals.

But oh, have I struggled with my weight. We all know how society views overweight people. This point of view is particularly punishing in Hollywood, where a size four is considered a bit on the chubby side . . . and a bit on the barely employable side. I laughed when I found out that the preferred size for starlets these days is a size zero. What kind of self-esteem is attached to a size zero? It's a size that implies that it would be better for a woman to just disappear. Larger women are described as size twelve and up. Size twelve is large? I'd be *ecstatic* to be a size twelve.

As any woman who has fought her weight knows, there are many months, years perhaps, when you just give up. At first there's relief, letting go of the anxious eye that looks at each meal in terms of calories, portion control, point values, and the balance between carbohydrates, proteins and fats. When you give up and give in, for a few days it feels great. You eat just to eat—eat whatever you fancy, and as much as you want. Soon, however, you can feel your body settling in for a lonely winter of just you and your food.

"I can't come to the phone right now. I'm having a meeting with my associates, Ben and Jerry. Call back next spring." After a wallow, I always find myself back on one kind of diet or another, and in the last sixty years I've tried some doozies.

The craziest ones always begin when you see a friend who has lost a big chunk of weight quickly, and you ask her what she's done to get such swift results. In Hollywood this could be anything from liposuction to crack addiction. Your alarm bells should go off any time some woman says she lost ten pounds in ten days, because you know from personal experience that, in order to do that, she's been engaged in some wacky gimmick, and the weight loss won't last. Nevertheless, you think, I'll give it a try. The chain of logic goes like this: *It's only ten days. I can do anything for ten days. And if I lose ten pounds. I'll start feeling so much better about my body that I'll never go back to that sick, disgusting, satisfying way I've been eating for the last three months or thirty years.*

The problem with this line of reasoning is that, in order to lose those ten pounds you switch from one sick, disgusting way of eating good food to another sick, disgusting way of eating, only, in the dieting version, the food you eat is truly bizarre and always expensive.

A few years back, one of my friends suggested that the way to begin weight loss was to cleanse the body of all toxins, something that always sounds like a fabulous idea. If my body and soul were toxin-free, I'd be clean and virginal, and the kinds of foods that weigh me down simply wouldn't appeal to me, or so the delusion goes. If there were no toxins in my body, I'd be lithe and have clear skin, like those women in the health food store who haven't touched sugar in five years and actually like to eat sea kelp. The problem isn't me. *I'm* good. The problem is those damn toxins.

She recommended that I purify myself by spending a day eating nothing but tomatoes. This sounded like an excellent eating plan, because I love tomatoes. I could eat them cold. I could heat them up. Whatever way I wanted to do it, as long as the only thing I ate that day was tomatoes.

I got ten big cans of tomatoes, the twenty-eight ounce kind that I used to make pasta sauce, and stacked them on the kitchen table in a pyramid. By bedtime I'd cut the pyramid in half, and by two o'clock in the morning I called my doctor. I thought I was dying. She asked me what was wrong, and I told her my heart was beating in a crazy rhythm that was keeping me awake and freaking me out.

"What did you do today?" she asked.

"I didn't do anything different," I said.

"Did you eat anything unusual?" she asked.

"All I ate today was tomatoes," I said proudly, expecting her approval. "I was cleansing my body of all toxins."

"How many?" she said with a strong hint of alarm in her voice.

"Every single toxin in my body," I said.

"No, how many tomatoes?"

"Well I've had several cans; five, I think."

"Doris, why would you do anything like that? You could kill yourself that way. An excess of potassium can send your heart all out of whack," she said.

It turns out I was cleansing my body of toxins by poisoning myself. I wanted to lose a little weight, and I almost lost all of it. My own personal *Attack of the Killer Tomatoes*.

Another time I saw a friend at the mall and she looked fabulous. She appeared to have lost about fifteen pounds since the last time I saw her, and she assured me she had done it without going on a diet. This is the other dark alley of weight loss, the one where a friend tells you she's taking a pill or wearing a special bracelet, and the pounds are falling off without her changing the way she eats. The idea always has some weak link to logic. The bracelet or the pill mysteriously boosts her metabolism, and the excess pounds quickly evaporate while she continues to gorge herself on forbidden foods.

That's the weight loss plan for me! Even though I know, when the friend describes her method, that it's illogical, the notion that you could lose weight by doing something that is unrelated to self-discipline is so appealing that I always figure I'll give it a try. What could it hurt? The truth is, it could hurt a lot.

In this case, my friend told me she'd been having deep-tissue shiatsu massage, and that the intense pressure of it was releasing her fat stores. They were rubbing the fat out of her, just forcing it into the bloodstream and out of her system. I made an appointment immediately. The masseuse dug into me and I was in so much pain I can't even describe it. This is good, I thought, as I endured the pummeling and the squeezing. In order for it to be effective, it's got to hurt. Logic, finally.

By the end of the day, I could not walk at all. The masseuse had gone so deep into my back that she inflamed my herniated disc, which swelled up and hit the sciatic nerve. I did not walk for four months, months I spent in bed using crutches to go the fifteen feet from my bed to the bathroom. Maybe her crippling technique would prevent me from sneaking into the kitchen for impulse snacks.

At that time my husband Bill was very ill with leukemia. He was in one room in his bed and I was in another. For a while our sweet neighbors brought over food, but eventually I had to hire a woman to cook for us. I can't remember how I picked her. When you're in pain, you don't spend a lot of time checking references.

"We just want something simple," I said to her over the intercom from my bedroom. "If you roast some chicken and some vegetables, and make a salad, that would be lovely. What vegetables do I have in the bin?"

"Okay, I have something and I don't know what it is," she said. "It's round and dark red. It looks kind of dirty."

"It's called a beet," I said.

"Oh yeah," she said. "I get those out of cans."

At this point I thought I should fire her, but she was so willing and so agreeable that I decided to teach this woman how to cook by remote. That is what I did: lying there in bed, I'd envision what she should be doing and direct her step by step, as if I was the host of a cooking show. She came in not knowing what a beet was and left knowing how to prepare all my specialties.

Besides my back pain, my other problem was that I was immobilized in bed. I was like a beached whale. This weight loss attempt had truly backfired, as I was gaining weight no matter how little I ate. In addition to the drugs my doctor had prescribed for pain, I had an acupuncturist who visited me once a week. She had inserted a staple in my ear and instructed me to jiggle it whenever I felt pain. Again, there was some logic to this. You're in pain, jiggle the handle. The jiggling was supposed to activate a non-drug way the body has of coping with pain, but I was so doped up I don't even know if I remembered to jiggle.

During one of our weekly appointments, I started complaining about my weight gain. She suggested a different staple for my other ear, one that would suppress my appetite. "Of course," Logic said. "My other ear." She was pleased to tell me that she'd just returned from China, where she had acquired some very expensive, high-quality staples specifically designed for this purpose. Normally I wouldn't be so gullible, but at that point I was willing to try anything. I was high on pain pills and ear jiggling. She started to insert a staple and it bent. She looked at me, enraged.

"You bent my staple!" she said. "I brought these from China. They are very, very good and very expensive."

"I'm not doing anything," I said. "I'm just lying here. I didn't bend it."

She got another staple and attempted to put it in. It bent. She was furious.

"You have bent my second staple," she sputtered. "I'm trying to tell you that these are very expensive and very special and I brought them all the way from China. I don't understand what you are doing here."

"I'm simply lying in this bed," I said, getting a little frightened of her. "How could I be breaking your staples?"

She put the third one in, and of course it bent. Again she gave me the spiel about how expensive they were and how special they were and how she brought them all the way from China.

"I don't understand what this means," she said.

"I think it's my body saying 'fuck you,'" I said.

Maybe I shouldn't have said it that way. She left, and I've never seen her since.

There is a time to diet, a time when a self-improvement campaign has a better chance of working, and times when it's bound to fail. When I was getting poked with those staples like a book report, my husband was dying, I couldn't walk, and I was on so much Percodan I couldn't see straight enough to watch television. At this low point I was also going to take food away? My body simply refused.

More than a year later, after Bill had died and I had really taken the time to mourn, I woke up one day blinking at the world like a newborn. The clouds had lifted and somehow I found that I could deal with the idea of getting back out into the world. I was able to look at myself in the mirror for the first time in a long time without seeing only my sorrow. I saw that I needed to lose some weight, and went back to my old friends at Weight Watchers.

Weight Watchers has always worked for me. The diet is sensible and the weight loss is modest-but-steady and nobody tries to staple me. I even enjoy the group meetings. When you do Weight Watchers in Hollywood you get some pretty hilarious characters as your group leaders. One day, about a month into the program, the topic of the meeting was trying to tell the difference between what you want and what you need, a crucial problem in weight loss. One of the reasons we end up at Weight Watchers is that most of us have a real problem with impulse control when it comes to food.

We see it; we eat it. Very little time elapses between the first glimpse of the high-calorie food and the first taste of it. If we had the ability to insert a little pause between impulses and action, most of us wouldn't be in this predicament. Maybe there would even be time to remember what we really want in life, and if eating that cake or plate of pasta would bring us any closer to that larger goal.

The leader went around the room asking us what we really wanted in life. One woman said she wanted to be a famous actress. Another woman said that she wanted to get off her diabetes drugs, because she was frightened that, as she aged, her condition would worsen and she'd have mobility problems. *What do I want?* I was thinking as she made her way around the room. *What do I really want?* I was satisfied with so many aspects of my life, but I still yearned, I still dreamed. If I could pick one thing, what would it be?

"Doris? Doris!" she said, trying to get my attention. "What do you want?"

"I want a man dipped in chocolate," I said. I brought down the room.

This was my weight-loss problem expressed in a single sentence. I didn't just want chocolate. I didn't just want a man. A wanted both, and at the same time. Too much is probably not enough.

The conclusion of this is not the traditional happy ending, which I think would be a revelation that leads to me getting food under control. Experience shows that when you have all the chocolate you want, the men tend to stay away. And when your life is filled with a man, you don't think too much about chocolate. The desires shift back and forth, and, at each stage, the real struggle is to appreciate what you have in that moment. Life is full of choice: Sleep? Food? Sex? When you grow older, only the order of priority changes.

If you can't get a man dipped in chocolate, this recipe will get you through the night.

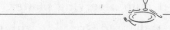

Flourless Chocolate Decadence

I pound bittersweet or semisweet chocolate, coarsely chopped

10 tablespoons (1¼ sticks) unsalted butter, cut into 10 pieces

5 large egg yolks

5 large egg whites

¼ teaspoon cream of tartar

I tablespoon sugar

1. Preheat oven to 325 degrees. Grease an 8×2-inch-round pan and line the bottom with wax or parchment paper.
2. Combine, in a large heatproof bowl, the chocolate and butter. Set the bowl in a large skillet of barely simmering water and melt, stirring often until the chocolate and butter are warm, melted, and smooth.
3. Remove from heat and whisk in egg yolks.
4. In another large bowl, beat egg whites and cream of tartar on medium speed until soft peaks form.
5. Beating on high speed, gradually add sugar. Beat until the peaks are stiff but not dry.

6. Use a rubber spatula to fold ¼ of the egg whites into the chocolate mixture, then fold in the remaining white.

7. Scrape the batter into the pan and spread evenly.

8. Set the pan in a large shallow baking dish or roasting pan, set the baking dish in oven and pour enough boiling water into it to reach halfway up the sides of the cake pan. Bake for exactly 30 minutes. The top of the cake will have a thin crust and the interior will still be gooey.

9. Set the cake pan on a rack to cool completely, then refrigerate until chilled overnight. To unmold, slide a thin knife around the cake to detach it from the pan. Invert the cake and peel off the paper liner, reinvert onto a serving platter. Using a doily or fine-mesh strainer, if desired, sprinkle with powered sugar. Store in the refrigerator, but remove 1 hour before serving. Serve with whipped cream and fresh berries.

Serves 8.

Chapter 21

Dinner at Roddy's

One of my closest friends, and someone I miss terribly, was the actor and photographer Roddy McDowell, the host of some of the most incredible dinner parties I've ever attended. You never knew who you'd be sitting next to when you were invited to Roddy's. Maybe it would be a great actor, like Tony Hopkins, Elizabeth Taylor, or Vincent Price. Or you could find an opera star or two among the guests, or often a painter, such as David Hockney. The table could be set for an intimate party of twelve or an enormous party of fifty. The only two things you could depend on were that the conversation would be memorable and the food would be inedible.

Roddy owned a charming house off of Laurel Canyon in Los Angeles, a magical place with walls filled with his stunning black-and-white photographs of Hollywood stars. You were asked to arrive for the lengthy cocktail hour around 7 P.M., and he always said dress was casual. I usually dressed *high* casual, in a simple black dress or pants with a colorful jacket and accessories. You never knew who you might meet at Roddy's, so you didn't want to look like a slob.

One of the great attractions of an evening there was how wonderful everyone looked in his subdued lighting. He lit the house only with tiny lights and loads of candles. One of his guests told me that part of the reason she was always delighted to accept an invitation to Roddy's was because she could wear something that needed to go to the dry-cleaners. The light at Roddy's was so dim that no wrinkle on your face or stain on your outfit would be visible.

You were greeted at the door by Roddy's butler, a servant of many years whose wife was the hapless cook. Every cook who ever worked for Roddy did the same appalling job with his standard menu: pounded, fried chicken in a flour base, gluey mashed potatoes, and cold, overcooked vegetables. The hors d'oeuvres were always the same—guacamole and chips. Dessert was usually a terrible store-bought pie.

Roddy's great skill as a host was the artful way he mixed people, which always led to a night of great conversation. He didn't just choose people at the peak of their careers. He'd invite people at all stages of life: those who were down on their luck, those who'd made it to the top, and those who had just started out. Writers and directors who had projects they were trying to get underway might find exactly the star they were looking for sitting across the table from them at Roddy's. People who were trying to jump-start their careers sometimes ended up in conversation with someone who could give them a boost. I was always excited like a little kid the day I got an invitation to Roddy's. You might find the people there intimidating in other circumstances, but at Roddy's they came as his friends and behaved that way. For people in Hollywood he created a real "Fantasy Island." Everything was magical, except the pie.

I was at Roddy's one night after a trip to Rome where I'd attended an opera. I'd come late to the opera and hadn't managed to snag a program. As I settled in my seat, I was trying to figure out who was the soprano on stage, but I was loathe to use my rudimentary Italian to find out from one of my neighbors.

Finally, I skewed up my bilingual courage and, in Italian, asked the young girl in the seat next to me the name of the star. "Aprile

Milo," my neighbor said, continuing in English. "She's a friend of mine from New York." I was telling this story to Aprile Milo herself, who happened to be a guest at Roddy's that night, when from across the room came a little voice: "I was that young girl you sat next to."

It was at Roddy's where I met a woman who was to become a close friend of mine, Coral Brown, who was an actress married to Vincent Price. Coral was an elegant woman, always perfectly turned out and carefully coiffed, with tailored clothes and pearls. What continually delighted me about her was that, although she looked like a million bucks, it was just a front for a wicked sense of humor. One night at Roddy's, Coral told the story of a trip to Fortnum and Mason's, one of London's premier department stores. A floorwalker approached her to ask if he could help her.

"What is your pleasure, Madam?" he asked.

"Fucking and kite flying," she said drolly. "But today I'm just looking for a pot of jam."

Once I was among the guests at a dinner party at Roddy's where everyone was British, except the Austrian film actress Luise Rainer and myself. Luise, who was quite old at that point and hadn't been in a film in many years, was seated to my left. She was very excited because she had a part in a film that was just about to be released and was encouraging the guests to come to the screening.

"You must come and see my film," she announced to the dinner guests. "I haven't done a film in fifteen, twenty-five, thirty, I don't know how many years. I will invite you. You must promise not to look at the photographs of me in the magazines, because there I look so old. I don't have the lines in my face that they show there."

I looked at her. I didn't know what mirror she was looking in, but I wanted to get one immediately.

She went around the table singling out each of the guests.

"What do you do?"

"I'm a producer," one guest said.

"Ah yes, you must come," she said. "And you?"

"I am a writer," another guest said.

"Excellent. You give me your number. I will call you to come and see my film."

She at last made her way to me.

"And you, darling, what do you do?" she said.

"I'm an actress," I said, at which point she turned her back to me and didn't speak to me again for the rest of the evening.

Okay, maybe everyone didn't behave as friends.

Roddy, however, was the best friend anyone could ever have. He really cared about you and remembered everything you'd ever told him about what was happening in your personal life and in your career, as well as being unfailingly loyal.

You knew your secrets were safe if you told them to Roddy. Stars trusted him with some of the most fascinating tales of old Hollywood. Some nights when we were out to dinner, just the two of us, he would delight me with some delicious story of an aged star many years in the grave that would reveal the true person behind the legendary character. After one of these dinners, I'd always urge him to write a book to collect these treasures.

"Roddy, that's chapter fifteen," I'd say. "You must write the book. You're the only one who can write the true story of old Hollywood. You're the only one who knew all those people."

"No, I can't do that," he said. "That would be a betrayal, and I could never do that to my friends."

He cared for his friends by protecting their feelings in other ways as well. We'd gone out to dinner with our mutual friend, Dr. Richard Wulfsberg. When Dr. Wulfsberg left, I felt a frightening chill come over me even before I turned to look at Roddy. When I caught his eye, he delivered the terrible news.

"I have terminal cancer," he said. "I won't make it till Christmas. I ask you not to tell anyone. My lawyer knows, my doctor knows, and you know."

"What about your sister? What about Elizabeth? What about all your friends?" I said. "Roddy, you can't do that to them. They need to know."

"No, they'll know in time," he said. "I can't tell them now, because they will act inappropriately."

He knew I wouldn't fall apart or make it difficult for him by becoming too emotional, and that I, too, could keep a secret.

It was an honor to be entrusted with this knowledge, but it was also very difficult for me. I was close to so many of his friends. I wanted to lighten my burden by sharing it with them, so we could all have a good cry. To do that would be a betrayal, the greatest sin as far as Roddy was concerned. Toward the end, the last four weeks, his secret got out and the whole world came to see him. People flew in from New York, Australia, England, everywhere. He received them grandly, sitting in his wheelchair attired in a smoking jacket, an ascot, and his morphine drip. And the dinner parties continued to the very end.

Sometimes it was just a plate on our laps, and other times it was a sit-down dinner. He oversaw the festivities in the same grand way he always had, telling stories and keeping up with the doings of his friends. The tone was never depressing, thanks to his great attitude. He was grateful for every moment right up until the end. You never saw him wince or abandon himself to self-pity or anger, so all of his guests met him at that level. As each person left the house after those last parties he gave them something: a household object, a piece of art or memorabilia. He gave me a beautiful little bisque lamp that unfortunately a friend of mine broke. I was glad it broke in a way, because every time I saw it I just went back to the sadness, and I really needed to let go.

Elizabeth Taylor, Roddy's best friend since childhood, held a memorial for him at her house. All the rooms were filled with people, and others of us crowded around the pool. We each in turn told our Roddy stories, wonderful, funny stories. When we were finished, she had a bagpipe player circle the pool. He went slowly through the house and finally faded off into the distance. Is there any sound more soulful than that of a bagpipe?

As the sound of the bagpipe faded away I raised my champagne glass and called out: "Hip-hip, hooray for Roddy!" Most of the others joined in the salute, but some looked at me as if this was the dumbest, craziest, rudest thing I could have done. My feeling was that my mourning was private and personal and took place at home. This was a chance to celebrate all those wonderful nights at his house and express my gratitude. There are some lives that need to be celebrated.

Roddy's life still is. His fabulous rose garden has been transplanted to the Motion Picture Home, the retirement home for actors.

At the memorial, Roddy's closest female friends pledged to get together for dinner every few months to celebrate Roddy. When we wanted to plan the first one, Suzanne Pleshette immediately identified our main problem. Not scheduling, not the guest list, nor the agenda.

"How the hell are we going to find someone to cook as badly as that?" she asked.

This is better than the guacamole served at Roddy's, but then that wouldn't be hard to do.

Guacamole

3 ripe avocados

½ red onion, finely diced

2 cloves garlic, minced

½ fresh jalapeño, stemmed, seeded, the ribs removed, and
    finely diced (Be sure to wear rubber gloves!)

2 roma tomatoes, pulp and seeds removed, diced fine

the juice of 2 limes

salt to taste

(optional: add a handful of chopped cilantro; I don't like
    cilantro, but many of us do)

1. Peel and remove the avocados' stones and place avocados in a bowl large enough to contain them.
2. With a potato masher, mash avocado until it reaches desired chunkiness or smoothness.
3. Add all remaining ingredients and stir gently to blend.

Makes enough to serve with a large bag of tortilla chips.

Part Seven

Turning Points

Chapter 22

The Riddler

I had the good fortune twenty-two years ago to buy a house in a neighborhood in the Hollywood Hills thick with oddballs—artists, actors, writers, and designers. The more our group got to know each other over the years, the more we realized what an incredible number of tastes and interests we had in common. We like good food, travel, art, museums—and more good food. One year we decided to solve the perennial problem about what to do for New Year's Eve by taking a trip to New Orleans, and we've spent New Year's Eve together in a different place every year since.

A few years before I started on *Raymond,* we rented a big van and headed to northern California, thinking the New Year would look a lot rosier if we'd spent the whole day before thoroughly researching the wines of the Napa Valley. I needed a boost. Despite the pleasure of this company of old friends, I was in a foul mood and not much looking forward to the New Year. I wasn't too sure about my future. I was alone, overweight, and out of a job. I call it being 4-F; in this town if you're *female, forty,* and *fat,* you're *finished.* Most disturbing of all, I was upset by how poorly I was getting along with my daughter-in-law, Jane.

My only child Michael is married to a fabulous woman—bright, beautiful, inquisitive, and strong—but at that time our relationship wasn't too fabulous. Both of us are stubborn with definite opinions about the way things should be done around the house. Just like my character, Marie Barone, those opinions were the source of a lot of friction.

As a result, Jane and I have had our share of little dustups over the years. Small things, really, but the unfortunate result was that whenever I went over to their house both of us were on our best behavior. Everything was couched in politeness, but there was no mistaking that a wall was going up between us. I was so worried that I'd say the wrong thing and set off an argument, I said very little and she said even less.

A few days before we began our trip to the Napa Valley, I'd been invited to dinner at my son's house. I welcomed the chance to spend time with my grandchildren, letting them show me the latest treasures in their rooms while Jane cooked.

They're all raised Catholic, but I'm Jewish by birth. You couldn't even say I'm a lapsed Jew, because I don't follow religion, but I do generate the required amount of guilt to stay Jewish. I sat down at the table and the family bowed in prayer. I tilted my head toward the plate to respect their tradition and my eyes fell on my daughter-in-law's meat sauce. Jane's sauce is, well—first of all she puts too much sugar in it, she cooks it too long, too, and the color is too dark, rather than the rich red of the sauce I make. I know better than to try and correct her on something this fundamental.

My grandson caught my stony expression and chided me: "Nanny, if you don't pray, you can't eat."

"I'm praying all right," I said, thinking to myself: I'm praying that God will get me through this sauce.

That behavior was what was bothering me on our New Year's trip. The only part of the situation with my daughter-in-law I had the power to change was how I behaved. What could I do to turn off my nagging, critical voice, a voice that seemed to just get louder with every passing year? I couldn't keep these feelings bottled up forever. If I didn't find a way to change, I ran the risk of alienating Michael and Jane and losing contact with my grandchildren. I was at a total loss where to even begin.

My friends and I started New Year's Eve at 10 in the morning at Winchell's Donuts. Donuts are always a good start, and even a bad donut is still pretty good. Besides, the very next day I would start to diet *again*. By 11:30 we were at the first winery, where we sampled five different years of Merlot. Then off to lunch at Mustard, one of my favorite restaurants, for a memorable lunch that I've pretty much forgotten because we had more wine there. After that, we had an appointment at Schramsburg Vineyards, producers of some of the world's finest champagne. It's an old winery (for California), with caves built into volcanic rock in the side of a mountain that keep the wine at the perfect temperature during the five to seven years it ages to perfection.

As the guide led us through part of the one and a half miles of caves, we saw a man moving very slowly from rack to rack fiddling with the bottles. The guide explained this man has a very important position in the winery. He's called the riddler. With a light, quick touch, he turns each champagne bottle just a bit: an eighth of a turn, or the distance between 12 and 2 on a clock face.

This tiny movement is essential to making fine champagne. The bottles are stored with the necks tilted down in large racks. The riddler twists the bottle thirty to thirty-five times in the two months that the bottles are stored in this fashion, so that yeast sediment and other junk can be sifted down and out through this tiny agitation. When he's finished, all the garbage has worked its way to the tip of the bottle. The vintners pop the plug, clean out the waste, add a little brandy or other flavoring and let the wine age to fine champagne.

As I watched the riddler making his way through the caves, it hit me: that is what we do in life. We're filled with resentments, envy, peevish little things, *junk*. We think that in order to make a change it's some monumental movement, as if you have to take an enormous boulder and move it up the side of a mountain. In fact, all that is required is to riddle from 12 to 2, to make a small and consistent adjustment in the way you look at things and how you act. Just this little shift—a little riddling—can change your perspective on everything in your life.

I decided to riddle my relationship with Jane. When I was invited to their house when I got back to LA, instead of looking at all the things Jane did that were different than the way I would do them, I looked at her for who she is and what she brings to our family. She is a very bright woman and a great mother. She loves my son and he loves her. She gave up a career as an electrical engineer to stay at home and raise my three beautiful grandchildren. Despite the work of raising three kids, she manages to find the time to teach music and math at the Catholic school my grandchildren attend. These are great and fabulous things, and it was important for me and the whole family that I focus on those.

This simple riddle in perspective transformed our relationship. There is no longer any hidden agenda on my part or on hers, which is fascinating. In my changing, she in turn did the same, and we didn't even talk about it. All the time, it was all in my attitude when I came through the door. Her sauce may not be to my liking, but it is delicious for her. When I go to visit them now, I sit and enjoy the fact that I'm having a meal with my family.

You don't need the judgments. You really don't. The human being that you are dealing with is doing the best he or she can, and we have to respect that. Their way may not be the way you want to do things, but nothing stops you from keeping right on with your ways of doing things and letting them do the same. Live and let live. If you just riddle that bottle and get out the junk, you are going to bubble with life.

My Meat Sauce

l large onion, chopped

4 cloves garlic, chopped

2 tablespoons basil

l tablespoon parsley

l healthy pinch oregano

salt and pepper to taste

l pound ground beef

two 28-ounce cans whole tomatoes with basil

l can tomato puree

1. Cover the bottom of a large pan with good olive oil, not that cheap crap from the 99-cent store, and turn the heat under it to medium. When the oil becomes fragrant, it's warm enough to add the garlic.
2. Add the garlic, the onion, basil, parsley, oregano, salt, and pepper. Sauté until onion is golden.
3. Add the meat and cook until brown, breaking it apart with a wooden spoon.
4. Add the tomatoes, crushing the whole tomatoes by hand. Cover and lower the heat, stirring occasionally for 15 minutes. Continue cooking uncovered for another 15 minutes. Serve over your favorite pasta.

Chapter 23

Success Isn't Always a Yes

In 1966 I was asked to do a new play at the Stockbridge Theater in Stockbridge, Massachussets, a comedy written by Elaine May and directed by Arthur Penn called *A Matter of Positions*. I was thrilled to be asked to premier this work. After all, Elaine May, half of the famous comedy team of Mike Nichols and Elaine May, was a brilliant comedian and writer, and I thought Arthur Penn directed some of the finest work I'd seen on the stage and the screen. If I did well in this production, it could really open doors for me.

My head filled with images of success. I described all the tantalizing possibilities to my husband Bill and my mother at dinner that night, but neither of them got very excited. They never said directly that I couldn't do it. Instead, they offered up nothing but doubts and difficulties. How could we afford to maintain two households? If I brought our housekeeper Olga—a woman who wore more blue eye shadow in a day than I've worn in my entire career on the stage—who could care for my husband? If I brought Olga with me to tend to Michael, who was eight at the time, we'd need to get a house in town. Olga's English wasn't good and she didn't drive. Houses in Stockbridge were much more expensive than those in the country. We simply couldn't afford to go into the hole financially so I could take this chance. And after all, it wasn't a sure thing, was it? It was too complicated. The whole household depended on my staying in one place and not disrupting everyone's life. Here was my opportunity to fly, and I was being chained down. I remember bursting into tears: "When is it going to be *my* turn?"

I knew my mother and husband were being sensible and practical, and I also knew that the right thing—the easy path—was to agree. It was nice to be asked to do the part, but I probably just couldn't accept. I got Bill to agree that we'd at least go up and take a look at the area. As we drove up the next morning, I was hoping that something magical would happen. I'd find a very cheap little house, and it would all work out that everyone would be happy.

I tried to maintain my optimism, but with each inappropriate and overpriced house we looked at, the possibilities seemed dimmer and dimmer. After a very long afternoon we called it quits. I phoned Arthur and told him it didn't look like I'd be able to take the part, and I asked him to recommend a restaurant so we could have a bite to eat before starting the long, sad drive, back to New York City.

We entered the dark restaurant a few minutes before it opened at five and took seats at the bar where we ordered whiskey sours. I hadn't even taken a sip before we were called to our table. As we settled in, I took that first sip and something a lot stronger than alcohol came over me.

"I'm going to do it," I said.

"You're going to do what?" he responded.

"Not your problem. *I'm* going to do it," I said.

"But . . ."

"Olga will stay with you in New York. She'll take care of your food and your clothes and all the things you need, and I will take Michael with me because he's my responsibility," I said.

"But . . ."

"I'm going to do it," I said for the third time, more firmly than before. I was convincing myself as well as convincing him.

In life, I think, women are always made to feel that they have to ask permission before they do anything. Someone else—your father, your teacher, your rabbi or priest, your husband, or even your children—has to give you the go-ahead. We wait for that in our lives, and it is so wrong it holds us up more than anything else. Between the guilt at asking permission and the fear of not being entitled, we freeze in place and our lives stay frozen around us. That's what was happening to me. I wasn't allowing myself to say yes. I was hoping the circumstances would say yes, and then I'd be lucky enough to just go along, too.

That was the "click" in my brain, saying that I would do it. I wasn't waiting for the perfect time, the perfect place, the perfect situation. I was going to *make* it work.

Not that it worked out perfectly. I rented a small apartment: just a living room, bedroom, and kitchen. Very small, but it was all I needed. I brought Michael with me to rehearsals during the week, hoping that his stepfather would come for visits. Unfortunately, my father-in-law became ill and Bill had to fly home to Texas to care for him. Without any support, I had a tough time keeping an eight-year-old boy entertained during the long rehearsals, but pretty soon the crew gave him the job of making smoke for one of the scenes. And on the weekends there were visits from my mother, who came to help out with Michael.

As most women know, having a visit from your mother is not always a relaxing experience. Before I went to pick up my mother at the bus station on Friday afternoon, I'd clean frantically and rush around town buying groceries so we could have a nice dinner and food for the rest of the weekend.

One Friday evening, after this mad dash to prepare for my mother's arrival, I arrived at the theater and collapsed in a chair. Elaine May was curious how I could have left the theater at lunchtime for an afternoon off and come back limp and exhausted. I told her how I'd spent my downtime and she offered me a great lesson in mother management.

"No, no, no," she said firmly. She instructed me to pick up my mother and take her to the apartment where I would be the first to slump in the chair. This would immediately arouse her maternal instinct. "Please, Mom, would you cook for me?" I was instructed to ask. "I have rehearsals all week, and it's hard to put a hot meal on the table for Michael at the end of the day. Could you cook some things and put them in the freezer so I could just warm them up during the week?"

This was a great plan, except for one thing. My mother was the worst cook I've ever met. She made the greasy spoon on the corner seem like Spago. She overcooked everything. She could burn salad. I didn't spend long hours learning recipes at my mother's side in the kitchen. I came to my first marriage free of cooking skills. That's why I didn't especially mind that our first apartment didn't have a real kitchen. We were in the same building as my mother-in-law, where we had dinner every night. (Marie Barone would have loved this arrangement!) I learned to cook by helping my mother-in-law and found, to my surprise, that I was a very fast learner. In fact, the only true cooking disaster to come from these hands was the time I left the giblet bag inside the Thanksgiving turkey. It didn't make the turkey inedible but it was disgusting to pull that wax package out of the cavity along with the stuffing. The teasing from my husband Michael's family went on for months.

I had a memorable cooking disaster on the set of *Raymond,* too. To give the scenes authenticity, I always handle real food on the set. If Brad wants a mortadella sandwich, I'm back there at the counter with real bread, mortadella, mayonnaise, lettuce, and cheese. The refrigerator on the set is always stocked with actual food: milk, soda, cheese, butter, eggs, Pop-Tarts, ice cream in the freezer, and special items for particular scenes.

The disaster came when I had to really make pancakes. I pour, turn, and serve pancakes at just the right moment in the scene while acting a fairly substantial part in the events. During rehearsal I did something completely out of character for Marie; I forgot to turn the pancakes over. They burned! Just like with Michael's family, the teasing about that went on for quite some time. Fortunately for all, I got the timing down perfectly on the day we actually filmed.

In some ways, though, my mother's lack of skill didn't really matter. Cooking for us made my mother so happy. She had a mission. While I was at the theater, she concocted dishes for Michael and me to work our way through—meal by dreadful meal—until she showed up again on Friday. No, they weren't the meals I would have cooked, but we didn't starve. The one dish my mother could actually cook well was pot roast. Cooking it was such a rare event for her, and it was always accompanied by the family wisdom. "You know what the secret is?" she'd inform us after the second bite. "Ginger snaps. I put ginger snaps in the sauce."

A Matter of Position wasn't a blockbuster. It didn't even go from summer stock to Broadway. But working with Elaine May in it led to two great movie roles in *A New Leaf* and *Heartbreak Kid. A New Leaf* with Walter Matthau has become a bit of a cult film. People still come up to me on the street and remind me of the wicked wink I gave Matthau when I played the addled heiress's housekeeper on the take. In the *Heartbreak Kid,* I didn't have as big a role as I had expected. Neil Simon, wrote the screenplay and Elaine May wanted to expand the mother's character so we did a lot of improvisational scenes to try and flesh her out. But most of the scenes were scrapped because Simon had not written them.

The experience of demanding my turn that summer was the real breakthrough for me as a woman and as an actress, because it showed me success isn't always a "yes."

When we think of success, we think of that moment when the

whole world seems to gather around and tell us, yes, we were right and things are going our way. In reality, success usually starts as a "no." People say you can't, you shouldn't, and, more often than not, they tell you not to bother even trying. Circumstances don't tend to cooperate either. Obstacles jump up in your way. You have to let go of some of the things you may be used to doing, such as cooking delicious dinners. When the world is saying "no," you must say "yes" to yourself. Saying "yes" to yourself is the first success, and all the others stem from that first one. A simple "yes," I'll go for it, I'll work out all the details in my way later leads to the "yes" of success.

In honor of all the imperfect meals my son and I consumed that hard summer in Stockbridge, I'm offering the recipe for the only meal my mother cooked to which I can say an enthusiastic "yes."

Mom's Pot Roast with Ginger Snaps

1 box ginger snaps

2 pounds chuck roast or stew meat, cut into 1-inch cubes

6 carrots, quartered lengthwise

3 russet potatoes, cut into 1-inch cubes

2 yellow onions, cut into large dice

3 stalks celery, cleaned, trimmed and cut into ½-inch slices

2 cloves garlic, minced

2 cups red wine

3 tablespoons vegetable oil

2 cups beef broth

2 cups water

1. Put the ginger snaps in a food processor and pulse until you have crumbs.
2. Put cookie crumbs into a large bowl and dredge the meat in the crumbs.
3. In a deep roasting pan, heat 3 tablespoons of vegetable oil and add meat. Turn meat until all sides are browned. Remove from pan and reserve.
4. In same pan add carrots, potatoes, onions, celery, and garlic, and sauté until onion is translucent and the other vegetables are beginning to soften, about 5 minutes.
5. Sprinkle in 1 cup of the remaining cookie crumbs and stir to coat.
6. Add wine and stir again.
7. Let alcohol burn off and reduce a little bit, about 3 minutes.
8. Add broth and water. Heat to a simmer.
9. Add meat and accumulated juices. If liquid does not cover meat, add equal parts broth and water until it does.
10. Lower the flame, cover, and let simmer for at least 2 hours.
    Serve with rice or pasta.

Serves 4–6.

Chapter 24

Raindrops

I knew that I wanted to be an actress from the time I was in kindergarten. In fact, I can date my ambition from my debut in a play in which I had the memorable role of Patrick Potato. My one line was: "I am Patrick Potato, and this is my cousin Mrs. Tomato." I heard laughter and I loved the happiness and warmth that it evoked in me. I was an extremely shy kid who barely spoke. Suddenly, all eyes were on me and I loved the attention and acceptance. It took a lot of determination to go from being a spud on stage to a role on Broadway. I never gave up, and that's what separated me from Mrs. Tomato, whose acting career peaked in kindergarten.

The major thing that moved me along in the world at first was my mother's job. She owned a public stenography business right in the heart of Broadway, a top-floor duplex in the former *New York Times* building where Seventh Avenue and Broadway merge at Forty-second Street. The office was easy for customers to find; we identified the building by telling them to look for the news ticker that flashed the day's events in six-foot-high letters of light that wrapped around the mezzanine level.

My mother's company typed most of the scripts for the plays and musicals and sides (excerpts of just their part) for the actors. So many Broadway stars came through that office. I remember seeing Danny Kaye, Jackie Gleason, Katherine Cornell, and even the great Maude Adams. The way they swept in the room, the way they held themselves, this air of excitement that made just their presence an event—I wanted all of that. They excited me the way rock stars excite kids today.

My mom worked long hours to keep that office going. Sometimes a whole week would go by without my seeing her, which is one of the reasons our Broadway evenings meant so much to me. My mother got free tickets to all of the shows, and I was her frequent companion. Sometimes she even let me play hooky from school to go to a matinee. I had my own special outfit for our nights on Broadway: a green coat with a squirrel collar and white Angora hat. To this day, when the house lights go to half before the curtain rises, my heart starts to race with excitement and a feeling that I'm privileged to be there.

Summers during high school when I filled in for girls on vacation in my mother's office, I'd walk down the Great White Way, or just stare out the office window, fantasizing about seeing my name on the theater marquees all around me. I didn't dare tell my mother this dream because I couldn't face the ridicule I was sure to get from her. It was just assumed that I would hang my high school graduation gown on the coat rack at the office and get right to work. I put a monkey wrench in these plans when I got married.

On a weekend visit to a high school friend who'd moved to Baltimore after she got married, I met a young Air Force pilot-in-training named Michael Cannata, who happened to live a block away. I shocked my entire family by marrying him a month later. Marriage seemed like a really good way of fulfilling two very pressing teenage needs: I wanted to get out from underneath Mom, and I wanted to get him on top of me. Back then, couples had sex after marriage—at least for the first couple of years.

Once I got out of my mother's house, my husband barely tolerated my attempts at an acting career, and the rest of the world seemed to agree. During my first acting class at NYU, the teacher's wife, an alcoholic, couldn't restrain herself from offering her assessment of my career, which was not good. She said I was a little, mousy, brown-haired thing who couldn't be heard and didn't belong on the stage. Her review sure did a lot for my self-esteem. I quit and went to the Neighborhood Playhouse and auditioned for the famous acting teacher, Sandy Meisner, who gave me a scholarship. (I am a survivor.) My mother had grudgingly agreed to allow me hours off here and there for auditions, as long as I promised to make up the time by working late typing scripts when I got back.

Although I had gotten small parts on television shows like *Studio One* and *Playhouse 90*, I hadn't yet fulfilled my Broadway dream. I'd read that Jean Dalrymple, one of a handful of female producers on Broadway, was mounting a revival of *The Time of Your Life*, and I ached to get just one little part in it to make my Broadway debut. There was a bit part as a prostitute—only three lines—which I wanted very badly.

One day, I looked up from my typewriter to see Jean Dalrymple herself in the office. She was a petite woman—only about five-foot-three—who wore beautifully tailored suits and her hair in a bun. She looked and sounded mousy, but inside was pure steel. I introduced myself and asked her if she might allow me to audition for the part. She brushed me aside.

"I'm not casting," she said. "You should get in touch with the director. If he says it's okay, then it's okay with me."

"And who is the director?"

"Sandy Meisner," she said.

You'd think that I'd be doing back flips at the idea asking one of my biggest supporters for this little job, but Sandy and I had not parted on good terms. When I was still in his class, he'd asked me to do a scene from Kelly's *The Show-Off*, first as written, then as an

English drawing room comedy, and finally as an Italian melodrama. I pulled off the comedy just fine, but I'd been too inhibited to let loose with all the histrionics of a melodrama. I made a huge mistake that afternoon. Rather than risk failure, I questioned the judgment of the maestro.

He laid into me in front of the whole class, and I was plastered against my seat biting my lip so hard I drew blood. The student to my left during this ordeal was Leslie Nielsen, whose arm bore the imprint of my fingernails for hours after the class was over. I'm sure he still has the scar.

The following week I came in and did *The Show-Off* as an Italian melodrama (and quite well, I might add), and quit the class.

I quit to show him and the class that no one treats me like that, or at least that was what I thought I was doing. The truth was that he frightened me and I backed away, using my bruised pride as a defense. My decisive action felt great for a few weeks—cowardice masquerading as courage—but soon I desperately missed the class and the breakthrough work we did there. The thought of calling Sandy Meisner to ask for this part brought up all my old insecurities and some new ones.

I picked up and hung up the phone about a dozen times before I skewed up the courage to call him. (I am a survivor.) His "yes" was immediate and sincere. "Doris, you'd be great in that," he said. "Of course you can have the part." What I didn't realize then was that the histrionics of student melodrama are a lot grander even than that of the Italians. Sandy had suffered this kind of treatment before from some of the greatest actors of our time, but he was willing to forgive the temper tantrums of those he believed in.

I was so happy, I was insufferable, bragging to my co-workers, husband, and mother about my big break. Weeks went by without a glimpse of the contract that would seal the deal. I didn't know what to do, and I had no one to confide in.

I called and called Jean Dalrymple's office trying to find out where the contract was, but no one there would give me an answer or put me in touch with Miss Dalrymple. Had I done something wrong? Was Sandy lying to me? No, that wasn't his style. Had they forgotten about me and given the part to the daughter or mistress of some backer? An actress' paranoia knows no bounds. When I read in *Variety* that rehearsals were scheduled to start in eight days, I panicked. I had to know. That day after work I decided I was just going to show up at Jean Dalrymple's house. I had been to her stylish townhouse in the East Fifties before to deliver scripts. I'd just stand there—all night if I had to—until she gave me an answer. Back then this was unfettered determination; now it's called stalking.

By the time I got to the East Side, it was raining. I rang the doorbell at the townhouse and Miss Dalrymple's sister answered through the intercom that Miss Dalrymple was not at home. I asked if I could come up and wait, but she said no, I could not. The townhouse didn't have a lobby or an awning for me to crouch under. I stood in the pelting rain hearing all my fears and insecurities. I'd protected this dream and worked toward it since kindergarten, seventeen years ago. I was determined that it not end in this rain-soaked doorway.

These sweet raindrops hit my forehead like blows from a hammer. With every raindrop that splattered on my forehead I thought: "I am going to get this part. I am going to get this part. I am going to get this part."

The street grew dark and it seemed I had been waiting a very long time, measured raindrop by raindrop. I jogged to the drug store at the corner to call home and say I'd be late. I started back to my post when it hit me that, with my luck, Miss Dalrymple had probably slipped back home just at the moment I was away. I went back to call from the pay phone and Miss Dalrymple herself answered.

"Oh,it'sDorisRobertsandIwantthreeminutesofyourtime. I'llberight there," I said, not giving her a chance to say no.

I sloshed up the stairs and into Miss Dalrymple's vestibule with my heart racing and my mouth running.

"I'vebeentryingtogetthisjobforsolong,andItalkedwithSandy,and
hesaiditwasright,andyousaidifIcouldgetSandythatIcouldhaveit,"
I blurted.

"You have it," she said, but I didn't hear it. I just kept on.

"ThisisapartIcando," I continued. "It'sonlythreelines,andyou
saidIcouldhaveitandSandysaid . . ."

"You have it," she repeated.

And I still didn't hear her! Finally she shouted: *"You have the
job!"*

As I left, she touched my arm tenderly and said softly: "You
know why you have the job, Doris? You did what I did as a young
woman. You didn't give up."

I have thought about those raindrops many times in the decades
since that long, wet evening. I'd been dreaming of acting since
childhood, and had allowed many things to distract me from getting
what I wanted. Dreams have a way of staying nothing more than
dreams, unless you muster the courage to act on them.

I think that, before that day in the rain, there was a good chance
that I might have given up, might have listened to my family's advice
that said the odds were against me and that it was wise to be more
sensible. I was certainly on the brink of allowing my pride to inter-
fere with what it was I really wanted in life, as I had in that class
with Sandy Meisner. It all changed for me that day in the rain when
I understood the power of this dream. I was willing to stand soaked
and humiliated and beg for it, that was how much it meant to me. I
had something to say, something to contribute, and clearly nothing
was going to get in my way. I am a survivor.

After getting stuck in the rain, you want a hearty meal. Here's a
meatloaf that makes strong men weep and feisty girls roar.

My Stuffed Meatloaf

2 pounds ground beef

2 eggs

1 medium onion, chopped

a couple of pinches of parsley

½ cup Italian bread crumbs

2 cloves of garlic, chopped

salt and pepper

8 ounces of ricotta cheese

a couple of pinches of dried basil

one 28-ounce can of whole peeled tomatoes with basil

1. Mix first six ingredients, salt and pepper to taste, and mold in standard-size loaf pan.
2. Scoop out the center of the loaf.
3. In a separate bowl, mix cheese and basil, salt and pepper to taste, and fill in the hole with this mixture.
4. Replace scooped-out meat to make a hat, covering the cheese mixture.
5. Top with tomatoes. Bake at 350 degrees for 45 minutes.
6. Sprinkle bread crumbs over the top and bake for another 15 minutes.

Serves 6–8.

Chapter 25

This Never Happens to Me

When I was a young woman in New York City analysis was all the rage. I was surrounded by a bunch of crazy actors, and hardly a conversation passed without someone quoting the personal revelation they had just had lying on the analyst's couch. I knew one actor who was so confused he was in group therapy alone. I, too, was at a point in my life where a lot of things didn't make sense to me, and I needed to resolve some long-standing conflicts. I decided that, even though it was outrageously expensive, considering the seventy dollars a week I made at my mother's public stenographer's service, I'd find someone to shrink my head.

I knew that I was unhappy, but I don't think I understood that I was angry. I didn't feel good about myself. It surprises people who know me now that, back then, I was sort of mousy. I had dull reddish-brown hair and a reticent manner. My mouth may have been closed, but my entire body was bursting with rage.

One of my friends recommended a prestigious, Vienna-trained female psychiatrist whose office was in a spare room in her grand old apartment on the Upper East Side. She was a powerhouse: a large, heavyset woman with a deep, heavily accented voice. Her senile father lived in the apartment, too. He didn't really understand that, when the door to her treatment room was closed, he shouldn't interrupt. He was the recurring bad dream in my therapy nightmare with this analyst.

Throughout the session, I could hear this poor man roaming around the apartment talking to himself. Frequently, while we were in there rummaging around in my gray matter, the analyst's father would wander into the room. Then the tone of her voice would change from soothing hypnotic tones to a sharp Germanic bark as she forced him out of the room with a powerful bellow: *"Heraus mit dir!"*

She was a big believer in the power of hypnosis. She would start off my trip into a deeper level of consciousness with the assessment: "You are very stronk unt younk." I shut my eyes as she requested, but I was too mousy to tell her that I wasn't completely under her spell. Most of my thoughts, while lying back on the couch with my eyes closed, were about her accent. If I ever had to play a Viennese analyst, I thought, I'll know that the *G* becomes a *K*.

But what did I know about analysis? I thought these antics were all part of the program and, besides, I was scared of her. Therapy is supposed to shake you up, right? I was certainly shaken up by this lady and her relationship with her dad. Little did I realize, but I'd picked what was probably the worst type of person to be my psychiatrist; she looked and sounded just like my big and formidable grandmother, and she was not giving or nurturing in any way, definitely not someone you'd want to confide in—more like someone you'd hire to collect a loan for you.

One day when I was on my way up to our session, I was changing trains at Forty-second Street when a man goosed me as I got into the car. He got his grab just before the doors shut and stood on the platform grinning at me through the subway windows as the train pulled out of the station. In analysis you are supposed to begin the session with the first thing that pops into your head, and this was the only thing on my mind when I lay back on the couch. I described my shame and my fury, but my analyst was calm, reflective, and a little too self-absorbed.

"This never happens to me," she said. Why would it? She looked like Ernest Borgnine in drag.

Besides, this wasn't about her, it was about me. I think I can do better than this, I thought.

I stopped therapy for a while, but my problems persisted. After a few months it all seemed so insurmountable that I decided to try analysis again, and I found Dr. Jonas, a much more moderate and reasonable man, someone with a soothing manner.

Things were going very well between us, but money was tight and I was having trouble paying him every week. I asked him if he'd allow me to keep coming for a while, even though I didn't have the money to pay him. He kept me on for six weeks, at which point he reached his limit. He told me he couldn't continue to see me unless I paid him.

I was upset but understood. Fortunately, I was meeting a friend for a cup of tea after my session with Dr. Jonas that day. As we were discussing my predicament, my legs went numb. I couldn't move. I couldn't stand. I panicked. What makes me a survivor was that, although I was terrified, I didn't surrender. I got angry at my doctor for abandoning me. This shifting of blame helped me to struggle to my feet.

I called Dr. Jonas back when I regained the full use of my legs. I said I wanted an appointment and I would bring the money. I borrowed from my mother and saw him the next day.

"Here is the money," I said, peeling off the bills onto his desktop.

"It wasn't about the money," he said. "You were going in a direction that was dangerous for you. I thought you were headed for serious depression if you continued on in that way. I forced you. I took a chance because I know how much you identify self-worth with money."

He was right about that. From my crib as a child, watching my mother lay the money on my grandmother's kitchen table to pay for her week of caring for me, I was obsessively focused on having enough money to feel safe and to put my relationships on a solid foundation. I still need to know I have enough money. I'm not one of those people who can live on credit. The house I'm living in today is the only home I've ever felt completely comfortable in, because I know it's mine. When the money is straight, I'm calm, more confident and secure. It took Dr. Jonas to point this out to me, and it show me what an important aspect of my character the craving for financial security is.

The real cause of the numbness in my legs, which had come back several times since that cup of tea, was hysterical paralysis, a physical manifestation of my fear of leaving my husband. The phrase I used frequently then was that I wanted to stand on my own two feet. If I was to leave my husband, I'd be standing on my own two feet, but Dr. Jonas pointed out, I had been doing so for a long time. My attitude was: "Okay, I'll take care of myself. Don't worry about me." Inside, I wouldn't acknowledge how afraid and insecure I was, which was what my legs were demonstrating for me.

So I left my husband, and with the complications related to that and the difficulties with Michael and my next husband, I was in analysis for a long time. At first I thought I'd go in to fix a specific insecurity I was concerned about. I didn't think I was signing up for years of therapy on couches from coast to coast. At a certain point you begin to wonder if it's helping, because you've forgotten the reason you started this whole thing in the first place. It's a habit, and it can be revealing and comforting, but will you ever be cured?

Yes, you can be.

A few years ago I went to see a production of a Russian play at The Old Globe Theater in San Diego. The play, about a village where the women were left behind when the men went off to war, was performed by an ensemble of Russian actors who had worked together for a long time. The audience wore headphones through which they heard a simultaneous English translation of the dialogue.

I was swept up by the predicament of the women on stage, but—more than that—I was enthralled by the women themselves. They could take an awful lot of heartache and bear tremendous burdens. When life wore them down, it was as if they would go into the ground for a minute to find their strength and emerge to celebrate. They were tough and indomitable. I thought: that's me. That's who I am. I'm a Russian peasant. I might as well be a villager milking a yak in *Fiddler on the Roof*.

The last thing I wanted from my early dealings with analysis was to see my ties to my Russian peasant past. What's sexy and commercially viable on the New York stage about being a Russian peasant?

However, through the strong performances of these women, I understood that the fundamental qualities that had served me well throughout my life were less a construct of my will and more a product of my genes. I looked so much like them, and they looked so much like my mother. I wasn't ashamed of it. I was proud of it. And more important than that, I finally knew who I was.

A lot of my difficulties in life sprang from this search for my identity. I was always trying on new ones. With each husband I thought I could slip out of the confines of myself and be Mrs. Cannata or Mrs. Goyen, and that that role and that relationship would give me a definition. Yet, even though I was asking for an identity, I chafed against the confines of the ones I chose.

Of course, I can name a lot of things about myself that do not please me. I'm not pleased that I'm fat. I'm not pleased about being short. I'm not pleased that I have pains in my lower back and my big toe. I'm not pleased with opportunities I failed to take advantage of, and I'm not pleased with the attitudes I had toward some people in the past. These are regrets, but I can say overall that today I am pleased with myself.

When I was going to Dr. Jonas, I quite literally could not stand on my own two feet. Even later, when I was self-supporting and successful, I still had trouble defining myself, being comfortable with my independent streak and my self-reliance. Now I can stand on my own two feet. I may get wobbly sometimes, but I'm standing, I'm not asking to be carried. I'm claiming my space. I'm not usurping anyone else's.

If I am rejected I have the capacity, like those Russian peasant women, to go underground for a while and come back up.

At first glance these statements might strike you as selfish, but in fact they are the opposite: a position of great generosity. Once you are no longer searching the world to find out who you are, you are better able to give to somebody else. You understand at last that you are not giving it away. The core of who you really are can't be squandered, its always there to draw from.

I wanted to include a German potato salad recipe in honor of my first analyst. Or maybe oatmeal and Maalox in honor of her father. But I hate German potato salad, so here's an Italian one instead.

Italian Potato Salad

4 medium potatoes

½ cup olive oil

2 teaspoons oregano

1 teaspoon salt

¼ teaspoon pepper

1 red pepper

½ cup red wine vinegar

1 large clove garlic, minced

½ cup red onion, thinly sliced

1 cup celery, chopped

½ cup kalamata olives, sliced or chopped

½ cup marinated artichokes, sliced or chopped

1 medium tomato, diced

½ cup white button mushrooms, quartered

1. Arrange potatoes is a baking dish.
2. Drizzle 2 tablespoons of olive oil, 1 teaspoon oregano, half of salt and pepper, and toss to coat.
3. Roast in a 350-degree oven for about 45 minutes or until potatoes are brown. Let cool completely.
4. Put red pepper under the broiler and turn until skin on all sides are charred. Transfer to a bowl and cover with plastic wrap immediately. Let cool. Run the pepper under cold water, rubbing gently until blackened skin is gone. Cut in half lengthwise and remove all seeds and fibers. Slice lengthwise into ¼-inch strips.
5. In a separate bowl, combine vinegar, garlic, and the remaining salt and pepper. Slowly whisk in oil and set aside.
6. In a large bowl, combine the potatoes, peppers, onion, celery, olives, artichokes, tomato, and mushrooms. Pour vinaigrette over and toss to coat.
7. Refrigerate until ready to serve.

Serves 6.

Chapter 26

Little Doris

For most of my life, I have been wakened regularly by a frightening dream of a man standing on the fire escape outside my bedroom. His heavy cape swathed him in darkness, and the fedora pulled low over his face obscured his features so that all I could make out in the black mass was a pair of burning eyes. Even in adulthood, every time I was visited by this nightmare, I sat up in bed terrified. In analysis I determined that this man must be a symbol of my father, the man who comes in the night and stays for only a menacing instant, but still makes his presence felt in frightening ways. Even into my later years, his image remained disturbing.

Then, a few years ago I was watching a movie late at night on television. The movie was *Death Takes a Holiday* starring Fredric March, a movie my uncle had taken me to see as a child. In it, March plays Death. At one point in the movie he appears in a dark cloak with a hat pulled low over his face so that all you can see are his eyes. I was amazed, and burst out into laughter and relief at the years of terror and dark thoughts I had constructed around this image.

The relief I felt doesn't diminish the power of the nightmare. My childhood self, Little Doris, had taken the terror inspired by this powerful image and matched it with the feelings she had about her villainous father to create a symbol of everything she feared. As much as I longed for Big Daddy to rescue me from the neglect I felt in my family, he wasn't much of a hero to my relatives. My longing was mixed with a fear that, if he did show up and snatch me away, it would be a kind of death.

All my adult life, memories of my childhood had made me extremely uncomfortable. I despaired of Little Doris, and in many ways I believed that there must have been a reason everyone ignored her. Inspired by the arrival of Fredric March in my bedroom late at night and late in life, I decided to try to get to know Little Doris.

I took out childhood photographs, the images of me that I'd seen hundreds of times over the years. So often had I shown these photographs to others that I'd stopped really looking at them. Now that I wanted to get to know her, I looked at Little Doris as if for the first time. She was a cute little girl. Why was she always scowling? What was she thinking? How did she take in the world? I wanted to get her to trust me, so she could explain to me how I got to be the person I am.

Little Doris did not make this process easy for me. She rejected every approach I made to her. I started a journal, writing to her as if I was a kindly adult who had just come across this adorable little girl and wanted to reach out to her. How do you feel? I'd write to her. What is going on with you? Her overwhelming emotion was rage.

I saw her sitting in a corner of a darkened cellar. She was turned to face the room so that she could see anyone who approached, but her attitude was far from welcoming. She was absolutely paranoid. I walked toward her, but as I got closer she kicked at me. I reached my arms out to her and she shrunk back. She wouldn't even let me put my arms around her.

I considered our first encounter a disaster, but I wasn't giving up. She fascinated me for what she showed me about Big Doris. She wasn't sophisticated enough to keep her mouth shut and hide her feelings of anger, distrust, and betrayal. It was all right out there on the surface. Anger had been a big force in motivating me to accomplish my goals as a young woman, but it had always been a quiet anger. When someone put me down or didn't give me a job, didn't give me the love and the attention I believed I deserved, I never said a word. The angrier I got, the more tightly my lips pressed together, while inside I vowed that I'd show them someday. Here I was in my sixties, successful and loved by my friends and my family, but Little Doris and her anger were still pretty much running the show.

I kept writing to Little Doris every night before I went to bed, and talking to her each morning when I walked around the Hollywood reservoir. I felt like a complete fool on those morning walks, gibbering away to my little-girl self. I remembered a woman I used to see on Seventy-second Street near my apartment on West End Avenue in New York who I thought was totally insane. She was nicely dressed and wore a smart new hat, but she always carried a baby doll close to her cheek, stroking it, constantly talking to it.

Props seemed to be the only visible difference between that woman and me during those morning walks. Sometimes the only difference between crazy and troubled is a nice outfit and lunch reservations. As I walked around the reservoir, I said to Little Doris: "I love you unconditionally. Believe in me. Trust me. You need nobody but me, honey, nobody but me. You don't need Big Daddy—just me. I'm going to take care of you." I was determined to unlock the secret Little Doris had to tell me.

The next time I approached Little Doris, she was in a sandbox and she still wasn't very happy to see me.

"Let me help you out," I said.

"No," she barked back. "No! You'll get me halfway up and then you'll let me go."

It took me a moment to recover and respond.

"Okay. I will make a cement step for you and you can get *your-self* out."

In my imagination, I fashioned a few small steps that allowed her to get out on her own. But she was still wary of me. I felt that if I could make her understand that she was safe and loved for exactly who she was, Big Doris would experience a profound release.

I decided that I had to level with her. I bet she wasn't buying all this kindness and gentle concern, so I took a new tack in my conversations with her: love mixed with disappointment. "You need no one except me," I told her. "I love you unconditionally. Unconditionally and forever. There are times when I don't like you, and times when you are a big pain in the ass, but I love you despite all of that. I will protect you. If you trust me and come along with me, life will be fabulous."

God, was she stubborn! Suddenly it dawned on me that I was telling her the things that *adult* Doris wanted to hear. I was talking in abstracts—unconditional love, trust, and security—real needs that could only be vague concepts to a small child. What Little Doris wanted, I decided, was to have fun.

"Come with me," I told her the next time we spoke. "I'm going onstage tonight. I've got a big part in a play, and hundreds of people are coming to see us. Come with me and I'll show you a good time." I felt her with me that night onstage. I felt—and I know this sounds completely crazy—a kind of playfulness, a freshness that made my performance that night feel as if I were saying the words for the first time. I felt the strength of her and the joy in her, and I realized that she had been right not to trust me until that point.

I had told Little Doris I loved her unconditionally, but in fact I didn't really try to know her. It was as if unconditional love was a policy decision I had made, and I was sticking to it. I pitied her and feared her for what she revealed about my childhood misery and how much of it I carried forward to today. I didn't embrace the positive qualities she had, that submerged playfulness and delight. In bringing her out with me onto the stage, I felt her fully, and I understood how much of Little Doris there was to love. She was tough. She was a survivor. All of those hostile qualities were the ones I saw when I looked at her, but that was such a limited picture of her and of myself. She was a beautiful and inventive child, and those loveable qualities were as much a part of the present day me as the anger and hostility.

The monologues on my early-morning walks changed after I took Little Doris out of the basement and onto the stage. I stopped crowing about how I loved her unconditionally. One memorable morning at 6:30 when no one was around, I walked the reservoir imagining that I was holding her in my arms. "You come with me," I told her. "I'll show you a great life. I'll show you fun and we'll have some laughs. Just trust me. If you trust me, you'll begin to trust other people in life, and it'll be much better." I know this sounds odd, but for some wonderful reason this imaginary creature I was holding in my arms sort of dissolved into a liquid and disappeared within my body.

I found myself becoming stronger because I was responsible for that little girl. Life is pretty tough most of the time, and, as an actress, part of getting work is getting frequent rejections. When I had Little Doris integrated into my being, I could acknowledge the emotions we adults try to bury because we are afraid they will distract us from getting on with the business of responsible living. After a disappointing day, it is easy to slip into a funk and be consumed by insecurities, or find yourself picking a fight with someone you love because the anger has to come out somewhere. Let's face it, sometimes it's hard to resist yelling at your husband for something he didn't do.

When I would come home at night, I always asked Little Doris how she felt.

"Terrible," she might say.

"Terrible?" I'd say, surprised. "What's so terrible?"

"I didn't get the part I wanted in that movie today," she'd say.

"Does that mean *you're* terrible?" I'd ask. "You were too blonde, or you were too thin, or too fat? It doesn't make any difference. It doesn't invalidate you."

I find my relationship with Little Doris enormously soothing. You may say it's just a trick of the mind, but splitting off my troubles and fears into her, and allowing her to articulate them, allows me the adult role of reassuring and reminding her that things really are all right. Little Doris is a truth teller, and she's not ashamed to be mean, or petty, or fearful. After all, she's just a little girl. Fortunately for both of us, she's a little girl who has me, and I know just how to comfort her. And Little Doris is teaching me more and more about how to have a good time. Together we're learning not only to have self-confidence, but to revel in self-worth.

I imagine Little Doris and me sharing this extremely simple and delicious Mud Pie.

Ice Cream Mud Pie

1 stick of unsalted butter
½ box graham crackers, pulverized into crumbs
chocolate ice cream, softened
whipped cream

1. Melt butter and combine with cracker crumbs, making a paste.
2. Press into a 9-inch pie pan.
3. Fill pie with ice cream. Cover and store in freezer until you are ready to serve.
4. Build a mountain of whipped cream on top just before serving.

Serves 8.

Chapter 27

Divas

When my son Michael was very young, I had a hard time working at my acting career. Michael's father was just starting his law practice and we didn't have much money—and certainly no extra money for childcare. My mother still worked full-time and wasn't around to to babysit. If I wanted to audition for a part, I'd have to call around to find a friend willing to watch Michael for a few hours, then haul him to the friend's place in time to make my casting call. In some ways, I feared getting a part because of the complicated arrangements I would have to make to accommodate my son and husband while I worked. I suspect, in retrospect, that worry influenced my auditions. I kept my dream of being an actress alive and my skills fresh by working on scenes at the Actors Studio.

The Actors Studio is the legendary acting and playwriting cooperative where greats like as Marlon Brando, James Dean, Al Pacino, and Marilyn Monroe honed their craft. You have to become a member of the studio before you can work with the actors, writers, and directors who test their work there. I was honored to be a member, and grateful for the Tuesday and Friday sessions where I could perform scenes with some of the finest actors of my generation—Martin

Balsam, Anne Bancroft, and Kim Stanley—and keep my acting moving forward during a very hectic time in my life.

After the sessions, everybody would cram into a little coffee shop nearby, and it was the social highlight of my week. We'd exchange gossip about the theater world and deliver our (often scathing) reviews of plays we'd seen on Broadway or off. There was one actor who always stood apart from the hubbub and the hilarity. Rod Steiger would walk into the coffee shop a little later than the rest of us and acknowledge the group with a nod. Then he'd settle into his favorite booth, order a cup of coffee, and bring out a book.

While I craved the wit and companionship of my fellow actors, Rod appeared to need no one. I envied how his still, distant presence was always in our thoughts as we chattered on. He reached out for his coffee without looking up from the page, oblivious to the glances we threw his way. Eventually some of us would seek him out. He might allow us to sit down, or just as frequently beg off with his book. He wasn't scrambling for the spotlight. The spot was trained on him, and he decided if you shared it with him. I was in awe of his self-confidence and wondered if I could possess such power.

After weeks of studying Rod, I brought a book to the coffee shop and chose a booth an appropriate distance from his. I opened my book to a pre-chosen page and traced my eyes over the words. This is not to say that I read those words. My anxiety made the letters unintelligible. I glanced up furtively to see if anyone was watching me, then rapidly back to the page if anyone actually was.

My act was not convincing. People walked past my booth to the group in the back. No one even said hello. Eventually I found myself buttonholing people walking by to see if they wanted to join me. Clearly, whatever Rod Steiger had was something that required more than simply sitting in a booth alone. Rod Steiger was a diva.

Diva is a Latin word for "goddess," but it has come to mean something different. The opera diva is the most common type. When a true diva makes her entrance on the vast stage of the opera house, among the towering scenery and the colorfully costumed cast, your eyes are riveted on her and her alone. Maria Ewing, who I saw in *Tosca* at the Los Angeles Opera, is a classic diva. Ewing strode confidently on the stage and captivated the audience as much with her presence as with her rich voice. She had on the most beautiful black beaded dress, a dress that hugged her curves and sparkled like fire under the lights. As her aria *Vissi D'Arte* came to a crescendo, she fell back against a flat wall on stage and slid to the floor.

The audience gasped before bursting into a rapturous ovation. "Oh my God, she's going to be in trouble with the wardrobe mistress about that," I thought. "The producers will be furious. How will they be able to get someone to repair that dress before the next performance? It must have cost a fortune!"

That's the difference between the diva and Doris. The diva doesn't care about the dress. The dress is for the crew to figure out and the producers to pay for—and pay gladly because of the amazing performance Maria Ewing delivered night after night. She and every other woman in the audience knew the value and delicacy of that dress and she used that fact brilliantly to portray a woman so overcome with emotion that she doesn't even care about her clothes. The diva doesn't let the material world get in the way of displaying her genius.

Another time, in a performance of *Salome*, Ewing used wardrobe in a dramatic and unexpected way. As she built to the end of her aria, she began to take off her veils. With each stitch of clothing she shed, her voice got stronger and her presence on the stage appeared to grow, electrifying the enormous opera house. She finished standing absolutely naked on the stage, singing with incredible power. There wasn't a single person napping through that aria, but I'm sure a few men needed one after that. We were dumbstruck that a performer had literally stripped naked before us, exposing everything she had in the service of conveying the song. The silence that followed hung in the air for a long time before it was broken with the roar of the audience's applause. Real divas share a showshopping characteristic: their silence fills up a room.

It's the false divas who give the concept a bad name, and I've certainly seen a lot of them during my acting career. The Actors Studio was full of demi-divas and divas-in-training, people who acted entitled to special consideration and handling, even though they hadn't earned the right to be elevated above the rest of us. These dimestore divas made a lot of demands, including that we forgive them when they were late or unprepared. Performers can forgive each other's excesses if the work that's delivered on stage makes up for special consideration. There is a big difference between being a diva and being a bitch, a distinction the false divas never understand, no matter how many times you write them a note and tape it to their dressing room door.

The director of the Actors Studio was Lee Strasberg, who, despite his short stature, light hair, and the funny snorts he punctuated every conversation with was a powerful presence. He *always* nailed what was wrong with a weak performance, and he was harsh if he thought an actor had done a sloppy job. In some of the classes, the members would comment on each other's performance at the conclusion of the scene. When Lee was in the room, we kept our mouths shut. What he had to say was so brilliant, we just hung on his words.

The first full-length production I did at the Studio was my first brush with my inner diva. We were working on a play called *Marathon 33*, by June Havoc, the sister of Gypsy Rose Lee, who in her youth was the famous Baby June immortalized in the musical *Gypsy*. June's play was about her experiences at the dance marathons during the Depression. She had competed in them when she was a fourteen-year-old kid, too old for vaudeville.

During the Depression more than 30 percent of the population was out of work, so all different types of people forced themselves through these thirty or forty days of humiliation in the hope of earning a little cash. College students and professionals who had lost their jobs were among those who would dance, sponsored by laundries or restaurants. Besides the modest fee from the sponsors, couples would get money from the audience, who would toss small change on the floor. Desperate contestants would scramble like rats for pennies.

Couples stayed in the competition as long as they kept their feet moving. As time wore on, the couples would slump together from exhaustion, barely shuffling along on the floor. When their feet stopped moving they were either disqualified or someone hit them on the back of the legs with a ruler to start them up again. The competition was cruel and punishing, and June captured it all memorably in this exhausting play.

My part was the winner, and my partner was a very large guy, Logan Ramsey, who I had to carry on my back for part of the play (something I believe contributed to my present back problems). The forty-seven actors rehearsed the play for a full year before we felt ready to put it up. Four hours before the premiere, Lee Strasberg strode through the crowd of actors seated cross-legged on the stage of the Anta Theater to give us his final critique. As he passed each one, he'd deliver a specific tip—this actor should be a little meaner or this one a bit louder. Then he came up to me.

"Doris, I don't know what to say," he intoned. "Nothing is working."

He moved on to the next actor.

I could feel my spirit, my energy, my blood sinking out of me down through the floorboards. It was like I was drowning. I not only had no energy, I had no hope. The other actors started edging away from me as if I were poison. When the stage manager told me to speak to Lee, I stuttered, "I . . . I . . . I can't." Lee came up to me, the last one still rooted to the stage.

"Doris, what is it, darling?" he asked.

"You said that nothing was working."

"What?"

"You said that you didn't know what to tell me because nothing was working."

"No, no, no," he said as if speaking to a wayward child. "The joke you do. I was talking about the joke."

In the play, my character told a joke about a house of ill repute where the madam opens the door and looks down to see a midget. She asks him what he wants. "I rang the bell, didn't I?" he says. That was the joke, one that was pretty hard to put across. Everyone had been giving me tips on how to tell the joke, but Lee was saying none of them was right. They way I had done originally before getting any advice, had been better.

He'd criticized me in front all of my fellow actors a few hours before opening night, but the explanation came after everyone had left. Suddenly my spirit returned. I was *furious*.

I called my husband and asked him to meet me for dinner that night. We went to the Capri, where I ordered baked clams and a whiskey sour. My husband was shocked. He knew my policy was never to drink before a performance. But this was no ordinary performance for me. I sat at the table brooding, dipping my bread into the clam juice and staring straight ahead.

After dinner I went to the dressing room that I shared with three other female members of the cast. As I was putting on my eyeliner, Lee came into the room and looked at my face in the mirror. "Aren't you going to give me a kiss for good luck?" he asked. I just kept looking in the mirror, stone-faced, applying my makeup. I was tending to the outrage deep in my core and I said, "No."

I came down the stairs very slowly on my way to the stage just before the performance. Lee and his wife Paula were standing at the bottom of the stairs.

"Go out and be a winner," she said as I passed.

I grabbed her wrist and, holding it firmly, drew her close to my face.

"Didn't you know I *am* a winner?" I said.

Well, that was perfect. The anger at being humiliated fueled my character. I was so full of piss and vinegar on the stage that night. I was one of the few actors singled out in the reviews for the quality of our performances.

Strasberg could have destroyed me that night. I could have been crushed by his casual condemnation and weak apology. Instead, I showed my belief in myself, and because of it my life changed. I left the Studio after the play had its run, determined that I would make it as an actress. For that night, I was a diva.

A few years ago, my acting teacher—the brilliant Milton Katse-las—asked me what it was I hated most about show business.

"Arrogance," I responded.

"Arrogance?" he said with amusement. "You'll never have it—and you could use a little. Look up the word."

What an arrogant dismissal, I thought. Dutifully, like the good student I am, I looked up the word in my dictionary when I got home. At first my eyes found *arrogant* with a meaning that justified everything I hated in the false divas I knew: asserting unwarranted claims of one's own importance, aggressive conceit, presumption or haughtiness, said the *Oxford English Dictionary*. Why would Milton think I needed more of any of that?

Milton has taught me to be fascinated by the original meaning of words. I kept reading the definition to discover that *arrogance* comes from the Latin word *arrogate*. In *arrogate* I saw what Milton, Rod Steiger, and Maria Ewing had in mind. The *OED* (Oxford English Dictionary) defines *arrogate* as "to ask or claim for oneself."

When an actress walks onto a stage, or a woman walks into a room, she makes an entrance only if she claims it for herself, i.e., if she is arrogant in the best sense of that word. She doesn't display the false arrogance of someone who is begging to be noticed, but displays instead the real sense of entitlement that a person of confidence and self-assurance inspires when she enters a room. This was the difference between me sitting in a coffee-shop booth and Rod

Steiger claiming an identical space. There was something about him that piqued curiosity. Whereas in my booth I was doing the coffee-shop equivalent of flagging down cars on the freeway.

Maria Ewing claimed the stage and used every bit of her talent to hold it. She gave a sold-out audience everything she had, but I got the sense that she would have done it whether the place was packed with adoring fans or completely empty. She *knew* her value, and if the rest of the world was smart enough to catch on to it they would have a memorable evening. If not, she would have a memorable evening, audience or no.

I don't know any women who were raised to think that their ambitions and talents were the most important focus, a valid life's work. Rarely do women begin the day with the question: What do I want to do today? What pleases me? Instead we wake up knowing everything we have to do for everyone else, and, if we are lucky, we wedge some time in for ourselves. If we want that, we have to claim it for ourselves. Claim it, own it, and never be ashamed of the diva that you were destined to be.

Here's my version of the baked clams I had just before my performance in *Marathon 33*.

Baked Clams

24 raw clams (make sure that all of the shells are closed;
   discard any clams with opened shells)

1 bunch fresh thyme

2 cups white wine

3 cups bread crumbs

2 tablespoons oregano

2 cloves garlic, minced

1 generous pinch crushed red pepper

½ cup Parmesan cheese

1 cup olive oil

salt and pepper to taste

1. Place clams into a stock pot with the thyme. Pour in wine and cook over low flame just until the clams have opened up. Discard all clams that do not open.

2. In separate bowl, mix bread crumbs, oregano, garlic, cheese, crushed red pepper, salt, and black pepper. Drizzle in oil until you've made a paste. If paste is too dry, add cooking liquid 1 tablespoon at a time until the paste is almost a liquid but not quite.

3. Arrange clams on a baking sheet and spoon a teaspoon of the paste onto the clams.

4. Give the clams a spritz of olive oil and bake in a 350-degree oven for 15–20 minutes or until bread-crumb mixture starts to brown.

Serves 2 as a main course or 6 as an appetizer.

Part Eight

Warnings

Chapter 28

Beware of Men Who
Feed You

There are moments when I think back on the shy, naïve Doris who took on the New York theater world of the 1950s and marvel at her innocence. How did that creature survive? Part of it was plain determination and tenacity in the face of failure. I walked boldly and blindly into compromising situations that wiser women would have read for exactly what they were. But I also know my genuine naïveté sometimes worked to my advantage.

Way back then, I had a part in a quality off-Broadway production of *The Death of Bessie Smith* at the Cherry Lane Theater, a small house that only the truly theater-hardy have the motivation to ferret out. The audiences were enthusiastic, but I harbored no illusion that big Broadway producers were among those seeing my performances. That's why, when I entered the dressing room before one evening's show and the stage manager told me that Lawrence Langner, the director of the New York Theater Guild, had called, my response was less than enthusiastic. Much less than.

"Yeah, sure he did," I said. "And the Tooth Fairy and Santa Claus are third-row-center tonight."

The New York Theater Guild was, at the time, the most prestigious production house on Broadway. It produced all the major plays, and every production it mounted was of the highest quality with first-rate sets, solid casts, and booked into the best theaters. The chances that the great Mr. Langner would hunt me down in this little theater on the fringe of Manhattan were slim. It would be as if the star of a college student's senior thesis film got a phone call from Steven Spielberg. I crumpled up the phone message, thinking that the stage crew was having a good laugh at my obvious dedication, earnest ambition, and hard work. I may have been naïve, but I was New York naïve and getting more world-weary every day.

A week later the stage manager gave me another phone message.

"Hey Doris, Lawrence Langner called again."

"Would you guys stop it," I said. "I don't find this very funny."

"Gee, Doris, Lawrence Langner calls and you don't return his phone call," the stage manager said, as his cronies cracked up behind him. "I thought you wanted a career in the theater."

"You guys are unbelievable," I said.

"So next time when he calls, should I just say that Miss Roberts does not accept calls from powerful and important producers?"

"Give me that number," I said, convinced I'd call and it would be a pizza joint or one of the guy's favorite strip clubs.

I called the number and the woman on the other end of the phone answered: "Good afternoon. New York Theater Guild. May I help you?"

"Can I speak to Lawrence Langner please?"

"Who may I say is calling?"

"Doris Roberts," I said, then blurted out. "Returning his call."

So the number was right! My heart sank as I waited for the next shoe to drop. What if it was some friend of the stagehands' who they had convinced to participate in this practical joke? Or worse yet, as I waited there anxiously, the receptionist was buzzing into a big meeting Mr. Langner was having with other producers. When she announced my name, he'd scowl at the interruption. If our paths were ever to cross again, he would probably not remember me, but have a vague sense that there was some reason he didn't like me. Then a male voice picked up the line.

"Doris, this is Larry Langner," he said. "What took you so long to call?"

"I didn't believe it was you calling," I said. "I thought the crew was playing a joke on me."

"Oh, all right," he said. "Look, I'd like you to come up to my office tomorrow. I think you are a marvelous actress, and there are some people I'd like to introduce you to up here. Do you have any time free tomorrow?"

Do I have time free tomorrow? I have morning, afternoon, and night free tomorrow.

"Yes, I think I have some time open before the evening performance."

"How about tomorrow morning at eleven? My office is on . . ."

"Thanks, Mr. Langner. I know exactly where your office is. See you at eleven."

Langner's office on Fifty-second Street was one of my own personal Broadway stations of the cross. I used to walk down that street when I was delivering scripts for my mother. When I passed by his building, I'd spit on the sidewalk in front of the door and say aloud under my breath: "Some day you'll know who I am."

That day had come much sooner than I could have ever imagined.

The next day I was face to face with Lawrence Langner, a tall man in his seventies with a confident bearing that felt to scale against the big windows of his enormous office. This time I made sure not to spit. Langner complimented me on my work. I was surprised he'd seen me in more than one play. Then he made a humbling admission.

"Fifteen years ago I would've made you a great star on Broadway," he said. "I don't quite have that power now. But I can open some doors for you."

He brought in people from other parts of the office, people who chose projects and talent for television and regional theater, as well as those who worked on the Broadway productions. As each new face entered his office, he made the same introduction. "This is Doris Roberts. She's a really marvelous actress who will be a big star some day. I want you to keep her in mind."

My head was swimming. Just when I was at the moment when thanking him seemed appropriate, he asked me if I might be free to lunch with him the next Thursday.

Yes, I said, I imagined I could arrange to be free.

The next Thursday I met Larry Langner for lunch at Maude Chez Elle, a lovely French restaurant near his office.

I wasn't quite sure what he was up to, taking me to lunch, although as a perpetually starving actress I was more than happy for the free meal with a man who could do my career a world of good. He didn't use the meal to tell me war stories of Broadway or gossip about the stars. He seemed completely fascinated by *me*.

I didn't consider myself to be so intriguing, but he had a fabulous way of drawing me out. He asked me all about my childhood and seemed to relish every anecdote and observation. I'd never had a man—even my husband—pay such close attention to the details of my life story. I began to think this was what a mentor was, someone who spotted you among the crowd and saw your unique qualities and your gifts, and helped you bring them out with his advice, direction, and contacts.

We got into the habit of having lunch together every third Thursday of the month for five months. On that fifth month, when he'd heard everything I had to recount in as much detail as I could muster, he closed the meal with a great piece of advice.

"Okay, I've heard everything about you," he said. "I know why you are the actress you are. Now you have to forget everything and just live."

This was excellent advice for actresses and everyone else, which I grew to appreciate later in life. All those stories and memories are always available to us. But day to day, moment to moment, it's better just to live.

I didn't have much time to ponder the deeper meaning of this statement as Mr. Langner asked me to come back with him to his office. He knew the great director Tony Richardson was about to direct a play in London, and he thought I'd be perfect in it. He wanted me to come back to the office with him to help him write a cable recommending me to Tony. He also wanted to send a recommendation to the legendary theater director Harold Clurman to indicate how appropriate I was for something he was working on.

After we sent the cables I was sitting in one of the chairs facing his desk thanking him for all his support when he came around the desk and tried to kiss me. I was shocked. I had no idea that these months of long lunches indicated anything more than a professional relationship. Certainly, I'd never given him any encouragement along those lines. Yet suddenly there were his lips as dry as parchment coming toward me. I leapt out of the chair and began to examine the framed playbills that decorated his office walls.

"Oh, Mr. Langner, I saw this production. Katherine Cornell was marvelous in this," I said.

He was at my back and his powerful arms began to encircle my waist.

"Now this is an interesting painting, Mr. Langner," I said, as I sprung over to a watercolor on the opposite wall. "How did you and your wife come across this?"

Silly me, thinking that if I mentioned his wife, the formidable Armina Marshall, it might remind him that he was married and make him stop this foolishness. The only time reminding a man about his wife stops him is if she's right behind him and you're pointing at her. I got no answer from the onrushing Mr. Langner, so I ricocheted to another painting.

"What is this one? You must tell me about this one," I said. I didn't know what else to do. I didn't want to jeopardize my relationship with him by saying what I really felt which was: Stop this, you silly old fool!

I sprinted to the desk and picked up a paperweight.

"Tell me the story behind this," I said brightly.

He sidled up to me and laid his arm over mine as if to take possession of the paperweight, but instead he grasped my hand. I broke free and stepped to his side of the desk.

"I love this pen-and-pencil set," I said, indicating the impressive heavy pair in the holder at the top of his desk. He came toward me, so I ducked around the other corner.

"I love this picture of your wife," I held the picture of Armina up in front of me as if it were a cross and Mr. Langner were Dracula. He took the picture and set it back down on the desk as I skittered to the window and took in the view.

"You must be very pleased to be able to look out of this window every day when you are working," I said. "It's such a wonderful view."

This went on for about ten minutes until I grasped how ineffective my evasion tactics were. I wasn't sure how to break this off without insulting him, short of surrendering. After another circuit around the room, I grabbed my purse and turned to face him. The intercom buzzed with his secretary announcing a call for him.

"Gee, Mr. Langner. It's so late now. I've got to be getting home," I said. "I don't know how I'll ever thank you for all the help you've given me."

This was a candid admission. Clearly, the way he wanted to be thanked was not the way I wanted to thank him.

I got home and collapsed on the sofa, wrung out from the workout I'd had in the famous producer's office. Just before I was about to leave for that evening's performance, the phone rang. It was Armina Marshall. I was quaking in my shoes.

"Where's Larry?" she demanded.

"I don't know," I said.

"Well, you were his last appointment. You must know where he is," she insisted.

"We had lunch at Maude Chez Elle and then we went back to the Theater Guild, which is where I left him," I said.

"Darling, he's the keynote speaker at a Kennedy benefit and no one can find him," she said.

It turned out that his pursuit of me had so exhausted him that he'd fallen asleep on the couch.

I never saw Lawrence Langner again. Harold Clurman hired me, in part based on Langner's recommendation, for an out-of-town production of a new play. When I got back to New York I attended Mr. Langner's funeral at Campbell's Funeral Parlor on Eighty-first and Madison. As I walked into the room, struck by how many of the greats of the theater were in attendance, the song they were playing was "I'll Be Seeing You In All The Old Familiar Places." I kept a safe distance from the casket, just in case.

I was still struck by how I could have misread those signals, signals I continued to misread for most of my life. I thought that when men took you out for a meal they were just trying to get to know you. I had the woman's view of what feeding another person a meal means: I welcome you and nurture you. I didn't understand that for many men the real objective in getting to know you is to know you through and through.

Going out for months before he made a move on me lulled me into believing that we had a higher, purer kind of relationship, the kind of relationship that is above sex. I know now that there are very few men who think any relationship is above sex. The older and more experienced me knows that sex is the question you answer first, and one you just might return to at a later date if he doesn't like the answer he was given. I also believed that Mr. Langner was way too old to be thinking sexual thoughts about a woman in her twenties. Keep in mind, this was before Viagra. And mace. He was a grandfather figure, or rather, a great-grandfather figure. Surely great-grandparents don't have sex, I would have said at the time. It would have horrified me to think that my grandparents were having sex. Now that I'm in my seventies, I understand exactly how naïve I was.

Larry Langner wasn't just feeding me for my health. As my late husband said: "Doris, if someone likes you or loves you, they want to know all the things about you, the sexual you, the person, the artist, everything. You can't say, 'just love the artist and not the rest of me.'"

I was thinking: here is a great producer who recognizes a budding talent. He's hanging on my every word because he cherishes my gift. Maybe—but he also cherishes my butt, which he wanted as a gift—unwrapped, and way before Christmas.

I don't mean this story to prevent young women from going out to dinner. That's why the title isn't: Avoid Men Who Feed You. *Beware* of men who feed you. Be on your guard. Sometimes it's just dinner. But, with most, they want to be fed right back.

Lamb is a deceptive meat, like the men who fed me. It is the easiest on the digestive system, but has the highest cholesterol.

Pan-Fried Lamb Chops
with Mustard Cream Sauce

1 generous pat of butter

1 shallot, chopped

2 sprigs fresh thyme

⅓ cup white wine

splash of vermouth

2 cups heavy cream

2 heaping tablespoons Dijon mustard

Lamb chops (rib or loin, whichever you prefer)

salt and pepper

1. To make sauce, melt butter in a saucepan.
2. Add shallots and thyme and cook until the shallots are translucent.
3. Add wine and vermouth. Reduce liquid by half over low flame.
4. Pour in cream and stir in mustard. Let sauce reduce over low flame by another one third.
5. Salt and pepper the lamb chops.
6. Melt some butter in a sauté pan and place the seasoned chops in the hot pan. Cook 3–4 minutes, depending how you like your meat cooked, then turn them and cook another 3–4 minutes.

To serve, drizzle the plate with a little bit of sauce, place the chops right in the sauce, then drizzle a little more sauce over the top.

Serves 4.

Chapter 29

Ode to My Father

The man who had the sperm with the tail that made the journey.

Chapter 30

Stop Waiting for Big Daddy

I only saw my father once. When I was eleven years old, my mother and I were on the corner of Forty-fifth and Broadway when I heard her gasp: "Oh my God! Here comes your father!" I looked up at a smiling, handsome man about six feet tall, with sandy colored hair and hazel eyes, who had crouched on one knee to greet me.

Even as a young girl I could understand what my mother had seen in him. He was beautifully dressed and carried himself with dash and dignity. He threw his arms open and looked at me with delight, as if I was his long-lost friend, not the daughter he'd abandoned ten years before.

"Oh, this is our little Doris May!" he said. "Aren't you a charmer. I want to take you to lunch tomorrow."

At that moment he was everything I'd dreamed about: He was more dashing than my schoolgirl fantasies and he was my genetic link to the stage. Through him I was related to Henry Lewis, a headliner on the Orpheum/Keith vaudeville circuit. Big Daddy was a powerful man who could not only sweep me up in his arms but carry me to Broadway. Despite that, something in me hesitated to run to him. I looked from him to my mother and saw her flat expression and the hurt look in her eyes. My feet stayed rooted to the ground.

My father was a mysterious figure to me, and I'd often tried to guess what he looked like. No matter how bad things got at home, my mother never said a negative word about my father. But she never said a good word, either, and there were no pictures of my father anywhere in our house or that of my grandparents. I picked up some things about him by eavesdropping on my mother's conversations with my aunts. I'd heard he had cheated on my mother throughout their marriage. I also learned some new words that would make a plumber proud, but I only use them when in labor or in really bad traffic. The story that stuck in my mind was how my father would walk past my crib and say: "That bastard. That's not my child."

My aunts told the story to show what a liar he was, but I didn't know what to do with this information. There he was, so handsome and charming, kneeling in front of me, I wondered if he *was* the one who was telling the truth. What else could explain why he had abandoned us? I thought it all had to be my fault. If I had been prettier, or a better baby, or smarter, my parents would still be married. I never shared these feelings with anyone, despite how strong they were inside of me.

Here was my chance to show him that I hadn't been a mistake. I *was* worth looking after and getting to know, even spoiling, the way my fantasy Big Daddy would.

I looked at my mother's unchanged expression. Although she appeared stoic, I knew it would have killed her if I accepted his invitation. Instead of following my heart, I mirrored her attitude. "No, I don't think so," I said. I never saw him again.

I spent a good part of my life waiting for Big Daddy and looking for him in every man I met, although you'd think that I'd be the last woman on earth to believe that a man was about to swoop down and come to the rescue. As a little girl, you believe in fairy tales, even though you know that they don't come true. Many of the women I know are still looking, despite how life has shown them over and over again that there is no Big Daddy to provide an instant solution to everything.

My curiosity about my father didn't die, nor did my craving for a Big Daddy. When I was married and my mother had remarried, I thought the subject might no longer be so hard for her to talk about. One afternoon, we were having lunch at Schraft's on Broadway and I asked her about my aunts' story, where my father denied that I was his child.

My mother said my father's philandering was pretty clear from the moment they married. He fell for a woman in East St. Louis and my mother found out about it. She called the woman, who was a devout Catholic, and told her that not only was she involved with a married man, but that he was also the father of a young baby. My father told his mistress I wasn't his child, and even tried to convince my mother. The aunts told this story to prove to my mother that, despite all the hardships she faced raising me alone, she was better off single than being married to a man who was so low that he would deny his own child.

My mother needed convincing. Despite his rotten behavior, my mother tried to woo him back. More than once, he went off with some other woman, but my mother always believed, when he came back, that this time he would straighten out if she could just keep him out of East St. Louis, West St. Louis, or the Midwest. She talked about once cooking a great dinner for him—probably her pot roast—and getting lovely candles and champagne to celebrate their reconciliation. He never came home that night. That was the cold, hard shattering of her idea that Big Daddy was going to rescue her. But it was not the end of mine.

A few years before my mother died, I asked her about him one last time. I decided that if she didn't want to discuss it, I would let it go for good.

"I don't want to harp at you or ever make you feel that I'm not grateful for all you did for me," I said, "but I would like to be able to just sit opposite my father in some coffee shop and absorb him and know who I came from."

She told me she would try to find his family.

A few weeks later, my mother came to my apartment unexpectedly in the middle of the afternoon. She sat at the kitchen table and asked me to fix her a drink, which wasn't something she normally did.

"I've found your father," she said. "He's in prison."

My mother had tracked down my father's sister—I hesitate to call her my aunt—who said my father was serving a prison sentence for embezzlement. I wasn't sure why my mother was taking this so hard. Finding out that he still hadn't changed his ways could have been a victory of sorts for my mom, but she was clearly shaken up by any brush with my father and his family.

She said his sister had invited us to visit her. I asked my mother if this would be all right with her and she said she would do it. She arranged for us to meet the woman in her huge apartment across from the Museum of Natural History planetarium on West Seventy-ninth Street.

When his sister talked about my father, it was clear how much she loved him. I think she was caught up in his charm, too. From the stories she told, I heard how she doted on him. Even though all of his get-rich-quick schemes failed, she lent him money the numerous times he fell on hard luck. It felt odd to sit there hearing these stories of a man who had lurched from one half-assed scheme to another, one failed relationship to the next, yet his sister spoke as if he was a great adventurer who'd led a colorful life.

I wanted to know about his other families. Maybe I had half brothers and sisters I'd never met. But, although my father had been married seven times, I was his only child.

When we left I was swimming in details. I had watched my

father's sister carefully, observing her charming manners and her elegance and trying to imagine which of her traits were similar to his. I couldn't help but wonder if I would have turned out differently if that family had been part of my life. Would I have absorbed that effortless style?

I also saw how hard it had been for my mother to see the opulent apartment of her ex-husband's sister. She lived only ten blocks from us, yet none of his family had been at all curious what had happened to my father's only child. Clearly, my mother recognized that they had been in a position to help her out during her tough times raising me, but they had refused to do so.

I thought back to that afternoon on the street corner, the one and only time I saw my father. He could have taken me to lunch, but it wouldn't have been a rescue. The most he could have done was distract me. He wasn't capable of saving me from danger. Clearly, he couldn't even take care of himself.

Ten days later my father's sister called me. She was very excited.

"I've been in touch with your father," she said. "He's so excited that I found you, or that you found the family, and would love to write to you and have you write to him. You've got to get permission from the warden to do that. Would you write to the warden or call his number?"

"No," I said. "I have no further use for that man."

I have no further use for that fantasy, is what I should have said.

The expectation that Big Daddy is coming to take all the problems away prevents you from building that strength in yourself, the confidence that you are not going to fall apart. I no longer wait for Big Daddy to rescue me. I do it myself every day.

In the late 1980s I was on *CBS Good Morning* promoting *Remington Steele*, and the host surprised me by mentioning my estrangement from my father.

"He's out there somewhere right now, Doris," she said. "If you could say anything to him, what would it be?"

Somewhere deep inside, this question touched my vaudeville lineage. I stuffed my thumbs in my ears and started my fingers waggling as I stuck my tongue out and produced a powerful raspberry. For weeks after that, people stopped me on the streets of New York and laughed as they delivered the same salute to me.

Make this refreshing tuna salad for a picnic with Mom.

Tuna Salad

2 cans tuna, drained and squeezed as dry as possible

1 stalk celery, finely chopped

1 half red onion, finely chopped

3 scallions, green parts only, minced

salt and pepper to taste

2 tablespoons mayonnaise

1. Mix all ingredients in a bowl until evenly distributed.
2. Grab your favorite bread and make a couple of sandwiches, and pick up a box of ginger snaps for dessert.

Generous lunch for 2.

Part Nine

The Love of My Life

Chapter 31

Blood Tests

The beginning of my love affair with my late husband was a scene right out of the movies. One day at the Actors Studio, Wynn Handman told me that William Goyen, a playwright from the Studio's writing and directing unit, was interested in approaching me about being in his play. "He's a huge fan of yours, Doris," Wynn said. "He sees all your work at the Studio, and he thinks you are brilliant, absolutely fabulous. He's written a play and he'd like you to read for it."

Rather than being complimented, I was furious.

"This man has seen my work at the Studio, thinks I'm brilliant, thinks I'm wonderful, and wants me to read for his play?" I snorted. "If he's seen my work and he loves it, why should I read for him? Tell him to go to hell."

Admittedly, this was a very bad time in my life, a time when my bark was about as bad as my bite. After twelve years of marriage, I had realized that my husband and I were in serious trouble, even though, to an outsider, our family probably looked fine. We were doing all the right things for all the wrong reasons—going to work, raising our child, attending family gatherings. I always had fun with him. He was like an adolescent, which made life with him a gas, but he never grew up. After I put him through law school, I thought the new job would force him to mature. Instead, he was still convinced life should always be a goof. When he walked out the door in the morning, he had a choice to make. If to the right was work and to the left was skiing, flying, or sailing, odds were he'd turn left.

My getting pregnant didn't change things, either. I realized I would always be on his back, always be answering the phone and saying the check would be in the mail. As this realization sunk in, there were fewer and fewer subjects we could talk about without conflict, and I felt the increasing distance between us. Yet, many things made it impossible for me to leave, or even consider it seriously.

First among these was my feelings about divorce. I was the product of a broken home. I knew the loneliness and insecurity that a child of divorce experiences, and I didn't want to do that to my son. Besides, I had made a commitment, I had taken a vow and I wanted to keep to my word, even if it made my life difficult. Maybe, if I worked at it harder, we could save our marriage. I hoped we might rekindle our love for each other if we could get away from the stresses of daily life. In a last ditch effort, we took a month-long family trip to Europe.

We shipped our ourselves and Volkswagen across the Atlantic on a Greek freighter, and we drove through Great Britain, France, and Italy. The trip only increased my sense that things were over between us. No matter what my husband wanted to do, I wanted to do something different. Maybe this was because I didn't know my right from my left when taking directions. In fact, years later I remarked to my son Michael how much of a chatterbox he had been during that trip. He explained why he talked all the time back then: because, the more he talked, the less his father and I argued.

When we got home, it was clear to me that the marriage was over, but neither of us wanted to deal with it. Our families would be outraged by a split-up, which would be seen on all sides as a betrayal. My husband came from a large and very traditional Italian family. God only knew what reprisals those characters would think up if I left my husband and took his son. How could I do that, anyway? I was an actress, and not a very successful one at that. I was terrified of trying to support myself while still finding a way to provide and care for Michael. I was paralyzed by the situation. In those days, anything that annoyed me, like that phone call from Wynn Handman, resulted in an angry comeback.

I was still steaming about this character, Goyen, wanting me to read for his play, when the doorbell rang. There was a torrential rainstorm that night, and I couldn't imagine that any sane person would want to be out in it. I came to the door in my chenille bathrobe, looking about as frowzy and beaten-down as I felt, my face pale, without a scrap of makeup. I might as well have had curlers in my hair. I opened the door, and there stood Bill, dripping wet with a limp copy of his play in one hand, his broken arm in a sling, and a taxi idling in the street behind him on St. Mark's Place.

The first sight of him huddled in the doorway took my breath away. Despite his scrunched up posture as he dodged the rain, the cut of his raincoat over his lanky frame gave off an air of sophistication and sex appeal.

"Miss Roberts, I'm William Goyen, the writer who wants you to be in his play. Oh God, I'm such a fan of yours," he said. "The work I've seen you do is just extraordinary. I didn't mean to insult you by asking you to read for this. Please forgive me. Please read this. I hope you want to do it. I'd be honored if you would."

More than his courtly manner, what struck me was his face. His mesmerizing gray-blue eyes shot through with dashes of green regarded me in admiration and concern. The thick lines of his strong features, his dark eyebrows and hair, drew the gentle face of an old soul.

I struggled to keep up the bearing of a grand star at a moment when I felt like a washerwoman. I was at the lowest point in my life and feeling very vulnerable. Yet, despite the fact that I looked like a total slob, Bill Goyen made me feel as though I was the only important person in the world. This handsome, gentle, wonderful playwright had chosen me and had taken the time and expended the energy to come to my house and apologize in the flesh, to ask me to read his play and hope I would want to do it. The idea that someone was awaiting my decision gave me an unexpected feeling of importance. At a moment when I felt my lowest, someone was paying attention to me. All of it contributed to this fairy-tale meeting.

"I'll read it and let you know," I said flatly and closed the door.

I read it and it *was* extraordinary. The play was called *Christy,* and it was set in Bill's home state of Texas on the occasion of a mother's funeral. My character was the drunken daughter who arrived late accompanied by her fifth husband. She brought with her a garish wreath for the grave, a horseshoe-shaped arrangement she'd gotten cheap from a florist at the racetrack. Her relatives, who were appalled at the faux pas, didn't understand its real purpose. Inside the wreath she had hidden her flask, and throughout the scene she sneaked sips. The play was both hilarious and sad, two qualities I came to love about Bill. Of course, I ended up doing the play.

During rehearsals, the cast was not allowed to speak with the playwright. We saw him in the audience at each run-through, but the director wanted us to communicate only with him, and he, if necessary, would speak with Bill. During the weeks of rehearsal Bill and I spoke only twice. I offered Bill a folded-up matchbook to use to scratch underneath his cast, a tool that had worked well for my son Michael when he had broken his arm a few years earlier. Bill was very grateful for the tip.

My stepfather passed away while we were working on the play and I missed a day of rehearsal to attend his funeral. That night, Bill was the only member of the cast who was thoughtful enough to call me at home to offer his condolences. I can't remember what he said, but I do remember holding the wall phone receiver in the kitchen and hearing this extraordinary soft and sweet Texas drawl soothing everything over. I was carried along by that voice that assured me that everything was going to be all right.

When the play premiered at the Studio, the house was packed with the toughest critics among them, Elia Kazan and Audrey Woods. They all loved it, and—after bathing Bill with praises the bigwigs asked him out to Sardi's to talk about it. The cast and I had previously planned to celebrate at Downey's, a less-expensive bar, where Bill agreed to meet us when he was finished with the others. We stayed at Downey's for two hours with no sign of Bill. Just as I was collecting myself to go home, he called and begged us to stay so he could come to thank us. One by one, the other members of the cast excused themselves to go home until it was just Bill and me. He asked if he could buy me dinner and I said yes, as if I had no need to go home, no baby and no husband.

We started with polite praise. I thanked him for creating such wonderful characters, particularly the one I played, and predicted great success for the play. He thanked me in return for how I'd made his character come alive. As the evening went on, we talked as if we had known each other all our lives. We were so comfortable with each other that the time raced by, until they kicked us out at closing. He took me home in a cab and, as I was getting out at my house, he invited my husband and me to a party he was having at his house that Sunday.

The party was great—filled with theater people. As my husband and I were leaving, Bill took me aside and pressed a copy of his short-story collection into my hand. "I wondered if you might look at them and see if anything strikes you," he said. The next morning around 11:30 I called him. My first words didn't seem kind.

"You bastard," I said.

"What?" he said.

"To cause me such pain," I said.

He *had* caused me pain, but if that was all that he had caused in me I would not have had such a strong reaction, and I wouldn't have raced through the book in just one sitting.

Like those dark gray-blue eyes, his stories were turbulent tales of loss and regret, shot through with green flashes of humor and, in the end, redemption. I had never read anything quite like what he wrote, nor even conceived of the East Texas world he brought so vividly to life on those pages. Once, when a journalist asked Bill what started him writing he said: "It starts with trouble. You don't think it starts with peace, do you?"

Yes, all of the stories started with trouble, but they also started with an unforgettable voice—similar to his voice in real life—unlike any I had heard before. He'd draw you in with a deceptively casual drawl, the language and manner of an encounter with a stranger you chatted with at a lunch counter. One of his stories started with:

> Do you remember the bridge that we crossed over the river to get to Riverside? And if you looked over yonder you saw the railroad trestle? High and narrow? Well that's what he jumped off of. Into a nothing river. "River"! I could laugh. I can spit more than runs in that dry bed.

In just those few sentences, he brought you into a different world, established who will guide you through it, and made you wonder why someone would end their life in a "nothing river." I was entranced by his writing, by his style, and by him. Yet I had been too preoccupied with the drama of my own life to understand how this added up to attraction.

While we were in rehearsal for Bill's play, my husband and I agreed to separate. We signed the papers necessary to file for a quick divorce in Mexico, and he promised to travel there and take care of it. He kept putting off the trip, and I never had enough money to go myself. I was frantically trying to get work to support myself and my son, so, despite the separation, we remained living in the same house. Finally, after a year and a half I saved up the money and carved out the time to go to Mexico. I told my husband that I was flying out to California to do a movie, and I would stop off in Mexico on the way to get the divorce.

I was on my way to the plane at LaGuardia Airport when I heard my name being announced over the loudspeaker. On the white courtesy phone was my lawyer telling me not to go to Mexico, because my husband had rescinded his consent to get the divorce. To get a quick Mexican divorce, both parties must agree. I was standing at the airport with the phone in my hand and my plane leaving in twenty-five minutes, eager to get it over with, to accept the end of my marriage and to move on to the next incredibly difficult phase of life. All my momentum was going in one direction, yet my lawyer was telling me to put on the brakes. I'd only be wasting my money and my time. I don't know what I thought I was going to do, or how I was going to do it, but I was going to get this accomplished. I got on the plane.

I landed in El Paso and went straight for the attorney's office, south of the border. Evidently the telegram my husband had sent withdrawing his consent hadn't arrived yet. I walked into the attorney's office, signed all the papers, and walked out a free woman. Thank God there was no Internet, or I'd probably still be married to that man.

When I got back to New York I moved out of the house right away and into a tiny, tiny room I rented on West Thirteenth Street. I couldn't take my son with me, because the room just wasn't big enough for both of us. I went to tend to Michael every day. Back then, St. Mark's Place was not the trendy spot it is today. It was filled with immigrant families—Polish, Irish, Italian—and maintained a very traditional atmosphere, where divorced women were considered one step removed from whores. As I walked with Michael to the park, women would spit at me as I passed. They'd make the horn sign, retracting the two center fingers of the hand so that the index and little finger jutted out to form the devil's horns. They were wasting their energy sending bad luck my way. I had plenty already. I had no money, I had no job, and I had no position in society. After a while, though, I had Bill.

Our attraction to each other had grown over the year and a half since my husband and I became legally separated. When I told him of my plans to finalize the divorce, Bill wanted to get married right away. I wasn't ready. I was so disillusioned with marriage and still experiencing the deep pain of the divorce, I just couldn't commit. He had no such ambivalence, though. When I turned him down and went to California, he left on a writing fellowship to Europe in an attempt to get me out of his mind.

When Bill returned, he moved to a new apartment on the top floor of a building on East Fiftieth Street. He asked me to come over one Saturday afternoon and help him shelve his many, many boxes of books. I arrived at the appointed time and rang the bell. No answer. I rang the bell several times, getting more and more impatient—until the fire department came to my rescue.

Bill's new apartment was across the street from the second biggest hook-and-ladder company in the New York City Fire Department, where a group of firemen had been amused by my very visible and mounting frustration. When they found out I was trying to meet up with my friend, they suggested that they pull the huge rig over to Bill's building and extend the ladder to his living room so I could climb up and bang on his window. As I was not wearing trousers, I declined.

The firemen's plan B was to turn on the sirens at full volume and shine their brightest light on his window, expecting that that would wake old Sleeping Beauty. When they turned on the noise and light, every window on the block flew open as the neighbors attempted to see what was going on. That is, every window except Bill's.

Eventually a man in a neighboring building performed the daredevil stunt of climbing from the roof of his building to Bill's and inside through the hallway so he could bang on Bill's door. I'll never forget the face of Bill, awakened from what had to have been one of the deepest sleeps of the last century. He poked his sleepy head out of the window to the theatrical scene of the entire fire company and all of his neighbors staring up at him with me in the center of it all, hand on hips and demanding to be invited in. As Bill said later, I always made great entrances.

In the end, the separation didn't work for either of us, a simple fact that brought us to Longchamps on a winter afternoon shortly after this memorable entrance.

Longchamps was a chain restaurant we frequented that featured a bar. We used to call the one on Madison Avenue "The Mother Grape," because it was the biggest one, and also because, typically, we drank there and never touched the food. One night at The Mother Grape two years after my divorce was final, Bill suggested we visit his doctor.

"He's around the corner," he said. "Why don't we go there and get blood tests, in case someday soon we might want to get married?"

This was not exactly the romantic marriage proposal every girl dreams of getting. But, considering our history on this subject, what did I expect? In a giddy mood of unstated promise, we went to the doctor and had our blood drawn.

At that time I was doing a little play called *The Color of Darkness* on East Fourth Street. Bill called me at the theater two days later between the matinee and the evening performance.

"If you're standing, sit down," he said.

"Why?"

"Well, the blood tests have both come back positive, which means we have venereal disease," he said.

I had no illusions that he had been faithful to me during our separation. I hadn't been faithful to him, either. We had broken up, after all, and whatever we did during that time apart was irrelevant, now that we were beginning to commit to a life together. Nonetheless, we both went crazy when we found out.

If I thought about him with another woman at all, it was another woman singular. The fact that he had the clap conjured in my mind more than one dalliance, perhaps dozens. Who was this man I was ostensibly promising to spend the rest of my life with? Did I really know him after all? I knew I had only had one affair, and I suspected that Bill was the one who had transmitted this disease to me. His suspicions were as strong as mine, and as hard to shake. This was terrible, hateful—the worst way possible to begin a marriage.

We fought all weekend like two insane people. Finally it was Sunday and we were both exhausted, but we were still in there slugging. "Well, we both have it, we'll both get cured," he said. I thought it was wonderful of him, a sign that our relationship was mature and we would put this (and the behavior that led to it) behind us.

On Monday he called me at home.

"If you're standing, sit down," he said.

"Oh no," I said. What could he possibly have to say that was worse than Wednesday's news?

"When my doctor got the report from the lab, he found out that they'd read him somebody else's results," Bill said.

"What are you saying?"

"Neither of us has VD," he said.

We laughed. We laughed until our sides ached, and at that moment, as well as at many moments in the future too numerous to count, I knew I would always love that man.

Six months later we were finally married in an eccentric Broadway ceremony. We took down the set for the play that was up at the American Place Theater and brought in some props to make the main stage look as though it had an altar. Wynn Handman, the man who had brought us together, appointed himself producer of the wedding. Elia Kazan's wife, Molly, arranged the music, and the legendary theater director Harold Clurman gave me away. In fact, we couldn't get him off the steps leading to the altar once he had performed his duty. I think he thought *he* was marrying me.

Two surprise uninvited guests were my former sisters-in-law. I had on an adorable little suit with a white mink collar accented with a white mink hat. As I came down the aisle one of them said sarcastically: "Well, don't you look pretty today, Doris?" I thought I was going to see blood on my white collar any minute. As I stood on the altar, I scanned the audience with one eye for a hit man. Still, nothing could keep me—the cynic—from feeling giddy as we began our fairy-tale romance.

I say fairy-tale romance without pretending that all of our life together was idyllic and "happily ever after." In fairy tales there is usually a monster who must be vanquished, or an enormous obstacle that has to be overcome. Bill and I had more than our share of those, but we also had a powerful and unshakeable love for each other that endured through every crisis. We were lovers, fighters, and friends. At our lowest moments, during times when we were quite literally at each other's throats, if I was riding on a bus and saw him walking down the street, my heart leaped in excitement to see him, and I was always proud to be on his arm. Although the life of two strong-willed, creative people was never easy, it was also never dull. He was more than I ever dreamed of having as a husband, the man who truly was the love of my life.

A spicy Mexican recipe to celebrate my independence.

Stuffed Roasted Chiles with Tequila Shrimp

I pound small raw shrimp, shells and tails removed

¼ cup red onion, diced

the juice of 4 limes

½ cup chopped cilantro

I clove garlic, minced

2 teaspoons chili powder

I cup tequila

½ cup corn oil

4 fresh poblano or Anaheim chiles (red or green bell peppers
   may be substituted)

2 ears corn

one 28-ounce can whole tomatoes

the juice of ½ orange

the juice of ½ lemon

2 cloves garlic

3 chicken boullion cubes

I shot of tequila

I cup shredded jack cheese

I cup shredded cheddar cheese

salt and pepper

1. In a bowl, combine shrimp, red onion, juice of two limes, cilantro, minced garlic, 1 teaspoon chili powder, 1 cup tequila, salt, pepper, and corn oil. Stir to evenly distribute and refrigerate.

2. On the stovetop or under the broiler, roast chilis until the skins are black on all sides. Remove from heat and put in a bowl and cover with plastic wrap immediately.

3. Husk the corn, remove silks and put under the broiler until they just start to color. Turn until all sides have some color. Scrape corn from cob and set aside.

4. In a food processor, blend the tomatoes, juice of the remaining two limes, orange juice, lemon juice, 1 teaspoon chili powder, two cloves garlic, boullion cubes, and a shot of tequila until smooth. Transfer to a sauce pan and cook over low heat. Let simmer.

5. When the chilis have cooled, run them under cold water to remove the charred skin, rubbing gently to aid in the process. Make a slit down the length of one side of the chilis, reach in, and remove the seeds and membranes.

6. When the shrimp have marinated for about a half hour, remove on with a slotted spoon, heat sauté pan and cook shrimp until just pink. Discard marinade. Let the shrimp cool.

7. In a bowl combine the shrimp with the corn and cheese and stuff the chilis with this mixture.

8. Arrange the chilis onto a baking sheet and bake at 325 degrees for about 20 minutes or until cheese melts and chilis are hot.

9. To serve, cover the bottom of two dinner plates with the warm, red sauce, and top with two stuffed chilis per plate. Drizzle more sauce over the chilis if you'd like.

Serves 2.

Chapter 32

The Quiet House

Although he was never a household name, like a television star, in the New York literary world of our youth, my husband, William Goyen, was a young man of bright promise. His first novel, *The House of Breath*, set in his birthplace of East Texas, had been extraordinarily well received, and his plays were a sensation in the world of the Actors Studio. When we met, he was moving effortlessly from one prestigious writing fellowship to the next, at theater companies around New York that were clamoring for his plays, and he had a novel underway that publishers were competing for. I was so honored and proud to be Mrs. William Goyen. His phenomenal success lulled me into the feeling that this was the norm, and not an aberration in the tumultuous ups and downs in the life of a writer.

I'd never been much of a reader as a child, simply because my mother was. You'd think that having a parent who read a lot would inspire that parent's child to read, but I resented books because they took my mother's attention away from me. My enormous respect for writers and for the written word had been reinforced by working on plays. I'd experienced the horror of trying to give life to badly written ones, as well the honor of being chosen to work on those that were well-crafted. Life had given me the gift of living with a man whose work I respected without question. I was amazed that Little Doris would find herself living in a nine-room apartment on West End Avenue in Manhattan, the wife of a prestigious and well-respected writer. My primary responsibility, I thought, was to protect my husband's creative gift and make his life as trouble-free as possible, because, God knows, writers bring enough trouble on themselves.

Bill was very disciplined. He got up at five every morning and sat in his study, waiting for the voice to come. That writing voice I loved so much, the hypnotic rhythms of his East Texas boyhood, was not easy to hear. It was not something that he could fake or force. He simply had to wait in the quiet room while the rest of the world was asleep. Often, he sat for weeks waiting for the voice to arrive.

I'd get up late after a night at the theater, and when Bill heard me stirring he'd break from work and we'd have breakfast together. Soon after, though, he'd return to his room to wait, or to write some more.

My contribution to his creative vigil was to ensure that the house was completely quiet while he worked. I didn't have friends over during the day. I didn't play music. When Michael was home from boarding school, I didn't allow his friends over, either. Bill had to concentrate undisturbed. Our grand apartment became a monastery.

The aspects of a man's character that you love can turn out to be the ones that infuriate you under different circumstances. Bill never compromised his vision for money. This was something I loved about him, but it also caused me distress that, during the years when his work went unrecognized, he turned down money-making offers that would have made our lives easier.

He wrote a fabulous musical about the life of the flamboyant evangelist Aimee Semple McPherson, the founder of the Foursquare Church whose kidnapping and mysterious reappearance seventy years ago remains unsolved. She was the first on-air evangelist to use the power of radio to build a nationwide following. She disappeared while swimming in the ocean off the coast of Los Angeles and was discovered more than a month later roaming the California desert wearing new shoes, a new outfit, and without her bathing suit. All of this made her a great subject for theater, and Bill did a fantastic job capturing her and the time she lived in. I felt sure he had a hit on his hands.

When the piece was premiering in Provincetown, we hired a bus to take all the people I knew in theater in New York to see it. I made elaborate trays of hors d'oeuvres and walked the aisle of the bus distributing drinks to ensure that everyone was in a great mood to enjoy a spectacular opening.

Jules Stein, one of the most successful Broadway producers of that time, expressed interest in mounting a production of *Aimee*. He asked Bill to his office so they could discuss some of the changes that would be necessary in the script for him to back it. Bill refused to change a word. I suggested (pretty strongly, I'll admit) that maybe this producer was giving him good advice and that Bill should at least listen to him. Bill turned down the producer, just as he later turned down offers to do screenplays and adaptations of other writers' work. "It's not what I do," he'd say simply.

What he did wasn't going very well all of a sudden, either. He wrote a book called *The Fair Sister*, about two African-American sisters, one of whom was light-skinned while the other was very dark. It was published in 1964, right at the crest of the Civil Rights Movement, and received a full-page review in *The New York Times* Sunday book section. The review started off praising Bill's work, but quickly transitioned to skewering him for addressing this sensitive topic while so much political turmoil was taking place on the issue of race. The reviewer attacked Bill for not writing a more political book, but that wasn't the book that Bill wanted to write. When his publishers saw the review, they stopped the presses. Only five thousand copies of the book were printed, despite the favorable reviews that followed in other newspapers.

When his next novel came out, the publisher didn't gather cover blurbs, the prepublication compliments from famous critics and other writers that authors post on the back of their books to encourage people to read it. Bill believed this oversight was the death knell of that book, which also didn't do very well. In the face of these failures, he took a job as an editor at the publisher McGraw-Hill to support us. He supported us quite well, but his spirits were sunk, as his early promise went unrecognized despite the beauty of his writing.

In the mid-1970s I started getting offers to work in television in Los Angeles. I thought that I'd only be out there for a month or two and then return to our apartment in New York. From the moment I hit town, the scripts piled up at my door. I had come to Los Angeles to work on *Maude,* but I quickly got offers for guest spots on other variety shows, such as *The Lily Tomlin Comedy Hour,* which continued to lengthen my stay.

For a few years I ran back and forth between the coasts. Bill would come to visit from time to time, but his antipathy toward Los Angeles was clear. It wasn't a writer's town, and he didn't believe he could find a community of like-minded souls with whom he could talk about writing and literature. I'd never before in my career had so much consistent and well-paid work, and I wanted to move there to give myself a chance. When my mother died in 1975, I felt as if we should try it out here for a while, and Bill agreed, but he didn't really settle in. He kept his teaching position at Princeton University and would fly back for his classes. It was a very unsettling time for both of us, as we felt unmoored without each other.

One Thursday afternoon, I saw in the entertainment newspaper *Variety* that the movie star Dolores Del Rio's home was for sale and decided I'd take a look. When I walked into the place it gave me the shivers, because it was so dark. Miss Del Rio did not like the sun. All the shades were drawn and the walls were painted dark colors. The real-estate agent urged me to go with him up to the top floor, which he promised was spectacular. I hated the house and saw no point in going any further. He asked me what it was I wanted in a house that this one didn't have.

I'd never really thought about it, but I surprised myself with my quick, specific answers. I said, "Well, I'm claustrophobic, so I don't like houses on top of each other. My husband's a writer, so it has to be big enough so he can work in peace and I can move around the house without bothering him. And I'd like it to be interesting, dramatic." He said he knew exactly the place for me.

He brought me up into the Hollywood Hills to a Spanish revival house that dominated an entire corner. Although it fulfilled my need for drama, the inside was a mess. The house stunk from the four cats that had been peeing on the floor for God knows how many years. The living room was a horrible mustard color I described to my friends as baby-shit brown. The owners weren't much for decorating, either. They had beaten-up sofa beds in every room, had the living room, with its soaring ceilings and huge fireplace, was dominated by an enormous, filthy bird cage whose occupant had flown the coop years ago. When I walked in the door I saw instantly what the place could be, and I fell in love.

Still, I had my doubts about what Bill would say about my buying a house. That next night I went to a dinner party where all I talked about was that house. My friends convinced me I should make an offer. Saturday found me in the living room of this wreck, making an offer that my real-estate agent dutifully carried upstairs to the kitchen to the couple who owned it, waiting patiently and toting their counter-offer back. In the end, I bought this enormous home with a huge garden and swimming pool for the now laughable price of $138,000. When they accepted my offer, I strode to the front of the house, uprooted the FOR SALE sign and threw it to the ground like Scarlett O'Hara in *Gone With The Wind*, proclaiming: "I'll never go hungry again."

I was right. I've never gone hungry since, but I almost was homeless. Even though it was the dawning of the feminist movement and the beginning of NOW, the bank wouldn't permit a woman to be the sole owner of a house. Bill didn't want to have anything to do with buying it. He didn't even want his name on the deed. If I was going to buy it, I had to do it on my own.

I'd made a lot of money doing a series of commercials for the air-freshener, Glade, so I had enough for a down payment; but the loan officer refused to sell me the house. "Let me get this straight," I said after weeks of evasion. "My husband can buy a house without my signature, but I need his permission if I want to do the same?" In the end I had to threaten the bank with talking on television about their discriminatory policy to get them to grant me a loan.

The day I was supposed to take possession, I visited the house to check out what I needed to do to get it in shape. The previous owners hadn't left. The man of the house, a body builder, was sitting at the kitchen table in his underwear with a copy of *TV Guide*, marking off the shows he wanted to watch that night. His wife sat at the dining room table with dozens of bottles of nail polish clustered around her as she methodically painted her nails, oblivious to me. They hadn't even packed a box. I was beside myself. When I confronted the former owner, he didn't even look up from his magazine. "Call me later," he said.

After all I'd gone through to get this house, the fact that he wasn't leaving made me insane. I punched him right in his massive forearm.

"You think that scares me? You think this muscle scares me? You don't scare me," I said. "You're going ass-over-elbow into the alleyway if you're not out of here by tomorrow. My trucks will be here at three."

My trucks! What trucks? All I had was a card table and four folding chairs.

The next day, when I drove up the hill with my table and chairs in the car, his truck was coming down the hill as I was going up.

He'd left, but he'd left his wife behind. She was seated in exactly the same place she'd been the day before, still painting her nails. On the table next to her was a handgun with a pile of bullets next to it. I grabbed the ammunition and tossed it into the shrubbery at the back door. I told the wife that if she and her husband were not out by the end of the day, I would charge them $250-a-day rent.

When I arrived the next day, I saw they'd left, but not without damage. He'd turned off the water and cut the telephone and power lines. I was furious, but the trouble didn't end there. When I got the power restored, the man I'd hired to refinish the floors arrived and had a heart attack in the middle of the job.

After the ambulance carted him away, I paced the barren, shabby house. God is against me, I thought. Whatever is wrong with this house is bigger and stronger than me. I seriously considered leaving. But, when my friends came that weekend they changed my mind. They descended on the house with food and wine and pitched in to give the inside a coat of paint. June Havoc, my old friend from the Actors Studio, opened the windows wide to blow out any lingering, scary spirits. We turned up the music and painted, danced, and drank until at last I felt I was in a house that was really my own.

That night, while I was putting food away in the refrigerator, I felt a kind of serenity and security I'd never experienced before. All my life I'd been living through someone else's goodwill, it seemed. From the moment I saw my mother slapping down the cash on my grandparent's kitchen table to pay them for caring for me, I understood how vulnerable I was. If I didn't act right, they could toss me out, and then where would I be? I felt the same throughout both of my marriages—not because my husbands made me feel that way, but because I couldn't support myself. Here I was in my house. *My* house! The words were like a mantra. The bank and I owned it and no one could kick me out. I *never* would go hungry again.

That weekend gave me a taste of what I wanted, what I had been denied in the monastery I had been running for Bill in New York. In that house I felt the beginning of the adult woman coming into her own. I started to feel that I was important. I thought I had traveled along through my career on luck, lucky to get the next job, lucky to keep working. Walking around in my own house—the Casa de Glade, as the plaque on the door says—I began to believe in my own success.

The next week, when Bill arrived from the East Coast, I took him to a restaurant at the beach for Sunday brunch. It was a wonderful meal, but I was just picking at my food because I knew I had something I had to settle with Bill. He confessed that he was tired of commuting back and forth between Princeton and Los Angeles and was tired of being separated from me. He wanted to put down roots in Los Angeles, get a teaching job, and write. This was great news, because I had missed him so much in the last few years, but I wanted him to know that things were going to be different in Los Angeles.

"You know, I've come to the conclusion that I no longer want to live in the shadow of the great man," I said.

He looked at me blankly.

"Who's the great man?" he asked in all sincerity.

"You," I said.

"None of this is my doing, Doris," he said. "It's all yours."

I had a hard time finding something to say. That's how I always thought of him. I was not Doris Roberts. I was Mrs. William Goyen. I thought that it was expected of me to think in those terms. He was not the one who said there couldn't be music in the house, or kids, or laughter and carrying on, because he was working. I was the one who did that. I created this illusion and supported it with my sacrifice.

Years back, in analysis, my psychiatrist had done a drawing of me that depicted my relationship to men. He drew me holding a table over my head, on top of which was a man sitting in a chair. My first reaction to this drawing was admiration of how strong I was. I was Atlas holding up my world. The next wave of my response was an embarrassment about the egotism. I am the one holding up the world! Next, I felt sorrow at the loneliness of the self-sacrifice. The person who holds up the world doesn't have anyone holding her up. She struggles with her heavy burden alone.

Women do this to themselves all the time. They make arrangements to support their partners—tasks they start off performing selflessly, so as to make the life of the couple run more smoothly. Somewhere along the way, the woman begins to resent the sacrifice and in turn resents the man for making her perform such tasks, tasks he never asked for. When she finally says she simply isn't going to do this anymore, and that things have got to change, the man is mystified by her anger. Who told her she had to do this in the first place?

This is precisely what happened with my great man, my man who didn't feel that great anymore. I told him I no longer wanted to keep a quiet house. In Los Angeles, I wanted to be able to have my friends over and I wanted to play music in the middle of the day, whenever I felt like it. He had to get an office outside of the house. He stunned me with how quickly and completely he agreed.

He got an office on the twelfth floor of an old office building on Hollywood and Vine, a place he just loved. He'd open the windows to hear the traffic and buses on that busy intersection and feel as though he had the best of New York in the middle of the beautiful Mediterranean climate of Los Angeles. I didn't need to keep a quiet house to be Mrs. William Goyen. I didn't need to hold up his world any more than he needed to hold up mine. We only needed to hold each other. That would be enough.

Here is a California antidote to the New York quiet house.

Avocado Stuffed with Spicy Lobster Salad

2 cups mayonnaise

¼ cup Dijon mustard

the juice of 1 lime

¼ cup chopped cilantro

½ jalapeño chili, seeds and membranes removed, and finely
   chopped

¼ cup of finely chopped green onion

½ cup of a red onion finely diced

the meat from 2 lobster tails, cooked

6 ripe avocados, peeled, halved and seeded

salt and pepper, to taste

1. In a bowl, mix the mayonnaise, mustard, lime juice, cilantro, jalapeño, green onion, and red onion, salt, and pepper.
2. Remove the lobster meat from the shell, coarsely chop, and put in bowl.
3. Mix in the dressing 1 tablespoon at a time until the lobster meat is evenly covered with a thin coat of dressing.
4. Spoon the lobster salad into the avocado halves and arrange on your serving platter. Drizzle some lime juice over the top and sprinkle some chopped cilantro to garnish.

Serves 6 for a nice lunch.

Chapter 33

To the Vine and the Palm, and for Doris

Once, shortly after we were married, Bill took me on a trip to his hometown in East Texas to meet his family and see firsthand the world he described so vividly in his stories. He wanted to show me the site of *The House of Breath*, his celebrated first novel that I had loved. As we drove closer to it my excitement grew; ever since I'd fallen in love with Bill and the book, I'd wanted to see this magical place. We took a left up a tiny street and, way at the end, on the left-hand side, was a house with a breezeway, just as he had described in the novel.

"There it is!" he announced. "This is where it all took place."

I scanned the unspectacular features of this house trying to uncover what he'd seen in it. None of the magic he described in *The House of Breath* was visible. His child's memory and adult imagination had filled this ordinary place and the everyday people of his Texas boyhood with his powerful dreams, and created unforgettable characters.

Bill used to say that all of life is loss, a statement that irked me because I couldn't agree with it. Yet, I also understood that, in order for him to create his fictional world, he gave so much of himself that he created a loss inside. He lived in that loss to create a world of magic, which in turn created meaning out of the brutality and chaos of his childhood. In his books, just as in his life as a writer, there was never a loss without redemption.

All of it took a terrible toll on him. When he would sit at his desk waiting to hear his characters speak, he was at a loss. Eventually they would speak, and he would be redeemed—but weeks or months could go by when they would remain silent, something that was difficult for both of us. He would fall into deep depressions and lash out at me in punishing ways, especially when he had been drinking. As the years went by and his failures piled up, he drank more and more.

In the New York apartment we had huge arguments, rows that sometimes lasted until late in the night. One night when I was watching television Bill burst in and switched it off.

"I want a divorce," he said.

I calmly walked over to switch the television back on.

"Well, Bill, it's 12:30 on a Friday night and I don't think any lawyers' offices are open now," I said. "Can this wait till Monday?"

He stormed out of the room, but he was back a few minutes later.

"And you're not getting a penny."

I assessed my penniless writer husband with a cool eye.

"That's okay, Bill," I said. "I don't want your penny."

He could be quite cruel in his responses if we argued while he was drunk, although he'd never remember it the next morning. One night I decided to trap him. I hid a tape recorder, which I turned on when he started to pick on me. The next day I produced the tape recorder at dinner.

"You don't believe me when I tell you how cruel you are," I said. "You'll believe me when you hear this."

What came out of the recorder surprised both of us. Instead of cruel rantings, we heard witty banter worthy of Noël Coward. Bill's drop-dead funny responses to my arguments sounded as if he'd plucked them right off a stage comedy. We were in hysterics listening to the two of us go at it, barely even listening to each other. I lost that argument.

One night at 3 A.M. we had such a row that I pulled off my wedding ring and slammed it down on the dining room table and glared at him.

"That's it. I'm out of this marriage," I said.

Bill grabbed my wedding ring off the table and threw it out the window of our twelfth-floor apartment. My heart leapt as my eyes followed the ring, and I suppressed a powerful impulse to go after it. I composed myself and held firm. We held our angry stares for a few seconds and took our positions at separate corners of the apartment.

Twenty minutes later the doorbell rang. The doorman stood meekly in the doorway, offering up my wedding ring. He said that one of our neighbors had been walking his dog when my wedding ring bounced onto the sidewalk before him. The man had scanned the building and saw that the only light on was coming from our apartment.

"The gentleman figured this had to belong to you," the doorman said.

As I put the ring back on my finger, our argument evaporated. I figured, for better or for worse, that Bill and I were married for life and we would face our problems together.

Our relationship began in a bar and grew during hours spent in fascinating conversation over cocktails, so it was hard for me to know when drinking moved from the way we amused ourselves to the solitary way Bill dealt with his pain. I suppose any woman married to an alcoholic could say that sentence. The truth is, I loved him so much that I made excuses for his behavior. In fact, I actively supported it, until one night I stopped drinking and he kept on.

We'd gone to Sardi's for a drink at the bar after I got off work, and I noticed that the man next to me had his arm in a sling. I asked him what happened to his arm.

"My monkey bit me," he said.

"I just found my newest best friend," I said to Bill.

We started drinking with him and his date and went on to all take a table for dinner. After dinner he suggested we have a nightcap. Back at the bar, he ordered us all Galliano Stingers. If you've never had a Galliano Stinger, my advice to you is not to. It is a drink that is so lethal it's hard to describe its effect. Although I'd had wine with dinner and a whiskey sour before, the Galliano Stinger was the final hammer blow to my equilibrium.

As the Galliano Stinger seeped into my bloodstream, my body slipped into an odd form of semiparalysis. I was perched carefully on the bar stool contemplating my next move. I don't mean my next move in my career or my plan to get my husband out of the bar. I mean the next move of my foot. "Okay," I instructed myself. "Take the heel of your shoe off the rung of the stool you're on and put it on the floor." I examined this complicated series of movements and came to the executive decision that I could not do it. "Just move your foot," I lectured myself. "Just put your damn foot on the floor."

I don't know how I got my foot to the floor, but I remember staggering out to the curb and being poured into the cab. We got home and somehow made it through the foyer and into the elevator. It took a while for Bill to get the key in the door, but I had a lot of patience for this action, as I planned how I was going to navigate through the doorway. He staggered into the apartment and tripped over the ottoman and I fell over him. That was how we woke up the next day, splayed around the floor like victims of a car wreck.

I have not had hard liquor from that day to this. Bill continued to drink, and, because I didn't, I saw his behavior much more clearly. That's when I knew he was an alcoholic, even though the world around him was telling us over and over again that he was not. Once, when his mother called and Bill had a hard time forming sentences, his mother asked me what was wrong with him. "He's drunk," I said.

"Oh no, Doris," she responded. "That's a horrible word. Don't ever use that word. He's not drunk."

The psychiatrist he went to at my urging assured us that drinking was not the problem, depression was. After all, Bill was still working every day. He'd work early in the morning and get drunk every night. The analyst told me that as Bill dealt with his depression, his drinking would decrease, so it was okay for him to continue drinking. Despite my feelings about this, I was in a completely codependent role. I'd even fix his martinis for him.

By the time we moved to Los Angeles I understood that, no matter which label we put on Bill's behavior, it was not changing. Cut off from his New York friends and isolated in an unfamiliar world, Bill's despair closed in on him. He lived all the failures of his life anew, this time inflamed by the dry weather and palm trees of Los Angeles. The warm climate and vegetation are similar to that of his Texas home, a place that brought too many painful memories. His drinking got steadily worse when he was here.

My attempts to talk to him about it only resulted in arguments or tears. I realized the only behavior I could control was my own. I went to Al-Anon, the support group for people who are intimately involved with an alcoholic. I found it enormously helpful in understanding how to take care of myself, how to control my own actions, and how to throw the responsibility for Bill's behavior back on his shoulders, so I didn't have to carry that burden.

All of this sounds sensible and almost too obvious. When you try to put it into practice, you break the patterns that have been established for years. It's astonishing how comfortable the familiar pain feels, when faced with the prospect of changing to a different one.

The night that Bill stopped drinking was a night I held my resolve.

Norman Lear, the television producer of such great situation comedies as *All In The Family, Maude,* and *The Jeffersons,* was hosting a big party at the grand old Hollywood restaurant, Chasen's, and had invited Bill and me. Everyone who was powerful in television was going to be there, which made it a very important evening for me. I knew we were in trouble from the moment we got there. Bill went immediately to the bar and ordered a martini.

"Well, that bastard," he said of one important producer he spotted across the room. "I've got something I want to say to *him*."

Although I was terrified of what he might do, I forced myself to do what had been drilled into my head at Al-Anon. I said to myself: take your eyes off him and do what you have to do. You cannot control him, and you are not responsible for his behavior. I started to work the room. I made a mental list of all the people I needed to greet to have made a success of the party. I went off to talk to a few executives, and returned to my husband, who had a fresh martini in his hand and had identified new targets for his rage.

I saw someone else I needed to chat up, and left Bill at the bar. I knew he was hurting, being in a room full of incredibly successful people, when he was struggling so hard with his writing. That night at Chasen's, I had to set aside my sympathy for the series of setbacks he'd endured and the pain they had caused. Although I was incredibly sympathetic, none of it was my responsibility, either. After I had made the rounds of all the people I needed to greet, I returned to Bill, who was still grumbling at the bar.

"Bill, I'm going home," I said, and started for the door.

I knew as I started for the door that, if I so much as turned my head back an inch to see if he was coming with me, he never would have followed. I headed straight for the door without looking back. When I was standing in front of Chasen's waiting for the valet to bring the car around, he showed up at my side. I focused completely on getting the car and going home. Bill mumbled under his breath about all the things he wanted to say to the others in the car line. The pop star who was a "bitch" (I agreed with him on that one); the producer who was a jackass; the writer who was a hack. I thought our car would never arrive.

When we got home, he fixed himself another drink. I held tightly to my Al-Anon training, which told me not to get angry with him for this, or for anything he had done that night.

"I don't want to live," Bill said.

"I know that, and there's nothing I can do to change that if that's how you feel," I said. "I wish I could. If there was something, I'd do it."

"I write a book and what happens to it?" he said. "It gets taken off the press. I write another book and they don't even send it out for blurbs. It's like giving birth to these babies and they die. They're stillborn. You get up to the top of the mountain and you go sliding back down. And it takes everything in the world to come back up. You write that next one and nothing happens. Who knows when I will write another one? Who knows?"

"I understand," was all I could say. "I absolutely understand, but there is nothing I can do."

We talked more and he got clearer and clearer, but not sober. Bill and I had had great talks in our years together, but nothing like this. We were open to each other in a way I'd never experienced with any other human being. It was as though our souls were touching and we were not afraid to reveal our deepest feelings, our deepest fears. The trust between us was complete, with a sensation of a pure understanding of the truth of who we were in the world and to each other. Around three in the morning, I told him I had to go to bed. He followed me. The next morning, around seven he woke me up.

"What's the name of that guy up the street who is in AA?" he asked.

"John," I said.

"Call John," he said.

"I can't do that Bill," I said. "You have to do that."

"Well, will you get me the number of AA?" he said.

"Bill, I can't do that," I said. "You have to do that."

He was capable of looking it up himself, but, in typical alcoholic fashion, he wanted me to do it so he could later blame me for pushing him into it if it didn't work. It took all the strength I had not to get out of that bed and find him the number. It was clear that only he could help himself do this, and that recognition of his problem started from this first step. I couldn't be an enabler of any kind, not in drink, and not in sobriety.

When the AA representative came to our house later that day he found Bill sitting dead drunk beside the pool, with a cigarette in one hand and a martini in the other. He looked elegant beyond belief, a grand figure of sophistication, even in his most addled state. They sat by the pool talking for hours and, by the time the AA volunteer left, Bill had committed to trying sobriety.

I divide my marriage into halves: the drinking half and the dry half. In the beginning of the dry part, it was all about AA. Bill went to meetings every day, and we talked about them and the issues they brought up about Bill and his past. Once the most intense part of that early sobriety was over, we had moved into our house and Bill began to write again.

In his office at Hollywood and Vine he heard the dark, sweet voice of East Texas more strongly than he had in years. He did some of his best writing in those sober years before he came down with leukemia. He made his peace with Los Angeles, too. In fact, one afternoon I caught him hugging a palm tree outside our house.

I cherish the dedication he wrote in *Arcadio,* the last novel he published before he died. "To the vine and the palm, and for Doris," is a poetic tribute to the life we were enjoying just before disease took him away from me.

Bill said that when he would fall into his dark despair what would bring him back was the ordinary things. He would be consumed by loss, yet he would look up and see people going about their business, paying their bills, and buying their groceries. "Despite my misery, life was going on!" he exclaimed to one interviewer. That was what I gave to Bill, a gift so commonplace that it hardly seemed like a gift at all, considering the world of art, culture, and travel he gave to me.

I suppose that is what made our marriage a perfect fit despite the turmoil. What we gave each other was something that we each had in abundance and could give of generously, and what we received from each other seemed nothing short of a miracle.

A delicious salad with hearts of palm.

Hearts of Palm and Fennel Slaw

    2 fennel bulbs, stalks and core removed
    ½ head of green cabbage
    ½ sweet onion, such as Vidalia or Maui
    I cup canned hearts of palm, sliced
    I cup apple cider vinegar
    I teaspoon celery seeds
    I teaspoon dry mustard, such as Coleman's
    ½ cup vegetable oil
    ½ head of red cabbage
    I basket cherry tomatoes
    salt and pepper

1. Shred fennel, green cabbage, and onion (cheese grater will do nicely), and combine them in a large bowl.
2. Toss in hearts of palm.
3. In a saucepan, bring vinegar to a boil. (Warning: this is gonna stink, but in the end it's more than worth it.)

4. Add the celery seed, dry mustard, salt and pepper. Stir and let reduce just a little bit.

5. Remove from heat and whisk in the oil.

6. Pour warm vinaigrette over vegetables. They will wilt a little, which you want.

7. Meanwhile, shred the red cabbage, and halve the tomatoes. When other bowl has cooled, garnish with tomatoes and red cabbage.

Serves 8.

Chapter 34

Last Days

As I mentioned earlier, Bill once said that when we refuse to look at a handicapped person, we take their light away. This is equally true for the way we treat those who are dying. Just at a time in their lives when a person needs to be reassured how much they matter, their friends and family find it extremely uncomfortable to be with them, let alone touch them. When Bill got ill, I vowed to myself that that would never happen. It was less of a vow than a need on my part to spend as much time with him as I could before there came a time when I would never see him again.

The same month Bill was diagnosed with leukemia, I came down with severe back pain from a herniated disc that was pressing on my sciatic nerve. The two of us were confined to separate bedrooms on the top floor of our house, with nurses attending to us and a person I hired to cook meals. After a few months of misery our conditions started to improve. Bill's leukemia appeared to go into remission and my back started to mend. The timing was fortunate, because, just as we turned this corner, I was cast in the part of the secretary Mildred Krebs in *Remington Steele,* which required me to travel to Mexico to film the first episode of the new season.

I strapped on my back brace and flew south, certain that my health would continue to improve while we worked. The warm weather and the swimming pool at the hotel would be good for my back. Also, the fact that Bill was getting better took a lot of stress off me. I was happy, too, to be working again, which always cheers me.

I called Bill each night at the end of shooting but never found him home. He'd call me the next day and, when I asked where he'd been, he'd say he'd been to an AA meeting. Knowing how vigilant he was about his sobriety, I never questioned it. What I didn't know was that he was in the hospital. His condition had taken a sudden turn for the worse and he didn't want me to feel compelled to return.

I was in shock when I got home two weeks later and found out the truth. I felt terribly guilty for abandoning him, but he wasn't interested in any of that. He said there was nothing I could have done to help him. He was well cared for at Cedars-Sinai, he assured me, and was receiving treatment for his condition. The last thing he wanted was to ruin my chances of getting a part in a television series. I moved into his hospital room and slept on a rollaway bed next to him.

This would be all well and good, if the care his doctors were giving him was in fact adequate, something that I was not convinced of at all. What had sent Bill to the hospital were fevers as high as 105 degrees that affected his epilepsy, sending him into grand mal seizures. Each night they put him to sleep on a bed of ice to cool him down, and each morning three doctors—an oncologist, a neurologist, and an expert in exotic diseases—came into his room to puzzle over his condition.

I always find myself making a fuss at the hospital. I don't care about their rules and procedures. I want my loved one taken care of, and I don't care whose feathers have to be ruffled to get those needs met. I was convinced the doctors hadn't explored every possibility for the cause of these fevers and seizures.

A friend of ours who came by the hospital for a visit was recounting her recent bout with the medical establishment. She'd had a severe pulmonary infection for which she was medicated. Every time she took the medication, she got so sick she finally told the doctors she wasn't going to take it anymore. She said she'd rather die than feel the way she did on that medication. The instant they took her off the drugs, she got better. Little had anyone realized that she was allergic to the medicine.

The idea of being allergic to the medicine stuck with me. The next morning, when the trio of doctors arrived I suggested that they should look into any possible allergic reaction Bill could be having to the drugs they had prescribed. The doctors shook their heads and said to me in a very patronizing way that there was no way he could be allergic to this medication. After all, hadn't he been on it for eight months? They assured me that it was a-million-to-one that what I believed was true.

"A-million-to-one shot?" I said, infuriated by this lax response when my husband's life was hanging. *"Take it."* Within days of being taken off the drugs, Bill's fevers disappeared completely although he still suffered from leukemia.

Having been brought to the brink of death, and then snatched back, put Bill in a frenzy to create with whatever time he might have left. He completed work on a collection of short stories called *Had I A Hundred Mouths* and a children's book called *The Wonderful Plant,* told from the point of view of a little boy who is very sick. I've always thought it would make a fabulous animated movie. As the boy nurses a plant that has been left for dead back to health, he discovers the wonderful world of colorful creatures who live around it and is restored to health himself.

Loss and redemption, but we knew that, for Bill, eventually loss would triumph. A little more than a year after we fought the doctors over his medicine, Bill became very weak and had to be readmitted to the hospital. It all felt different this time. It felt to me as if he was dying, something I saw in the look in his eyes. In our first battle he had steel in his eyes, as well as outrage. We were battling the insanity of the situation and the inadequacies of those around him. This time all I saw was fear and hopelessness, as if he were simply resigned. I was the one who had to be strong, in the hope that he would take strength from me.

I went to work directly from the hospital and returned every night. I took the rollaway bed on the nights when it was not possible for me to sleep in the bed with him. I was relieved to have a job to go to. While I was at work I could think about other things and pretend all the rest of it was not happening. It was just underneath the surface though, and would rush up as soon as I had an idle moment. I remember many times starting to cry as I sat in my trailer during a break between scenes. I'd lean over as far as I could so that the tears would not ruin my dress or my makeup.

I thought I was being professional and concealing my feelings so I could get on with my work, but Pierce Brosnan—the Remington in *Remington Steele*—wasn't fooled by my brave front. We were on the set waiting for the crew to adjust the lighting for a scene when he turned quietly to me. "Life is so strange, Doris," he said, placing a loving hand on my shoulder. "Here I am waiting for the arrival of my first child, and here you are saddened by the fact that your husband is dying."

It was the gentlest of touches, but it made a strong connection between us. He acknowledged what I was going through, something that most people felt very uncomfortable even being near, much less mentioning, but he was also putting it in perspective. I love him for that simple, well-timed gesture of concern.

Despite this it was important to me to think that I was maintaining a façade for Bill. Each night when I left the set I'd compose myself on the drive to the hospital, so I could present a cheerful face to my dying husband.

When you are fighting for someone else's life, you hang on to a slender hope, bolstered by a huge amount of denial. I was resolute and optimistic, taking any small sign of improvement as the beginning of an upward trend. Every day I asked the nurses for the number of normal white blood cells in his lab report, a daily barometer of his body's ability to fight disease. Leukemia causes the body to produce an overabundance of mutated white blood cells that are ineffective in combating illness.

"He's got seventeen today," one of them would say.

"Great, great, that's up from yesterday," I'd say, because the day before he only had fifteen. So this was an improvement in my mind. In fact, a healthy person has hundreds. But I wanted hope, so I held on to whatever I could get to keep myself going.

The nurses had seen this kind of behavior before, and they feared I was heading for a big fall when Bill's condition took a precipitous turn for the worse. One of them was kind enough to speak to me about it. She asked me to have a cup of coffee with her in the nurses' break room.

"You know," she said softly. "It's possible he's not going to make it."

I looked into her eyes. I knew exactly what she was telling me, and I fell apart. From that day on I accepted that he was dying, and I tried to make his last days as peaceful and loving as possible.

The way people behave around a dying man reveals a lot about their character. Some of my friends would call me up and prattle on about how they just went up for a job and they didn't get it even though they thought they did a good reading. The unreality of it all. I was sitting there with my husband dying, and this person was telling me about her career! Other friends were angels. Some of them would come and kick me out of the room. Julie Harris was one and Charlotte Rae was another. Julie would come and sit with Bill to force me to go get my hair done, or just breathe in some fresh air. I am still grateful for those acts of generosity.

As Bill's condition worsened, I decided to decorate his suite and make it a place to celebrate his life, instead of a place of death. I had the reviews of his just-published book of short stories, *Had I A Hundred Mouths,* blown up into big posters and placed around his room. When he woke up, the first thing he saw were his praises.

> (His) voice was a bard's voice, singing dark narratives in lines rich and rhythmic enough to transform stories into ballads . . . I would place *Had I A Hundred Mouths* and *In the Icebound Hothouse* among the greatest short stories of the century.—*The New York Times Book Review*

> These selected stories should not only broaden acknowledgement of Goyen's work, but also emphasize and underscore the remarkable and unique beauty and oddness of his vision.—*USA Today*

We didn't spend a lot of time on memories, though. We lived each moment we could as best we could in that room.

One afternoon, about two weeks before he died, we were holding each other in his bed.

"I worry about you," he said. "I worry about what will happen. . . ."

Then he stopped in midsentence as a sly smile crept over his face.

"On second thought, that will be your problem," he said.

Oh, we laughed. We laughed so hard over that. It got us through to another level of acceptance.

That last week, when he started to die, his room got very crowded with all the friends and family who'd come to visit. His suite became a place where his friends gathered, and where hospital staff who had ended their shift would stop by before going home, a perpetual party taking place around Bill, which comforted me enormously, as I know it did him.

A few days before he died, one of the staff took me aside to raise an issue about our finances. When Bill had checked in, they'd put him in a room that was so small he could barely move in it. He had been incensed by this and threw his tray across the room. One of the biggest suites in the hospital was open, so they transferred him there as a courtesy. The hospital staffer had to tell me that my insurance was not covering this bigger room, and, as he was staying for an extended period, we would have to pick up the cost from now on. The cost was phenomenal, something like $500 a day. I didn't even blink.

"That's where he wants to be," I said. "If it takes every penny we've earned, or more that we'll have to borrow, I will find the money for him."

She looked at me for a moment and walked away. A few minutes later she returned.

"You know something, honey, you have enough on your mind," she said. "Let's forget I said any of this."

His last day, his friends knew he was dying. The word telegraphed through the community of his AA friends and his writing friends, as well as friends of mine. People crowded in the room, seated on the sofas that lined the walls and the chairs we'd corralled from the break rooms, empty rooms, and the cafeteria. People were even sitting on the windowsills.

I was oblivious to the crowd around us. I laid in bed with Bill, stroking him and telling him how much he meant to me. I had a chance to be there for him completely. I'd never had a chance to be that way for anyone before. It was so intimate. All our troubles from the past seemed small compared to how much we had given each other and how much life we shared. He had been my lover, my mentor, and my friend. I told him how he had changed my life and how it was hard to imagine what my life would have been if we had not met. The moment he died, I was holding him in my arms. I felt the last bit of electricity leave his body. I had thought that moment would be a whoosh, as his spirit flew out of his body, but in fact it was exactly as Eleonora Duse had portrayed it in *Cenere*. I had seen years before. It was like a flower closing.

I envy the way people from Arab countries mourn their dead. They wail and scream and rock their bodies until they have fully expressed their grief. Our stoical way of holding it in and going about our business doesn't serve us well, and I think it forces us to carry the pent-up anguish with us longer.

My particular way of mourning and honoring Bill was to go on tour, if you can believe that. His short story collection was so well-received that I didn't want it to sink like so much of his writing had in the past. I used my position as a star on a popular television show to get on all the talk shows and discuss his book.

When I would appear on the talk shows, the hosts would frequently ask me how I could do this. How could I go around the country talking about him? Wasn't that painful for me? Usually, I found that there were other people in the audience who were in the same position as me, grieving over someone they loved, and I would talk directly to them, as I do to any of you who are reading this and have recently lost someone close to you.

There's a time to mourn, no question about it, and you must give yourself that time. But then there is a time when you must put the coffee cup down and get back out into the world, or you will die with them. We're remarkable, us human beings, and we have great recovery power. But life is wonderful and you have to approach it from that point of view. The worst thing in life is to settle. The best thing is to stay open and continue to draw life in.

If nothing else, go back and do something for other people. The minute you get back and start doing something, life begins again. Of course it's different. You're not going to get that person back. You're not going to have him or her to share your life with.

I traveled around the country for a year talking about Bill, and then one day I decided I was through. I don't mourn him much anymore. I celebrate his gift to me and to the world, and I remember the beautiful light that shone upon him until that precious moment when his flower closed.

Like Bill, a great finish. This was a dessert he loved.

Crème Brulée with Raspberry Coulis

For the coulis:

2 baskets fresh raspberries (frozen will do in a pinch)

the juice of ½ a lemon

I heaping tablespoon of confectioners sugar

1. In a food processor, blend all ingredients until as smooth as possible.
2. Strain mixture and chill.

For the brulée:

6 large egg yolks

6 tablespoons sugar

1½ cups heavy whipping cream

1. Preheat oven to 325 degrees.
2. Whisk yolks and sugar until blended.
3. Slowly and gently whisk in cream. Pour into either individual ramekins or into a quiche pan. Place container or containers

into a large baking dish and fill dish with water until the containers are half drowned.

4. Bake until custard is set in the center, about 30–40 minutes. Let cool on wire rack.

5. Fire up your broiler. Sprinkle a coat of sugar on the custards and place under broiler until sugar begins to caramelize.

6. Cool, then chill until the sugar hardens (several hours).

7. Drizzle coulis over the top or alongside when ready to serve.

Serves 4.

Part Ten

Aging

Chapter 35

Finally Forty

The real anxiety about aging begins when you turn forty, the gateway to middle age. Some women grow into maturity. Those who don't have it thrust upon them at forty.

Saying that a woman is "in her thirties" has a different feel altogether than saying she is a forty-year-old woman. After all, that's when shop clerks start calling you "Ma'am." What happened to my face that I'm suddenly no longer "Miss"? "In your thirties" life is full of play and possibility, but forty has a solemnness to it, with hormones starting to fluctuate and weight shifting steadily south. Fight as you might against the signs of aging, they will start to show up in your forties, and the efforts to keep them at bay become more conscious and time-consuming. Suddenly, you start to regret missed opportunities and fear that there are some dreams that you may never realize, because you haven't got the will or you haven't got the time. Those who say that age is just a number are very far, on one side or the other, from forty.

As I approached the big four-oh, I fell into a deep funk, even though I was happily married, working steadily in the theater, and proud of my preadolescent son. It wasn't so much about what I felt at forty, but what others would think of me if they knew I was so old (although now, in my seventies, I laugh at the idea that forty is anywhere near old).

This anxiety was obvious in my new relationship with the mirror. There were three light bulbs over the mirror in my bathroom, but only one of them was working. This was a mature alteration on my part. In that kindly, dim light, I could barely see the hairline wrinkles that were starting to form. I had a specific pose I took when I stood there, one with my chin tilted slightly higher, so there wasn't a bit of a sag in any part of my neck or face. I also had a particular way of angling my head so that my eyes were the center focus and distracted my gaze from other tiny flaws. Arranged that way, I could stand in front of that mirror for a long time, examining my skin to reassure myself that it was virtually wrinkle-free. Everything was fine, I could tell myself in front of this fabulous mirror, as long as I didn't begin my morning with that day-destroying sentence: "You look pretty good for a forty-year-old."

At the time, I was starring in a Broadway play called *Bad Habits* and wishing that I'd had more of them. Why wasn't I having more fun? Actually, I was happy; but shouldn't I have had more fun in the past, when irresponsible behavior wouldn't have hurt anyone but me? One of my co-stars, F. Murray Abraham, sensed my gloomy mood and asked me what I wanted for this milestone birthday. I told him the one thing I really wanted was a follow spot, the spotlight in the theater that is trained on a main character and has an operator dedicated to keeping the light on the actress wherever she goes. "I don't want better billing," I told him. "I don't want more money. I want a follow spot. A follow spot makes you a star."

That request encapsulates the essence of turning forty, a sense that you haven't really gotten the notice that you deserved. By the age of forty, you've struggled, loved, been dumped, succeeded in some things, and failed in others. You've lived a significant portion of your life and begun most of the relationships that will be with you for the long haul. Has anyone really noticed me? Could anyone have taken in the whole thing? Most important of all, had I? So much of life whooshes past with us barely understanding its significance, so many rich moments just seem to evaporate. At forty you have the first glimpse of realizing how precious all of it has been, and, if you're like me, you desire to take that follow spot and illuminate not just the high points but the ordinary ones as well. You want to make sure that you are the star of your own play. After all, life is not a dress rehearsal.

Needless to say, I was heading for a pretty miserable birthday. Amazingly, my husband saw this coming and understood the delicacy of the situation. Like every woman throughout history, I said I wanted nothing: no celebration, no gifts; no acknowledgement whatsoever. The most I could stand was a quiet night home with just him and Michael. I was proving how great an actress I was in this memorable performance as the birthday martyr.

But my husband knew if we spent the evening having a quiet dinner with an expensive bottle of champagne, my obvious craving for attention would go unsatisfied. The struggle between celebration and despair would be tipped to the negative and he'd pay the price for months to come. He wasn't going to let me slink off into a cave to shrivel up and die. He organized a huge party at our apartment on Seventy-third Street and West End Avenue and invited dozens of our friends from the theater world to a late-night celebration that would begin after that evening's performance.

The evening started well enough. When I got to the theater, I couldn't get into my dressing room because Murray had hunted down a follow spot, a piece of equipment so huge that it took up most of the room. I was simultaneously pleased and dismayed that he'd also included amber gels. Gels are thin sheets of colored film that lighting technicians place in a frame in front of the spotlight to set a mood on the stage. The amber ones bathe the subject in a warm light that is the kindest to wrinkles. In my later years, I've seriously considered getting these for my home.

When I got to the apartment, a huge cheer rose up from the assembled guests. While I had been pounding the boards on Broadway, my guests had been pounding back martinis. When I walked through the door it was as if I was taking a second curtain call. The actors and singers crowded around the piano singing show tunes. My mother arrived beautifully dressed and full of joy, but her mood dropped to cold judgment when she saw the look on my face. I'd taken one look at all the merriment and my face was set in a scowl. Despite my husband's efforts and the presence of all of my close friends, I was unhappy with myself and angry at the world. My mother grabbed my arm and hustled me off to the bedroom.

"What is the matter with you?" she said. "You are behaving very badly."

"Oh, buzz off," I bit back.

"What are you? Crazy?" she said. "What more do you want? I've never seen you behave like this. Bill has brought all your friends here to celebrate your birthday. He's got flowers, and great food, and liquor. Everyone's having a good time and you, you're sulking. What is the matter with you?

"I'm forty!" I said.

"No you're not," she shot back. "You're thirty-nine."

"I'm *what?*"

"You're thirty-nine," she said. "I was wondering why you were making such a big deal out of your thirty-ninth birthday. But you know, I thought it was a big deal to you that this is your last birthday in your thirties."

"I'm forty," I insisted.

"Honey, I should know," she said. "I was there, too."

The truth of the matter was that I had been lying about my age so much since I was a teenager that I honestly didn't know how old I was. I graduated from high school early and I lied about my age so I could get work. When I was fifteen, I was passing myself off as nine-teen. I had monkeyed around so much with my age that the only person who really knew how old I was was my mom.

She was right. And the moment I realized this I was suddenly taller, thinner, and my hair was thicker with a lustrous sheen. My skin had the dewy springiness of a woman in her thirties, and I felt my breasts rise up without the benefit of the underwire. As I ran my fingers through my thick, beautiful hair, the formerly flapping upper arm flesh tightened with a new resolve to hang on to my youth. I considered adding another light bulb to the bathroom mirror to observe my transformation.

This made for a great evening, something to really celebrate. It was as though the governor had called to give the prisoner a pardon from middle age. We sang and reveled until the small hours of the morning and into the next day. I believed, when I looked in the special mirror, that I looked a little younger. I *did* look younger. All the stress of turning forty and the deepening frown lines of disappointment were definitely not doing much good for my skin. After all, I was still in my thirties and I had nothing to worry about.

A few years ago I turned seventy and decided I was finally ready to celebrate my fortieth birthday. I hired a restaurant and invited a hundred friends to mark the fact that I was finally mature enough to accept middle age. Like Jack Benny, I held on to that thirty nine—in my case, for thirty years. All my anxiety about turning forty made me understand that age was something you believed or didn't believe, and that the number mattered much more to you than to those around you. The party favor at my recent fortieth birthday was a silver-plated luggage tag that said in engraved letters "Finally Forty." I'm finally forty, and I've still got a lot of places to go.

Bill served this cornbread and chili combination at my "fortieth" birthday party.

Mexican Cornbread with
Texas Chili for a Party

<u>For the cornbread:</u>

1 ¾ cup yellow corn meal

1 teaspoon baking powder

¼ teaspoon baking soda

1 teaspoon salt

3 jalapeño peppers

1 cup buttermilk

2 eggs

1 cup creamed corn

1 cup grated cheddar cheese

⅓ cup vegetable oil

1. Combine dry ingredients, add milk.
2. Add unbeaten eggs, one at a time.
3. Stir in corn, fold in grated cheese.
4. Refrigerate.
5. As the batter is chilling, heat oven to 350 degrees. Pour oil into an 8×12-inch baking dish and heat in oven.
6. When oil is hot enough (when a drop of water sizzles), pour chilled batter into hot oil and bake for 20–30 minutes or until a fork comes out clean when pierced.

<u>For the chili:</u>

2 pound ground beef

1 large chopped onion

1 teaspoon chopped garlic

1 tablespoon shortening or bacon grease

2 teaspoon ground cumin

¼ cup chili powder

2 tablespoon flour

1 tablespoon salt

½ teaspoon pepper

2 cups canned pinto or kidney beans

2 cups canned diced tomatoes

1 cup water

1. Put meat, onion, and garlic in hot fat.
2. Cover and let simmer for an hour. If dry, add a little water.
3. Add cumin seeds, chili powder, flour, seasonings, and stir well. Add beans, tomatoes, and water, and stir again.
4. Cook very slowly for an hour.
5. Transfer to an ovenproof baking pan.
6. Pour cornbread batter over the chili and bake for 30 minutes in a 400-degree oven.

Serves 8–10.

Chapter 36

We're Still Having Sex and We've Got All the Money

Once, back in the 1970s when my husband Bill and I were having a huge argument, I called my mother at two o'clock in the morning. She was then in her seventies and lived ten blocks away. "Mom, I'm sorry I woke you at this hour, but Bill and I are having a terrible fight and I cannot stay here another minute," I said. "Can I come stay with you?"

There was dead silence on the other end of the phone. Any apple-cheeked American mom would have said to her distraught daughter: "What's wrong? What is it? What can I do? Come over right away, darling." Instead, I got dead silence. In that uncomfortable void, the unthinkable occurred to me.

"Uh, is there somebody there?" I asked in an incredulous voice.

More awkward silence filled the line.

"Uh-huh," she said quietly.

"Oh, my God! Never mind," I said. "I'll call you tomorrow."

I returned to the living room in a state of shock.

"Bill, we're going to have to settle this fight. I can't go to my mother's. She's got a *man* at her house," I said. I knew that whatever we were fighting about was not going to make me as uncomfortable as meeting the man who spends the night at my mom's.

Most children are horrified by the mental image of either of their parents engaged in lovemaking. When you add to that the notion of elderly parents in the throes of passion, the universal reaction of young people (and by this I mean younger than fifty) is a childish: "Eeewww." Or a more adult, "Oh my God." The listener is as grossed out as if he or she had just stepped barefoot on a slug. The other insulting response to discussing senior love life with people who are middle-aged or younger is the way they smile condescendingly—the same smile they might use when informed that their second-grader has a hopeless crush on someone else in the class. Sweet but pointless. It ain't gonna sell underwear. So what's the point? I guess the point is that sex is a beautiful part of life. And even when it's not beautiful, it's still a part of life.

When I think back on the shocking news that my mother was engaged in an intimate relationship with a man while she was in her seventies, I wasn't just upset that my mother was having sex, although that was hard enough to take. Mostly it was the mental image of those two elderly bodies going at it. The movie love stories and media images of love are always of two young people mixing it up in a world where no wrinkle or scar would dare enter. The young people are "hot"; their bodies are attractive, and two hot bodies in a dimly lit room is pretty much all you need to show. When the elderly are depicted in love, it's all about tenderness: the gnarled, spotted hands clasped before the sweet walk on the beach, or the frail little couple toddling down the country path. All of the love, none of the making.

Late in life, love is neither icky nor precious, just as youthful lovemaking isn't always hot. Despite Madison Avenue's opinion, sex is not just for pretty people. In fact, in my experience, as you age sex keeps getting better and better. Once I passed fifty, I started having the best sex of my life. Those of you who find this subject uncomfortable can stop reading right now. Any of you who plan to make it past fifty, read on. There is hope. More than hope, honey—it's a blast.

When I was young and in shape, the age when Hollywood might find my passions worth displaying, I was a pretty distracted lover. There was my baby, of course. Few women can abandon themselves to the act of love when they have one ear trained on the movements of the baby in the next room. The other factor was exhaustion. After a day at work, the emotional roller coaster of trying to be an actress, the demands of an active child, and the responsibilities of running a household, I was beat. When you're younger, you put so much energy into being something others would like to have sex with (attractive, successful, great ass) that there is no energy left to enjoy sex. Plus, you either have a child, or you're acting like one.

Many times when my husband got that gleam in his eye, I thought: "Oh no, not again. You put that thing away." It wasn't that I didn't love him. Far from it, in fact. It's just that I had been up with the baby at six in the morning, gotten my husband out the door to work, cleaned the house, wrangled a babysitter so I could go to an audition, auditioned, retrieved the baby, made dinner, and gotten the baby off to bed—and came out of the nursery to old gleam-in-the-eye. Oh boy, I'd think, someone else needs me to give. In that condition, how could sex be any more than a duty? I wanted it to be what it should be: an expression of the connection we had. As any woman who has been in that situation can verify, sex under those circumstances many times demonstrates the opposite of a connection; it shows how far you and your husband have drifted apart since the baby came between you. After all, this was the guy who was first for so many years, and he clearly enjoyed that ranking. Dinner could go cold on the table, the house could be a swamp, but at least he was getting laid, which meant all was in the right order. That gleam is a simple request to be moved a few places up in ranking. He probably would have settled for third, just before feeding the dog.

Besides all the things I had on my mind then, my technique

wasn't what it is today, either. When seniors say wistfully: "If I knew then what I know now . . ." people imagine we are talking about the insights about people's character and motivations, the knowledge we've gained about the way the world really works. Don't fool yourself that we're talking about career choices, sweetheart; we're talking about sex. If I could go back and give my youthful self the sexual knowledge I've gained in the last twenty years, I fancy that young Doris' life would have been radically different. I'm not complaining about who I am and where I've ended up, but I know I'd have felt a lot more powerful, happier, and loved, and I would have had a lot more fun. I'm not as good as I once was, but I'm as good once as I ever was. Thirty minutes of "yes!" is better than twenty years of: "Was it good for you?"

I can only speak for myself and my friends in saying this. I believe that the difference when you are older is that you're free. First of all, you're free from the shame society has taught you about your body. When I was a little girl my grandmother would bathe me in a basin in the kitchen. After my bath was over she'd stand me up on the kitchen counter to dry me. As my grandfather walked past, he'd wag his finger at me and say: "Shame, shame, shame." Looking back, I am horrified that anyone would give an innocent child that kind of message about her beautiful naked body. I carried his message with me most of my young life, and it took me years of analysis to overcome it.

When you're a senior, though, who cares? Everyone around you has started to sag, so where's the shame? That is, unless you are punishing yourself by holding on to the image of yourself as a young person and comparing that body to the one you're maneuvering today. The only shame is in not getting as much out of life as you can in the time you've got left. The victory is to still be in the game at my age, not to be the winner. Move it or lose it, baby, and I don't intend to freeze up now.

The best part about having sex when you're older is that you know what you want. When I was younger I took my health and vigor for granted as well as my toned skin and muscles. Now I can't take any of it for granted. I'm conscious of my heart rate, my blood pressure, my backaches, and the way my energy fluctuates throughout the day. I think sometimes I'm like those new cars who tell you when the tire pressure is low or the oil needs to be changed. When I open my eyes in the morning, I hear, "Check hip, back stiff, blood pressure low, see dealer immediately." A tune up, an oil change, some bran, and I'm good.

The upside of this self-knowledge is a satisfying understanding of precisely what turns me on. My willingness to explore is much greater than it was earlier on, and most of the men I've been with later in life have really known what they were doing. With the worry about getting pregnant or being caught in the act by your children out of the way, lovemaking can be much more spontaneous. And if your children are still walking in on you when you're in your seventies, they should get their own place or keep their mouths shut.

Free in my own home or free in a hotel room, free of obligation, I've found it much more fun. I know I haven't got that much more time left, so I'm not as shy about asking for what I want as I was before. The incredible gift of still being capable of intimacy comes with the bittersweet understanding that this in fact could be the last time you ever make love, so make the most of it. Get what you want, give all you can, and really enjoy yourself, honey, because this moment is all you've got. And if this *is* it, what better way to go.

Freedom from obligation is an important part of the mixture. When I was younger, sex was frequently a tool of entrapment, part of an elaborate game between men and women, with underlying worries about commitment. What does it *mean* that we're having sex? Have I given this precious part of myself away too soon? Will he still respect me, or, now that he got what he wanted, is he out the door? Are we going to get married? Is this the beginning of something? Is this bad sex—the bad sex that means our relationship is in trouble?

I'm not asking any of those questions now, which makes the act of love a more pure and complete expression. Frankly, I have more to express, now that I'm freed of obligation. So we *can't* get into some of the elaborate sexual acrobatics? No one's got the strength anymore to take me up against a wall, and it would probably throw my back out anyway. My lover's knee problems may rule out doggie-style, and that's a definite loss. But there are many compensating aspects, including humor. We know who we are and where we are at in life, so we might as well laugh.

Laughter is great foreplay. I had great sex with one man under conditions that would horrify younger people. We had started fiddling around and were just moments before the main event when he had to pause to suit up. He needed to wear an elastic sleeve on his left knee to protect it from strain—in my set, when someone dons a strap-on, it's usually a back brace. Thus attired, he looked more like he was going in for surgery than sex. A gift of being older, in this case, was how hard we laughed at our generation's "sex toys." From that laughter came acceptance, tenderness, and true intimacy that carried forward into a sweet and satisfying act of love.

And when I'm having sex I don't feel my mortality. There's an old line from World War II about bad sex: "Shut your eyes and think of England." Sex was your wifely obligation, and engaging in it was part of your duty to the nation to keep bearing children, whether the act of love was pleasurable to you or not. As an older person, I can shut my eyes and think of Doris, simultaneously in the room with the wonderful man who is stroking me and holding me, and back across time with some of the great lovers I've had decades before. I'm not looking for the love of my life or the answer to my prayers. I'm ecstatic to be alive and still loving, decades past the point when I thought it was possible. I'm a long way from "last call." I smile at the memory of my mom and her late-night visitor, just as I know she would be smiling at me if she saw the way I carry on her legacy now that I'm at her stage in life.

This is a dish that can simmer slowly while you do your cooking in a different part of the house.

Sausage and Peppers

8 hot or sweet Italian sausages

3 green bell peppers

2 yellow onions

4 tablespoons olive oil

1. Put 4 tablespoons of water in the bottom of a big frying pan and heat until steaming. Add sausages to pan and brown on all sides.
2. Cut the bell peppers in half, remove the seeds and the membranes, and cut into ½-inch strips.
3. Cut onions into ½-inch slices and toss in a bowl with the peppers, olive oil, salt, and pepper.
4. In a separate frying pan, add onions and peppers, and cook until brown and caramelized.
5. Pierce sausages with a fork and let their juices run out. Add pepper and onion mixture to the sausage pan. Toss until the sausage has mixed in with the other ingredients.
6. Cover cook on low flame for 30 minutes.

Serves 2 if you've worked up an appetite, or 4 otherwise.

Chapter 37

Still Kicking

I remember when I was in my twenties looking down at my mother's hands with fear. I noticed her hands, which had supported me through a very rough childhood, were suddenly pale and furrowed with deep lines. The skin on the back was translucent and as thin and wrinkled as crepe. Crepe, the fabric of funerals. My mother was dying, I thought. The juices were leaving her body and her life force was draining away with it. This must be what it's like to see yourself getting old, I reasoned, which is something I'll never have to do. It starts with the hands and then it takes over your body. I trembled at the idea that I would have to live without her.

At the time, my mother was in her late fifties. She went on to live to be eighty-one.

As my reaction to my mother's hands demonstrates, old really depends on where you stand. You've all heard six-year-old kids say things like, "My mom is *really* old. She's thirty." A young friend of mind said sarcastically that he was about to turn eighteen and "getting closer and closer to ninety." He's right in a way. Every day of our lives we edge closer and closer to ninety, but that doesn't mean we are old. It means you're young enough to worry about being old.

That's why old people look wise—they're finished worrying. Everything's happened and they're still here.

Now that I'm in my seventies, I've got a much different perspective on age. I'm at the peak of my career, at the height of my earned income and my tax contribution. I stopped claiming my TV children as dependents. When my grandchildren say I rock, they're not talking about a chair.

Yet, society considers me discardable. My peers and I are portrayed as dependent, helpless, unproductive, and demanding rather than deserving. In reality, the majority of seniors are self-sufficient, middle-class consumers with more assets than most young people, and more time and talent to offer society. This is not just a sad situation, *this is a crime!* Half off on a movie shouldn't mean half off on our dignity. The senior discount doesn't mean you should discount seniors.

In the next twenty-five years, more than one hundred and fifteen million Americans will be fifty and over. They will become the largest older population in history. To thrive as a society that is fair and respectful to all its members, we must address the devastation, cost, and loss that we as a nation suffer because of age discrimination.

Age discrimination negates the value of wisdom and experience, robs us of our dignity, and denies us the chance to continue to grow, to flourish, and to become all that we are capable of being. We all know that medical advances have changed the length and quality of life for us today. We have not, however, changed our attitudes about aging nor have we addressed the disabling myths that disempower us. I would like to have the word *old* deleted from our vocabulary and replaced with the word *older*. Unlike dairy products, we don't have an expiration date. My contemporaries and I are denigrated as *old*: old coots, old fogies, old codgers, old geezers, old hags, old-timers, and old farts.

The Arab countries have a saying: If you don't have an old person in your home, rent one. Other countries understand the value of the senior perspective on life, and people there turn to their elders for wisdom. In this country, older people are dismissed as reflections of an out-of-date set of values. If society found a way to embrace the gift of a vigorous old age, it would find a richness there that is astonishing.

In truth, the minute you are born, you are getting older, and your later years can be some of life's most productive and creative. For the last one hundred years the average age of the all the Nobel Prize winners has been sixty-five. Frank Gehry designed Seattle's hip new rock museum at age seventy. Georgia O'Keeffe was productive well into her eighties. Add to the list Hitchcock, Dickens, Bernstein, Fosse, Wright, Matisse, Picasso, and Einstein, just to mention a few people who produced some of their best work when they would be considered over the hill by current standards.

The entertainment industry—these image makers—are the worst perpetrators of this bigotry. We must change the negative stereotypes of aging that exist in the media. When I testified about ageism before the Senate Committee on Aging in 2002, a Yale professor discussed her eight-year-study of the damage caused by negative images of the elderly in the media. Her study found that seniors who were exposed to positive images of their age group lived 7.6 years longer. Imagine that! When you're my age, that works out to a more than 10-percent increase in your time on earth.

This horrible perspective on the elderly is a fairly recent phenomena. When I was a young woman, some of the most powerful and popular actresses were women past the age of forty. Women such as Joan Crawford, Bette Davis, Katharine Hepburn, and Barbara Stanwyck continued to work, getting better and better at their craft as they got older. Now, many of my friends—talented actresses in the forty-to-sixty-year-old range—are forced to live on unemployment or welfare because of the scarcity of roles for women in that age bracket.

I've been fortunate to be one of a handful of actresses who has continued to work throughout my career, but it has not been easy. When I was in my forties I heard of a great part on a new series called *Remington Steele*, but I wasn't considered for it because I was thought to be too old. Because I was very persistent and knew the casting director, I read for it and got it!

The roles for women my age frequently show seniors in insulting and degrading ways. They're cartoons of the elderly. There is a coalition to protect the way every other group is depicted in the media, but no one protects the image of the elderly. I recently turned down a movie role where I was supposed to play a horny grandmother who spewed foul language, exposed herself, and chased after young boys. Although I turned down the job, of course someone took the part.

Hollywood clearly is clueless when it comes to understanding today's seniors—it's blind to the advances in medicine and self-care and the increases in personal income, which have made us a force to be reckoned with and a market to be exploited. Twenty years ago it was accurate to show a senior coming in for his check-up dragging his oxygen tank. Today he would be dragging his golf clubs.

Yes, there is energy, excitement, and enthusiasm in the young, but there isn't any less of it in those in their senior years. It is small comfort to know that those who have perpetrated ageism will some day face it themselves. Nobody feels old until he or she is treated that way.

As General Douglas MacArthur once wrote:

Youth is not a time of life, it's a state of mind. Nobody grows old by merely living a number of years. People grow old by deserting their ideals. Years wrinkle the skin, but to give up enthusiasm wrinkles the soul. Worry, doubt, self-distrust, fear, and despair—these are the long, long years that bow the head and turn the growing spirit back to dust. You're as young as your faith, as old as your doubt, as young as your self-confidence, as old as your fear.

I am a person who's young in spirit, full of life and energy, and eager to stay engaged in the world and fight ageism, the last bastion of bigotry. I'm lucky, because, at least right now, I don't have any severe health problems. I don't move as fast as I once did, but I'm still moving. I forget a lot of things, but this is not something that is unique to people in their seventies. I hope my presence and the way I present myself can be a learning opportunity for younger people, especially those only twenty years younger than I am. As I said to the world when I won an Emmy for my work on *Everybody Loves Raymond,* "I'm seventy-one tonight and I'm still kicking!"

My hope and my wish is that everyone, no matter what they're doing at seventy-one, can live in a world where they are encouraged to feel the same way.

Open yourself a bottle of champagne (the older, the better) and toast to your continued longevity.

Afterword

I trust you've enjoyed the stories I've recounted in this book. I hope I've given you a laugh or two. I'm no life lessons expert, but the one thing I know is that when you keep your sense of humor about things, the heaviest burdens lighten and the darkest hours pass like a minute. Plus, you get more oxygen in your lungs. So see, I've already helped you!

The writing of this book has been an incredible journey for me, one that has shown me that in the end, all the different characters I've met and the diverse experiences I've had are more than just a collection of disconnected events; they're a story. And while my story does feature some exciting locals and famous people, it's a story not all that different than those of most of the strong women I love, including Marie Barone. A story where family comes first, relationships are paramount, and every encounter is a struggle to do the right thing while still remaining true to who you are.

Yes, I'm still hungry, dear, but I'm no longer hungry for it all at once. That way there's no chance to savor. I expect for the rest of my life I will have men and I will have chocolate and every once in a great while when the stars are in perfect alignment, I'll have both.

Index